A RULE FOR CHILDREN AND
OTHER WRITINGS

THE
OTHER VOICE
IN
EARLY MODERN
EUROPE

A Series Edited by Margaret L. King and Albert Rabil Jr.

RECENT BOOKS IN THE SERIES

TULLIA D'ARAGONA
Dialogue on the Infinity of Love
Edited and translated by Rinaldina Russell
and Bruce Merry

CASSANDRA FEDELE
Letters and Orations
Edited and translated by Diana Robin

VERONICA FRANCO
Poems and Selected Letters
Edited and translated by Ann Rosalind Jones
and Margaret F. Rosenthal

MARIE LE JARS DE GOURNAY
"Apology for the Woman Writing"
and Other Works
Edited and translated by Richard Hillman
and Colette Quesnel

LUCREZIA MARINELLA
The Nobility and Excellence of Women,
and the Defects and Vices of Men
Edited and translated by Anne Dunhill
with Letizia Panizza

ANNE-MARIE-LOUISE D'ORLÉANS,
DUCHESSE DE MONTPENSIER
Against Marriage: The Correspondence
of La Grande Mademoiselle
Edited and translated by Joan DeJean

FRANÇOIS POULLAIN DE LA BARRE
Three Cartesian Feminist Treatises
Introductions and Annotations
by Marcelle Maistre Welch
Translation by Vivien Bosley

SISTER BARTOLOMEA RICCOBONI
Life and Death in a Venetian Convent:
The Chronicle and Necrology
of Corpus Domini, 1395–1436
Edited and translated by Daniel Bornstein

MARÍA DE SAN JOSÉ SALAZAR
Book for the Hour of Recreation
Introduction and Notes by Alison Weber
Translation by Amanda Powell

ANNA MARIA VAN SCHURMAN
"Whether a Christian Woman Should Be
Educated" and Other Writings
from Her Intellectual Circle
Edited and translated by Joyce L. Irwin

LUCREZIA TORNABUONI DE'MEDICI
Sacred Narratives
Edited and translated by Jane Tylus

JUAN LUIS VIVES
"The Education of a Christian Woman":
A Sixteenth-Century Manual
Edited and translated by Charles Fantazzi

Jacqueline Pascal

A RULE FOR CHILDREN AND OTHER WRITINGS

❧

Edited and translated by
John J. Conley, S.J.

THE UNIVERSITY OF CHICAGO PRESS
Chicago & London

Jacqueline Pascal, 1625–61

John J. Conley, S.J., is associate professor of philosophy at Fordham University. He is the author of *The Suspicion of Virtue: Women Philosophers in Neoclassical France* and coeditor of *Prophecy and Diplomacy: The Moral Doctrine of John Paul II.*

The University of Chicago Press, Chicago 60637
The University of Chicago Press, Ltd., London
© 2003 by The University of Chicago
All rights reserved. Published 2003
Printed in the United States of America
12 11 10 09 08 07 06 05 04 03   1 2 3 4 5

ISBN: 0-226-64831-1 (cloth)
ISBN: 0-226-64833-8 (paper)

Library of Congress Cataloging-in-Publication Data

Pascal, Jacqueline, 1625–1661.
 [Selections. English. 2003]
 A rule for children and other writings / Jacqueline Pascal ; edited and translated by John J. Conley.
   p. cm. — (The other voice in early modern Europe)
 Includes bibliographical references and index.
 ISBN 0-226-64831-1 (alk. paper) — ISBN 0-226-64833-8 (pbk. : alk. paper)
 1. Jansenists—France—History—Sources. I. Conley, John J. II. Title.
III. Series.

BX4735.P3
[A25 2003]
282'.092—dc21

2002040862

To the memory of my beloved sister Nancy Maureen Conley
(1961–67)

CONTENTS

ACKNOWLEDGMENTS

This book could not have been written without the assistance of numerous people who encouraged the research, the translation, and the publication of the works of Jacqueline Pascal.

I thank the Folger Institute for a grant to participate in the seminar on gender and sanctity led by Dr. Alison Weber of the University of Virginia. The seminar permitted me to develop my first paper on Jacqueline Pascal. I also thank the Society for the Study of Women Philosophers, where I presented a paper on Jacqueline Pascal's subversion of virtue theory. The meetings of the Society also permitted me to gauge the interest among professional philosophers for a translation of her work on education.

I thank Fordham University for a sabbatical (1999–2000) that permitted me to consult manuscripts and rare printed material in several Parisian libraries, and I thank the staffs of the following libraries for their professional courtesy: Bibliothèque nationale de France; Bibliothèque Mazarine; Bibliothèque de la Société de Port-Royal.

I also recognize my debt to the French editors of the works of Jacqueline Pascal: Père Pierre Guerrier, Victor Cousin, Armand Prosper Faugère, and Jean Mesnard. I owe a particular debt to Mesnard, whose magisterial edition of the works of the entire Pascal family has provided contemporary Pascal scholars with a detailed map of Jansenist culture.

Perhaps the greatest debt is to a small circle of Jansenist laywomen and nuns, such as Gilberte Pascal Périer and Mère Angélique de Saint-Jean, who managed to preserve the manuscripts of Jacqueline Pascal in the face of a century of censorship, confiscation, interdict, imprisonment, and exile. Thanks to their determination in the midst of persecution, Jacqueline Pascal can still speak to us of the rights of conscience and of the formation of conscience in the shadow of the cross.

THE OTHER VOICE IN
EARLY MODERN EUROPE:
INTRODUCTION TO THE SERIES
Margaret L. King and Albert Rabil Jr.

THE OLD VOICE AND THE OTHER VOICE

In western Europe and the United States, women are nearing equality in the professions, in business, and in politics. Most enjoy access to education, reproductive rights, and autonomy in financial affairs. Issues vital to women are on the public agenda: equal pay, child care, domestic abuse, breast cancer research, and curricular revision with an eye to the inclusion of women.

These recent achievements have their origins in things women (and some male supporters) said for the first time about six hundred years ago. Theirs is the "other voice," in contradistinction to the "first voice," the voice of the educated men who created Western culture. Coincident with a general reshaping of European culture in the period 1300–1700 (called the Renaissance or early modern period), questions of female equality and opportunity were raised that still resound and are still unresolved.

The other voice emerged against the backdrop of a three-thousand-year history of the derogation of women rooted in the civilizations related to Western culture: Hebrew, Greek, Roman, and Christian. Negative attitudes toward women inherited from these traditions pervaded the intellectual, medical, legal, religious, and social systems that developed during the European Middle Ages.

The following pages describe the traditional, overwhelmingly male views of women's nature inherited by early modern Europeans and the new tradition that the "other voice" called into being to begin to challenge reigning assumptions. This review should serve as a framework for understanding the texts published in the series "The Other Voice in Early Modern Europe." Introductions specific to each text and author follow this essay in all the volumes of the series.

[handwritten margin note: Other Voice emerges vs. a backdrop of men]

TRADITIONAL VIEWS OF WOMEN, 500 B.C.E.–1500 C.E.

Embedded in the philosophical and medical theories of the ancient Greeks were perceptions of the female as inferior to the male in both mind and body. Similarly, the structure of civil legislation inherited from the ancient Romans was biased against women, and the views on women developed by Christian thinkers out of the Hebrew Bible and the Christian New Testament were negative and disabling. Literary works composed in the vernacular of ordinary people, and widely recited or read, conveyed these negative assumptions. The social networks within which most women lived—those of the family and the institutions of the Roman Catholic Church—were shaped by this negative tradition and sharply limited the areas in which women might act in and upon the world.

Greek Philosophy and Female Nature

Greek biology assumed that women were inferior to men and defined them as merely childbearers and housekeepers. This view was authoritatively expressed in the works of the philosopher Aristotle.

Aristotle thought in dualities. He considered action superior to inaction, form (the inner design or structure of any object) superior to matter, completion to incompletion, possession to deprivation. In each of these dualities, he associated the male principle with the superior quality and the female with the inferior. "The male principle in nature," he argued, "is associated with active, formative and perfected characteristics, while the female is passive, material and deprived, desiring the male in order to become complete."[1] Men are always identified with virile qualities, such as judgment, courage, and stamina, and women with their opposites—irrationality, cowardice, and weakness.

The masculine principle was considered superior even in the womb. The man's semen, Aristotle believed, created the form of a new human creature, while the female body contributed only matter. (The existence of the ovum, and with it the other facts of human embryology, was not established until the seventeenth century.) Although the later Greek physician Galen believed there was a female component in generation, contributed by "female semen," the followers of both Aristotle and Galen saw the male role in human generation as more active and more important.

1. Aristotle, *Physics* 1.9.192a20–24, in *The Complete Works of Aristotle*, ed. Jonathan Barnes, rev. Oxford trans., 2 vols. (Princeton, 1984), 1:328.

In the Aristotelian view, the male principle sought always to reproduce itself. The creation of a female was always a mistake, therefore, resulting from an imperfect act of generation. Every female born was considered a "defective" or "mutilated" male (as Aristotle's terminology has variously been translated), a "monstrosity" of nature.[2]

For Greek theorists, the biology of males and females was the key to their psychology. The female was softer and more docile, more apt to be despondent, querulous, and deceitful. Being incomplete, moreover, she craved sexual fulfillment in intercourse with a male. The male was intellectual, active, and in control of his passions.

These psychological polarities derived from the theory that the universe consisted of four elements (earth, fire, air, and water), expressed in human bodies as four "humors" (black bile, yellow bile, blood, and phlegm) considered respectively dry, hot, damp, and cold and corresponding to mental states ("melancholic," "choleric," "sanguine," "phlegmatic"). In this scheme the male, sharing the principles of earth and fire, was dry and hot; the female, sharing the principles of air and water, was cold and damp.

Female psychology was further affected by her dominant organ, the uterus (womb), *hystera* in Greek. The passions generated by the womb made women lustful, deceitful, talkative, irrational, indeed—when these affects were in excess—"hysterical."

Aristotle's biology also had social and political consequences. If the male principle was superior and the female inferior, then in the household, as in the state, men should rule and women must be subordinate. That hierarchy did not rule out the companionship of husband and wife, whose cooperation was necessary for the welfare of children and the preservation of property. Such mutuality supported male preeminence.

Aristotle's teacher Plato suggested a different possibility: that men and women might possess the same virtues. The setting for this proposal is the imaginary and ideal Republic that Plato sketches in a dialogue of that name. Here, for a privileged elite capable of leading wisely, all distinctions of class and wealth dissolve, as, consequently, do those of gender. Without households or property, as Plato constructs his ideal society, there is no need for the subordination of women. Women may therefore be educated to the same level as men to assume leadership. Plato's Republic remained imaginary, however. In real societies, the subordination of women remained the norm and the prescription.

The views of women inherited from the Greek philosophical tradition

2. Aristotle, *Generation of Animals* 2.3.737a27–28, in *The Complete Works*, 1:1144.

became the basis for medieval thought. In the thirteenth century, the supreme Scholastic philosopher Thomas Aquinas, among others, still echoed Aristotle's views of human reproduction, of male and female personalities, and of the preeminent male role in the social hierarchy.

Roman Law and the Female Condition

Fulcrum of
Roman law
men rule
all

Roman law, like Greek philosophy, underlay medieval thought and shaped medieval society. The ancient belief that adult property-owning men should administer households and make decisions affecting the community at large is the very fulcrum of Roman law.

About 450 B.C.E., during Rome's republican era, the community's customary law was recorded (legendarily) on twelve tablets erected in the city's central forum. It was later elaborated by professional jurists whose activity increased in the imperial era, when much new legislation was passed, especially on issues affecting family and inheritance. This growing, changing body of laws was eventually codified in the *Corpus of Civil Law* under the direction of the emperor Justinian, generations after the empire ceased to be ruled from Rome. That *Corpus*, read and commented on by medieval scholars from the eleventh century on, inspired the legal systems of most of the cities and kingdoms of Europe.

Great
subordination
to men

Laws regarding dowries, divorce, and inheritance pertain primarily to women. Since those laws aimed to maintain and preserve property, the women concerned were those from the property-owning minority. Their subordination to male family members points to the even greater subordination of lower-class and slave women, about whom the laws speak little.

Pater-familias
Father had
absolute
authority

In the early republic, the *paterfamilias*, or "father of the family," possessed *patria potestas*, "paternal power." The term *pater*, "father," in both these cases does not necessarily mean biological father but denotes the head of a household. The father was the person who owned the household's property and, indeed, its human members. The *paterfamilias* had absolute power—including the power, rarely exercised, of life or death—over his wife, his children, and his slaves, as much as his cattle.

Male children could be "emancipated," an act that granted legal autonomy and the right to own property. Those over fourteen could be emancipated by a special grant from the father or automatically by their father's death. But females could never be emancipated; instead, they passed from the authority of their father to that of a husband or, if widowed or orphaned while still unmarried, to a guardian or tutor.

Marriage in its traditional form placed the woman under her husband's authority, or *manus*. He could divorce her on grounds of adultery, drinking wine, or stealing from the household, but she could not divorce him. She could neither possess property in her own right nor bequeath any to her children upon her death. When her husband died, the household property passed not to her but to his male heirs. And when her father died, she had no claim to any family inheritance, which was directed to her brothers or more remote male relatives. The effect of these laws was to exclude women from civil society, itself based on property ownership.

[margin, handwritten: women were excluded from society through no property ownership!]

In the later republican and imperial periods, these rules were significantly modified. Women rarely married according to the traditional form. The practice of "free" marriage allowed a woman to remain under her father's authority, to possess property given her by her father (most frequently the "dowry," recoverable from the husband's household on his death), and to inherit from her father. She could also bequeath property to her own children and divorce her husband, just as he could divorce her.

Despite this greater freedom, women still suffered enormous disability under Roman law. Heirs could belong only to the father's side, never the mother's. Moreover, although she could bequeath her property to her children, she could not establish a line of succession in doing so. A woman was "the beginning and end of her own family," said the jurist Ulpian. Moreover, women could play no public role. They could not hold public office, represent anyone in a legal case, or even witness a will. Women had only a private existence and no public personality.

[margin, handwritten: women existed only privately in Roman law]

The dowry system, the guardian, women's limited ability to transmit wealth, and total political disability are all features of Roman law adopted by the medieval communities of western Europe, although modified according to local customary laws.

Christian Doctrine and Women's Place

The Hebrew Bible and the Christian New Testament authorized later writers to limit women to the realm of the family and to burden them with the guilt of original sin. The passages most fruitful for this purpose were the creation narratives in Genesis and sentences from the Epistles defining women's role within the Christian family and community.

Each of the first two chapters of Genesis contains a creation narrative. In the first "God created man in his own image, in the image of God he created him; male and female he created them" (Gen. 1:27). In the second, God created Eve from Adam's rib (2:21–23). Christian theologians relied principally on Genesis 2 for their understanding of the relation between man and woman, interpreting the creation of Eve from Adam as proof of her subordination to him.

The creation story in Genesis 2 leads to that of the temptations in Genesis 3: of Eve by the wily serpent and of Adam by Eve. As read by Christian theologians from Tertullian to Thomas Aquinas, the narrative made Eve responsible for the Fall and its consequences. She instigated the act; she deceived her husband; she suffered the greater punishment. Her disobedience made it necessary for Jesus to be incarnated and to die on the cross. From the pulpit, moralists and preachers for centuries conveyed to women the guilt that they bore for original sin.

The Epistles offered advice to early Christians on building communities of the faithful. Among the matters to be regulated was the place of women. Paul offered views favorable to women in Gal. 3:28: "There is neither Jew nor Greek, there is neither slave nor free, there is neither male nor female; for you are all one in Christ Jesus." Paul also referred to women as his coworkers and placed them on a par with himself and his male coworkers (Phil. 4:2–3; Rom. 16:1–3; 1 Cor. 16:19). Elsewhere Paul limited women's possibilities: "But I want you to understand that the head of every man is Christ, the head of a woman is her husband, and the head of Christ is God" (1 Cor. 11:3).

Biblical passages by later writers (though attributed to Paul) enjoined women to forgo jewels, expensive clothes, and elaborate coiffures; and they forbade women to "teach or have authority over men," telling them to "learn in silence with all submissiveness" as is proper for one responsible for sin, consoling them, however, with the thought that they will be saved through childbearing (1 Tim. 2:9–15). Other texts among the later Epistles defined women as the weaker sex and emphasized their subordination to their husbands (1 Pet. 3:7; Col. 3:18; Eph. 5:22–23).

These passages from the New Testament became the arsenal employed by theologians of the early church to transmit negative attitudes toward women to medieval Christian culture—above all, Tertullian (*On the Apparel of Women*), Jerome (*Against Jovinian*), and Augustine (*The Literal Meaning of Genesis*).

The Image of Women in Medieval Literature

The philosophical, legal, and religious traditions born in antiquity formed the basis of the medieval intellectual synthesis wrought by trained thinkers, mostly clerics, writing in Latin and based largely in universities. The vernacular literary tradition that developed alongside the learned tradition also spoke about female nature and women's roles. Medieval stories, poems, and epics also portrayed women negatively—as lustful and deceitful—while praising good housekeepers and loyal wives as replicas of the Virgin Mary or the female saints and martyrs.

Women also praised in comparison w/ religious figures

There is an exception in the movement of "courtly love" that evolved in southern France from the twelfth century. Courtly love was the erotic love between a nobleman and noblewoman, the latter usually superior in social rank. It was always adulterous. From the conventions of courtly love derive modern Western notions of romantic love. The tradition has had an impact disproportionate to its size, for it affected only a tiny elite, and very few women. The exaltation of the female lover probably does not reflect a higher evaluation of women or a step toward their sexual liberation. More likely it gives expression to the social and sexual tensions besetting the knightly class at a specific historical juncture.

The literary fashion of courtly love was on the wane by the thirteenth century, when the widely read *Romance of the Rose* was composed in French by two authors of significantly different dispositions. Guillaume de Lorris composed the initial four thousand verses about 1235, and Jean de Meun added about seventeen thousand verses—more than four times the original— about 1265.

The fragment composed by Guillaume de Lorris stands squarely in the tradition of courtly love. Here the poet, in a dream, is admitted into a walled garden where he finds a magic fountain in which a rosebush is reflected. He longs to pick one rose, but the thorns prevent his doing so, even as he is wounded by arrows from the god of love, whose commands he agrees to obey. The rest of this part of the poem recounts the poet's unsuccessful efforts to pluck the rose.

Women depicted negatively in the literature of courtly love

The longer part of the *Romance* by Jean de Meun also describes a dream. But here allegorical characters give long didactic speeches, providing a social satire on a variety of themes, some pertaining to women. Love is an anxious and tormented state, the poem explains: women are greedy and manipulative, marriage is miserable, beautiful women are lustful, ugly ones cease to please, and a chaste woman is as rare as a black swan.

Shortly after Jean de Meun completed *The Romance of the Rose*, Mathéolus penned his *Lamentations*, a long Latin diatribe against marriage translated into French about a century later. The *Lamentations* sum up medieval attitudes toward women and provoked the important response by Christine de Pizan in her *Book of the City of Ladies*.

In 1355 Giovanni Boccaccio wrote *Il Corbaccio*, another antifeminist manifesto, though ironically by an author whose other works pioneered new directions in Renaissance thought. The former husband of his lover appears to Boccaccio, condemning his unmoderated lust and detailing the defects of women. Boccaccio concedes at the end "how much men naturally surpass women in nobility" and is cured of his desires.[3]

Women's Roles: The Family

The negative perceptions of women expressed in the intellectual tradition are also implicit in the actual roles that women played in European society. Assigned to subordinate positions in the household and the church, they were barred from significant participation in public life.

Medieval European households, like those in antiquity and in non-Western civilizations, were headed by males. It was the male serf (or peasant), feudal lord, town merchant, or citizen who was polled or taxed or succeeded to an inheritance or had any acknowledged public role, although his wife or widow could stand as a temporary surrogate. From about 1100, the position of property-holding males was further enhanced: inheritance was confined to the male, or agnate, line—with depressing consequences for women.

A wife never fully belonged to her husband's family, nor was she a daughter to her father's family. She left her father's house young to marry whomever her parents chose. Her dowry was managed by her husband, and at her death it normally passed to her children by him.

A married woman's life was occupied nearly constantly with cycles of pregnancy, childbearing, and lactation. Women bore children through all the years of their fertility, and many died in childbirth. They were also responsible for raising young children up to six or seven. In the propertied classes that responsibility was shared, since it was common for a wet nurse to take over breast-feeding, and servants performed other chores.

Women trained their daughters in the household duties appropriate to their status, nearly always tasks associated with textiles: spinning, weaving, sewing, embroidering. Their sons were sent out of the house as apprentices or students, or their training was assumed by fathers in later childhood and adolescence. On the death of her husband, a woman's children became the responsibility of his family. She generally did not take "his" children with her to a new marriage or back to her father's house, except sometimes in the artisan classes.

Women also worked. Rural peasants performed farm chores, merchant wives often practiced their husbands' trades, the unmarried daughters of the urban poor worked as servants or prostitutes. All wives produced or embellished textiles and did the housekeeping, while wealthy ones managed ser-

---

3. Giovanni Boccaccio, *The Corbaccio, or The Labyrinth of Love,* trans. and ed. Anthony K. Cassell, rev. ed. (Binghamton, N.Y., 1993), 71.

vants. These labors were unpaid or poorly paid but often contributed substantially to family wealth.

Women's Roles: The Church

Membership in a household, whether a father's or a husband's, meant for women a lifelong subordination to others. In western Europe, the Roman Catholic Church offered an alternative to the career of wife and mother. A woman could enter a convent, parallel in function to the monasteries for men that evolved in the early Christian centuries.

In the convent, a woman pledged herself to a celibate life, lived according to strict community rules, and worshiped daily. Often the convent offered training in Latin, allowing some women to become considerable scholars and authors as well as scribes, artists, and musicians. For women who chose the conventual life, the benefits could be enormous, but for numerous others placed in convents by paternal choice, the life could be restrictive and burdensome.

The conventual life declined as an alternative for women as the modern age approached. Reformed monastic institutions resisted responsibility for related female orders. The church increasingly restricted female institutional life by insisting on closer male supervision.

Women often sought other options. Some joined the communities of laywomen that sprang up spontaneously in the thirteenth century in the urban zones of western Europe, especially in Flanders and Italy. Some joined the heretical movements that flourished in late medieval Christendom, whose anticlerical and often antifamily positions particularly appealed to women. In these communities, some women were acclaimed as "holy women" or "saints," whereas others often were condemned as frauds or heretics.

In all, though the options offered to women by the church were sometimes less than satisfactory, they were sometimes richly rewarding. After 1520 the convent remained an option only in Roman Catholic territories. Protestantism engendered an ideal of marriage as a heroic endeavor and appeared to place husband and wife on a more equal footing. Sermons and treatises, however, still called for female subordination and obedience.

THE OTHER VOICE, 1300–1700

When the modern era opened, European culture was so firmly structured by a framework of negative attitudes toward women that to dismantle it was a monumental labor. The process began as part of a larger cultural movement that entailed the critical reexamination of ideas inherited from the ancient and medieval past. The humanists launched that critical reexamination.

[Handwritten marginal notes: "Convent was an alternative to the family role"; "Convents had an intellectual climate"; "Good attentive if allowed to choose"; "Church restricted women w/ supervision"; "Options by the Catholic church were few"; "Protestantism placed man: wife on equal footing yet still called for female subordination"; "Needed to dismantle tradition of negative attitudes = ideas"]

The Humanist Foundation

Originating in Italy in the fourteenth century, humanism quickly became the dominant intellectual movement in Europe. Spreading in the sixteenth century from Italy to the rest of Europe, it fueled the literary, scientific, and philosophical movements of the era and laid the basis for the eighteenth-century Enlightenment.

Humanists regarded the Scholastic philosophy of medieval universities as out of touch with the realities of urban life. They found in the rhetorical discourse of classical Rome a language adapted to civic life and public speech. They learned to read, speak, and write classical Latin and, eventually, classical Greek. They founded schools to teach others to do so, establishing the pattern for elementary and secondary education for the next three hundred years.

In the service of complex government bureaucracies, humanists employed their skills to write eloquent letters, deliver public orations, and formulate public policy. They developed new scripts for copying manuscripts and used the new printing press to disseminate texts, for which they created methods of critical editing.

Humanism was a movement led by males who accepted the evaluation of women in ancient texts and generally shared the misogynist perceptions of their culture. (Female humanists, as we will see, did not.) Yet humanism also opened the door to a reevaluation of the nature and capacity of women. By calling authors, texts, and ideas into question, it made possible the fundamental rereading of the whole intellectual tradition that was required in order to free women from cultural prejudice and social subordination.

A Different City

The other voice first appeared when, after so many centuries, the accumulation of misogynist concepts evoked a response from a capable female defender: Christine de Pizan (1365–1431). Introducing her *Book of the City of Ladies* (1405), she described how she was affected by reading Mathéolus's *Lamentations*: "Just the sight of this book . . . made me wonder how it happened that so many different men . . . are so inclined to express both in speaking and in their treatises and writings so many wicked insults about women and their behavior."[4] These statements impelled her to detest herself "and the entire feminine sex, as though we were monstrosities in nature."[5]

4. Christine de Pizan, *The Book of the City of Ladies*, trans. Earl Jeffrey Richards, foreword by Marina Warner (New York, 1982), 1.1.1, pp. 3–4.
5. Ibid., 1.1.1–2, p. 5.

[Handwritten margin notes:] Humanism caused a re-analysis of all texts & ideas ∴ there was a re-ready of the traditions that had placed women in subordination

[Handwritten margin note:] Pisan

The rest of *The Book of the City of Ladies* presents a justification of the female sex and a vision of an ideal community of women. A pioneer, she has received the message of female inferiority and rejected it. From the fourteenth to the seventeenth century, a huge body of literature accumulated that responded to the dominant tradition.

The result was a literary explosion consisting of works by both men and women, in Latin and in the vernaculars: works enumerating the achievements of notable women; works rebutting the main accusations made against women; works arguing for the equal education of men and women; works defining and redefining women's proper role in the family, at court, in public; works describing women's lives and experiences. Recent monographs and articles have begun to hint at the great range of this movement, involving probably several thousand titles. The protofeminism of these "other voices" constitutes a significant fraction of the literary product of the early modern era.

The Catalogs

About 1365 the same Boccaccio whose *Corbaccio* rehearses the usual charges against female nature wrote another work, *Concerning Famous Women*. A humanist treatise drawing on classical texts, it praised 106 notable women, ninety-eight of them from pagan Greek and Roman antiquity, one (Eve) from the Bible, and seven from the medieval religious and cultural tradition; his book helped make all readers aware of a sex normally condemned or forgotten. Boccaccio's outlook nevertheless was unfriendly to women, for it singled out for praise those women who possessed the traditional virtues of chastity, silence, and obedience. Women who were active in the public realm—for example, rulers and warriors—were depicted as usually being lascivious and as suffering terrible punishments for entering the masculine sphere. Women were his subject, but Boccaccio's standard remained male.

Christine de Pizan's *Book of the City of Ladies* contains a second catalog, one responding specifically to Boccaccio's. Whereas Boccaccio portrays female virtue as exceptional, she depicts it as universal. Many women in history were leaders, or remained chaste despite the lascivious approaches of men, or were visionaries and brave martyrs.

The work of Boccaccio inspired a series of catalogs of illustrious women of the biblical, classical, Christian, and local pasts, among them Filippo da Bergamo's *Of Illustrious Women*, Pierre de Brantôme's *Lives of Illustrious Women*, Pierre Le Moyne's *Gallerie of Heroic Women*, and Pietro Paolo de Ribera's *Immortal Triumphs and Heroic Enterprises of 845 Women*. Whatever their embedded prejudices, these works drove home to the public the possibility of female excellence.

The Debate

At the same time, many questions remained: Could a woman be virtuous? Could she perform noteworthy deeds? Was she even, strictly speaking, of the same human species as men? These questions were debated over four centuries, in French, German, Italian, Spanish, and English, by authors male and female, among Catholics, Protestants, and Jews, in ponderous volumes and breezy pamphlets. The whole literary genre has been called the *querelle des femmes*, the "woman question."

The opening volley of this battle occurred in the first years of the fifteenth century, in a literary debate sparked by Christine de Pizan. She exchanged letters critical of Jean de Meun's contribution to *The Romance of the Rose* with two French royal secretaries, Jean de Montreuil and Gontier Col. When the matter became public, Jean Gerson, one of Europe's leading theologians, supported de Pizan's arguments against de Meun, for the moment silencing the opposition.

The debate resurfaced repeatedly over the next two hundred years. *The Triumph of Women* (1438) by Juan Rodríguez de la Camara (or Juan Rodríguez del Padron) struck a new note by presenting arguments for the superiority of women to men. *The Champion of Women* (1440–42) by Martin Le Franc addresses once again the negative views of women presented in *The Romance of the Rose* and offers counterevidence of female virtue and achievement.

A cameo of the debate on women is included in *The Courtier*, one of the most widely read books of the era, published by the Italian Baldassare Castiglione in 1528 and immediately translated into other European vernaculars. *The Courtier* depicts a series of evenings at the court of the duke of Urbino in which many men and some women of the highest social stratum amuse themselves by discussing a range of literary and social issues. The "woman question" is a pervasive theme throughout, and the third of its four books is devoted entirely to that issue.

In a verbal duel, Gasparo Pallavicino and Giuliano de' Medici present the main claims of the two traditions. Gasparo argues the innate inferiority of women and their inclination to vice. Only in bearing children do they profit the world. Giuliano counters that women share the same spiritual and mental capacities as men and may excel in wisdom and action. Men and women are of the same essence: just as no stone can be more perfectly a stone than another, so no human being can be more perfectly human than others, whether male or female. It was an astonishing assertion, boldly made to an audience as large as all Europe.

The Treatises

Humanism provided the materials for a positive counterconcept to the misogyny embedded in Scholastic philosophy and law and inherited from the Greek, Roman, and Christian pasts. A series of humanist treatises on marriage and family, on education and deportment, and on the nature of women helped construct these new perspectives.

The works by Francesco Barbaro and Leon Battista Alberti—*On Marriage* (1415) and *On the Family* (1434–37)—far from defending female equality, reasserted women's responsibility for rearing children and managing the housekeeping while being obedient, chaste, and silent. Nevertheless, they served the cause of reexamining the issue of women's nature by placing domestic issues at the center of scholarly concern and reopening the pertinent classical texts. In addition, Barbaro emphasized the companionate nature of marriage and the importance of a wife's spiritual and mental qualities for the well-being of the family.

These themes reappear in later humanist works on marriage and the education of women by Juan Luis Vives and Erasmus. Both were moderately sympathetic to the condition of women without reaching beyond the usual masculine prescriptions for female behavior.

An outlook more favorable to women characterizes the nearly unknown work *In Praise of Women* (ca. 1487) by the Italian humanist Bartolommeo Goggio. In addition to providing a catalog of illustrious women, Goggio argued that male and female are the same in essence, but that women (reworking the Adam and Eve narrative from quite a new angle) are actually superior. In the same vein, the Italian humanist Maria Equicola asserted the spiritual equality of men and women in *On Women* (1501). In 1525 Galeazzo Flavio Capra (or Capella) published his work *On the Excellence and Dignity of Women*. This humanist tradition of treatises defending the worthiness of women culminates in the work of Henricus Cornelius Agrippa *On the Nobility and Preeminence of the Female Sex*. No work by a male humanist more succinctly or explicitly presents the case for female dignity.

The Witch Books

While humanists grappled with the issues pertaining to women and family, other learned men turned their attention to what they perceived as a very great problem: witches. Witch-hunting manuals, explorations of the witch phenomenon, and even defenses of witches are not at first glance pertinent

Witches-
hostility;
prejudice
towards
women

Witch
theory was
accepted in
intellectual
circles;
was
grossly
exaggerated.

to the tradition of the other voice. But they do relate in this way: most accused witches were women. The hostility aroused by supposed witch activity is comparable to the hostility aroused by women. The evil deeds the victims of the hunt were charged with were exaggerations of the vices to which, many believed, all women were prone.

The connection between the witch accusation and the hatred of women is explicit in the notorious witch-hunting manual *The Hammer of Witches* (1486) by two Dominican inquisitors, Heinrich Krämer and Jacob Sprenger. Here the inconstancy, deceitfulness, and lustfulness traditionally associated with women are depicted in exaggerated form as the core features of witch behavior. These traits inclined women to make a bargain with the devil—sealed by sexual intercourse—by which they acquired unholy powers. Such bizarre claims, far from being rejected by rational men, were broadcast by intellectuals. The German Ulrich Molitur, the Frenchman Nicolas Rémy, and the Italian Stefano Guazzo all coolly informed the public of sinister orgies and midnight pacts with the devil. The celebrated French jurist, historian, and political philosopher Jean Bodin argued that because women were especially prone to diabolism, regular legal procedures could properly be suspended in order to try those accused of this "exceptional crime."

A few experts such as the physician Johann Weyer, a student of Agrippa's, raised their voices in protest. In 1563 he explained the witch phenomenon thus, without discarding belief in diabolism: the devil deluded foolish old women afflicted by melancholia, causing them to believe they had magical powers. Weyer's rational skepticism, which had good credibility in the community of the learned, worked to revise the conventional views of women and witchcraft.

Women's Works

Women
writing
was a
claim to
dignity

why not
may w. writes?
① No Ed
② Limited
Public
Roles
③ Cultural Silence

To the many categories of works produced on the question of women's worth must be added nearly all works written by women. A woman writing was in herself a statement of women's claim to dignity.

Only a few women wrote anything before the dawn of the modern era, for three reasons. First, they rarely received the education that would enable them to write. Second, they were not admitted to the public roles—as administrator, bureaucrat, lawyer or notary, or university professor—in which they might gain knowledge of the kinds of things the literate public thought worth writing about. Third, the culture imposed silence on women, considering speaking out a form of unchastity. Given these conditions, it is remarkable that any women wrote. Those who did before the fourteenth century were almost always nuns or religious women whose isolation made their pronouncements more acceptable.

From the fourteenth century on, the volume of women's writings rose. Women continued to write devotional literature, although not always as cloistered nuns. They also wrote diaries, often intended as keepsakes for their children; books of advice to their sons and daughters; letters to family members and friends; and family memoirs, in a few cases elaborate enough to be considered histories.

A few women wrote works directly concerning the "woman question," and some of these, such as the humanists Isotta Nogarola, Cassandra Fedele, Laura Cereta, and Olympia Morata, were highly trained. A few were professional writers, living by the income of their pens; the very first among them was Christine de Pizan, noteworthy in this context as in so many others. In addition to *The Book of the City of Ladies* and her critiques of *The Romance of the Rose*, she wrote *The Treasure of the City of Ladies* (a guide to social decorum for women), an advice book for her son, much courtly verse, and a full-scale history of the reign of King Charles V of France.

Women Patrons

Women who did not themselves write but encouraged others to do so boosted the development of an alternative tradition. Highly placed women patrons supported authors, artists, musicians, poets, and learned men. Such patrons, drawn mostly from the Italian elites and the courts of northern Europe, figure disproportionately as the dedicatees of the important works of early feminism.

For a start, it might be noted that the catalogs of Boccaccio and Alvaro de Luna were dedicated to the Florentine noblewoman Andrea Acciaiuoli and to Doña María, first wife of King Juan II of Castile, while the French translation of Boccaccio's work was commissioned by Anne of Brittany, wife of King Charles VIII of France. The humanist treatises of Goggio, Equicola, Vives, and Agrippa were dedicated, respectively, to Eleanora of Aragon, wife of Ercole I d'Este, duke of Ferrara; to Margherita Cantelma of Mantua; to Catherine of Aragon, wife of King Henry VIII of England; and to Margaret, duchess of Austria and regent of the Netherlands. As late as 1696, Mary Astell's *Serious Proposal to the Ladies, for the Advancement of Their True and Greatest Interest* was dedicated to Princess Anne of Denmark.

These authors presumed that their efforts would be welcome to female

[margin annotations:] women wrote letters; devotional literature · A few women were professional writers! · May women were patrons of writing

patrons, or they may have written at the bidding of those patrons. Silent themselves, perhaps even unresponsive, these loftily placed women helped shape the tradition of the other voice.

The Issues

The literary forms and patterns in which the tradition of the other voice presented itself have now been sketched. It remains to highlight the major issues around which this tradition crystallizes. In brief, there are four problems to which our authors return again and again, in plays and catalogs, in verse and letters, in treatises and dialogues, in every language: the problem of chastity, the problem of power, the problem of speech, and the problem of knowledge. Of these the greatest, preconditioning the others, is the problem of chastity.

THE PROBLEM OF CHASTITY. In traditional European culture, as in those of antiquity and others around the globe, chastity was perceived as woman's quintessential virtue—in contrast to courage, or generosity, or leadership, or rationality, seen as virtues characteristic of men. Opponents of women charged them with insatiable lust. Women themselves and their defenders—without disputing the validity of the standard—responded that women were capable of chastity.

The requirement of chastity kept women at home, silenced them, isolated them, left them in ignorance. It was the source of all other impediments. Why was it so important to the society of men, of whom chastity was not required, and who more often than not considered it their right to violate the chastity of any woman they encountered?

Female chastity ensured the continuity of the male-headed household. If a man's wife was not chaste, he could not be sure of the legitimacy of his offspring. If they were not his and they acquired his property, it was not his household, but some other man's, that had endured. If his daughter was not chaste, she could not be transferred to another man's household as his wife, and he was dishonored.

The whole system of the integrity of the household and the transmission of property was bound up in female chastity. Such a requirement pertained only to property-owning classes, of course. Poor women could not expect to maintain their chastity, least of all if they were in contact with high-status men to whom all women but those of their own household were prey.

In Catholic Europe, the requirement of chastity was further buttressed by moral and religious imperatives. Original sin was inextricably linked with the sexual act. Virginity was seen as heroic virtue, far more impressive than, say, the avoidance of idleness or greed. Monasticism, the cultural institution that dominated medieval Europe for centuries, was grounded in the renunciation of the flesh. The Catholic reform of the eleventh century imposed a similar standard on all the clergy and a heightened awareness of sexual requirements on all the laity. Although men were asked to be chaste, female unchastity was much worse: it led to the devil, as Eve had led mankind to sin.

To such requirements, women and their defenders protested their innocence. Furthermore, following the example of holy women who had escaped the requirements of family and sought the religious life, some women began to conceive of female communities as alternatives both to family and to the cloister. Christine de Pizan's city of ladies was such a community. Moderata Fonte and Mary Astell envisioned others. The luxurious salons of the French *précieuses* of the seventeenth century, or the comfortable English drawing rooms of the next, may have been born of the same impulse. Here women not only might escape, if briefly, the subordinate position that life in the family entailed but might also make claims to power, exercise their capacity for speech, and display their knowledge.

THE PROBLEM OF POWER. Women were excluded from power: the whole cultural tradition insisted on it. Only men were citizens, only men bore arms, only men could be chiefs or lords or kings. There were exceptions that did not disprove the rule, when wives or widows or mothers took the place of men, awaiting their return or the maturation of a male heir. A woman who attempted to rule in her own right was perceived as an anomaly, a monster, at once a deformed woman and an insufficient male, sexually confused and consequently unsafe.

The association of such images with women who held or sought power explains some otherwise odd features of early modern culture. Queen Elizabeth I of England, one of the few women to hold full regal authority in European history, played with such male/female images—positive ones, of course—in representing herself to her subjects. She was a prince, and manly, even though she was female. She was also (she claimed) virginal, a condition absolutely essential if she was to avoid the attacks of her opponents. Catherine de' Medici, who ruled France as widow and regent for her sons, also adopted such imagery in defining her position. She chose as one symbol the figure of Artemisia, an androgynous ancient warrior-heroine who combined a female persona with masculine powers.

Power in a woman, without such sexual imagery, seems to have been indigestible by the culture. A rare note was struck by the Englishman Sir Thomas Elyot in his *Defence of Good Women* (1540), justifying both women's participation in civic life and their prowess in arms. The old tune was sung by the Scots reformer John Knox in his *First Blast of the Trumpet against the Monstrous Regiment of Women* (1558); for him rule by women, defects in nature, was a hideous contradiction in terms.

The confused sexuality of the imagery of female potency was not re-served for rulers. Any woman who excelled was likely to be called an Ama-zon, recalling the self-mutilated warrior women of antiquity who repudiated all men, gave up their sons, and raised only their daughters. She was often said to have "exceeded her sex" or to have possessed "masculine virtue"—as the very fact of conspicuous excellence conferred masculinity even on the female subject. The catalogs of notable women often showed those female heroes dressed in armor, armed to the teeth, like men. Amazonian heroines romp through the epics of the age—Ariosto's *Orlando Furioso* (1532) and Spenser's *Faerie Queene* (1590–1609). Excellence in a woman was perceived as a claim for power, and power was reserved for the masculine realm. A woman who possessed either one was masculinized and lost title to her own female identity.

THE PROBLEM OF SPEECH. Just as power had a sexual dimension when it was claimed by women, so did speech. A good woman spoke little. Excessive speech was an indication of unchastity. By speech, women seduced men. Eve had lured Adam into sin by her speech. Accused witches were commonly ac-cused of having spoken abusively, or irrationally, or simply too much. As en-lightened a figure as Francesco Barbaro insisted on silence in a woman, which he linked to her perfect unanimity with her husband's will and her unblem-ished virtue (her chastity). Another Italian humanist, Leonardo Bruni, in ad-vising a noblewoman on her studies, barred her not from speech but from public speaking. That was reserved for men.

Related to the problem of speech was that of costume—another, if silent, form of self-expression. Assigned the task of pleasing men as their primary occupation, elite women often tended toward elaborate costume, hairdressing, and the use of cosmetics. Clergy and secular moralists alike condemned these practices. The appropriate function of costume and adorn-ment was to announce the status of a woman's husband or father. Any further indulgence in adornment was akin to unchastity.

THE PROBLEM OF KNOWLEDGE. When the Italian noblewoman Isotta Nogarola had begun to attain a reputation as a humanist, she was accused of incest—a telling instance of the association of learning in women with un-chastity. That chilling association inclined any woman who was educated to deny that she was or to make exaggerated claims of heroic chastity.

If educated women were pursued with suspicions of sexual misconduct, women seeking an education faced an even more daunting obstacle: the assumption that women were by nature incapable of learning, that reasoning was a particularly masculine ability. Just as they proclaimed their chastity, women and their defenders insisted on their capacity for learning. The major work by a male writer on female education—that by Juan Luis Vives, *On the Education of a Christian Woman* (1523)—granted female capacity for intellection but still argued that a woman's whole education was to be shaped around the requirement of chastity and a future within the household. Female writers of the following generations—Marie de Gournay in France, Anna Maria van Schurman in Holland, Mary Astell in England—began to envision other possibilities.

The pioneers of female education were the Italian women humanists who managed to attain a literacy in Latin and a knowledge of classical and Christian literature equivalent to that of prominent men. Their works implicitly and explicitly raise questions about women's social roles, defining problems that beset women attempting to break out of the cultural limits that had bound them. Like Christine de Pizan, who achieved an advanced education through her father's tutoring and her own devices, their bold questioning makes clear the importance of training. Only when women were educated to the same standard as male leaders would they be able to raise that other voice and insist on their dignity as human beings morally, intellectually, and legally equal to men.

The Other Voice

The other voice, a voice of protest, was mostly female, but it was also male. It spoke in the vernaculars and in Latin, in treatises and dialogues, in plays and poetry, in letters and diaries, and in pamphlets. It battered at the wall of prejudice that encircled women and raised a banner announcing its claims. The female was equal (or even superior) to the male in essential nature—moral, spiritual, intellectual. Women were capable of higher education, of holding positions of power and influence in the public realm, and of speaking and writing persuasively. The last bastion of masculine supremacy, centered on the notions of a woman's primary domestic responsibility and the requirement of female chastity, was not as yet assaulted—although visions of productive female communities as alternatives to the family indicated an awareness of the problem.

During the period 1300–1700, the other voice remained only a voice, and one only dimly heard. It did not result—yet—in an alteration of social patterns. Indeed, to this day they have not entirely been altered. Yet the call for justice issued as long as six centuries ago by those writing in the tradition

[Marginal handwritten notes: "Women were seen as incapable of learning"; "Women only needed to learn of chastity & domestic duty"; "Only when women had education similar to men could they offer a voice to counter them"; "Other Voice was one of protest"; "Women were capable of thought"; "1300-1700 still only a voice"]

of the other voice must be recognized as the source and origin of the mature feminist tradition and of the realignment of social institutions accomplished in the modern age.

W e thank the volume editors in this series, who responded with many suggestions to an earlier draft of this introduction, making it a collaborative enterprise. Many of their suggestions and criticisms have resulted in revisions of this introduction, though we remain responsible for the final product.

PROJECTED TITLES IN THE SERIES

[handwritten margin note: Other voice was the origin of the mature; modern feminist tradition]

Madeleine de Scudéry, *Orations and Rhetorical Dialogues*, edited and translated by Jane Donawerth with Julie Strongson

Justine Siegemund, *The Court Midwife of the Electorate of Brandenburg* (1690), edited and translated by Lynne Tatlock

Gabrielle Suchon, *"On Philosophy" and "On Morality,"* edited and translated by Domna Stanton with Rebecca Wilkin

Sara Copio Sullam, *Sara Copio Sullam: Jewish Poet and Intellectual in Early Seventeenth-Century Venice*, edited and translated by Don Harrán

Arcangela Tarabotti, *Convent Life as Inferno: A Report*, introduction and notes by Francesca Medioli, translated by Letizia Panizza

Arcangela Tarabotti, *Paternal Tyranny*, edited and translated by Letizia Panizza

Laura Terracina, *Works*, edited and translated by Michael Sherberg

Katharina Schütz Zell, *Selected Writings*, edited and translated by Elsie McKee

INTRODUCTION

THE OTHER VOICE

You begin your search for Jacqueline Pascal by taking the Paris suburban train from Gare Saint-Michel to Saint-Rémy-lès-Chevreuse. Then you walk along the valley of the Chevreuse to the ruins of the convent of Port-Royal. Soeur Jacqueline worked and died here, but her remains have disappeared. When Louis XIV ordered the destruction of the convent in 1710, even the cemetery was razed.

In the small museum on the site, an oil portrait labeled *Jacqueline Pascal* depicts a squarely built nun seated demurely on a chair. But the portrait is apparently a fraud: an artist painted the Port-Royal religious habit over an earlier portrait of a laywoman wearing a pearl necklace.[1]

It is in her writings alone that Jacqueline Pascal survives. They present her model of education for women, rooted in her direction of the convent school at Port-Royal. They defend the right to pursue a vocation against paternal authority. Forged in the controversy over Jansenism, they justify the freedom to dissent from church condemnations. In her works Jacqueline Pascal gives voice to the broader struggle of Port-Royal to exalt the intellectual and moral rights of women against royal and episcopal commands to silence.

THE LIFE OF JACQUELINE PASCAL

On October 5, 1625, Jacqueline Pascal was born into a family of the *noblesse de robe* in Clermont-Ferrand. Her father Étienne, a lawyer and judge, pursued mathematical research. Her mother, Antoinette Begon, died shortly after

1. For a discussion of the detective work surrounding the alleged portrait of Jacqueline Pascal, see Thérèse Picquenard, "Portrait dit de Jacqueline Pascal," *Chroniques de Port-Royal*, no. 31 (1982): 104–5.

Jacqueline's birth. Her sister Gilberte (1620–87) and her brother Blaise (1623–62) accompanied her through their education at home, which their father personally directed.

In 1631 Étienne Pascal moved his family to Paris, where he plunged into the intellectual debates of the city's burgeoning salons and academies. Charged with teaching her sister to read, Gilberte Pascal records Jacqueline's precocious taste for poetry: "We began to teach her to read at age seven. My father had given me this responsibility. But I encountered many obstacles, because she had a great aversion to this. Whatever I tried, she wouldn't do her lessons. Then one day by chance I read some verse out loud. She liked the rhythm so much that she said: 'Whenever you want me to read, make me read a book of verse. Then I'll do my lessons as much as you want.'"[2] By age eight, Jacqueline was writing poetry herself. At eleven she became the talk of Paris salons when she and two other young girls wrote and performed a complete five-act play. Acclaimed as a literary prodigy, at age twelve Jacqueline published a book of poetry.[3]

In 1638 her poetic fame became national. Queen Anne of Austria, the wife of Louis XIII, summoned her to court at Saint-Germain-en-Laye to thank her for her recent poem on the queen's pregnancy.[4] Jacqueline astonished the court by composing spontaneous poems at the request of Mademoiselle de Montpensier[5] and of the Duchesse d'Aiguillon.[6]

In the same year tragedy struck the Pascal household. Disgraced over a financial dispute with Cardinal Richelieu, Étienne Pascal fled into exile outside Paris. Jacqueline succumbed to smallpox. After her recovery, her poetry and her correspondence assumed a more austere and religious tone.

In 1639 Jacqueline managed to rehabilitate her family's political fortunes. Performing in a play at the home of the Duchesse d'Aiguillon, the niece of Cardinal Richelieu, Jacqueline charmed the cardinal. Pleading her father's case, Jacqueline persuaded Richelieu to pardon him and personally reconciled them in an interview shortly thereafter. To show his new favor, Richelieu appointed Étienne Pascal supervisor of taxes in Rouen.

2. Gilberte Pascal Périer, *Mémoire composé et écrit de la main de Madame Périer, touchant la vie de la Soeur Jacqueline de Sainte Euphémie Pascal sa soeur*, in Jacqueline Pascal, Gilberte Pascal Périer, and Marguerite Périer, *Lettres, opuscules et mémoires de Madame Périer et de Jacqueline, soeurs de Pascal, et de Marguerite Périer, sa nièce, publiés sur les manuscrits originiaux par M. P. Faugère*, ed. Armand Prosper Faugère (Paris: Auguste Vaton, 1845), 54–55. Hereafter cited as *LOM.*

3. Jacqueline Pascal, *Vers de la petite Pascal* (Paris, 1637).

4. See Jacqueline Pascal, "Epigramme sur le mouvement que la reine a senti de son enfant, présentée aussi à Sa Majesté," *LOM,* 121–22. The queen was carrying the future Louis XIV.

5. See Jacqueline Pascal, "Épigramme à Mademoiselle, faite sur-le-champ par son commandement," *LOM,* 123.

6. See Jacqueline Pascal, "Autre Épigramme à Madame d'Autefort, faite le même jour sur-le-champ, par le commandement aussi de Mademoiselle," *LOM,* 123.

In the provincial salons of Normandy, Jacqueline's reputation as a poet grew. Guided by Rouen's leading writer, the dramatist Pierre Corneille, in 1640 Jacqueline won the coveted Prix de la Tour for her poem "On the Conception of the Virgin."[7] Her brother Blaise also began to receive national acclaim for his mathematical genius. To help his father streamline the burdensome job of calculating the tax records of the province, the adolescent Blaise devised a counting machine that performed the four basic mathematical operations.

Although Jacqueline Pascal would later abandon writing poetry as incompatible with her religious vocation, her formation as a poet influenced her later work. Many of her letters and later prose works bear the trace of the epigram: the concise, proverb-like phrase that is a central feature of her adolescent poetry. She also developed a taste for another fashionable salon genre: the moral portrait. Her *Memoir of Mère Marie Angélique*[8] and numerous letters carefully evoke the moral temperament of a particular person.

The Rouen years also witnessed a religious turning point for the Pascals: their entry into the Jansenist movement. In 1646 Étienne Pascal fell and broke his hip. By expert manipulation of the bones two folk practitioners managed to heal the fracture. Religiously motivated in their service to the sick, the healers explained their attachment to the Port-Royal convent in Paris. They discussed the militant Augustinian theology of the convent, centered in the theories of the late bishop Cornelius Jansenius[9] as interpreted by the convent chaplain, Saint-Cyran,[10] and by the convent's leading theological ally, Antoine Arnauld.[11] Previously perfunctory in their Catholic prac-

---

7. See Jacqueline Pascal, "Sur la conception de la Vierge," *LOM*, 130–31.

8. See Jacqueline Pascal, *Relation de la Soeur Jacqueline de Sainte Euphémie Pascal, concernant la Mère Marie Angélique, LOM*, 223–27.

9. Cornelius Jansenius (1585–1638), professor of theology at Louvain, appointed rector of Louvain in 1635 and bishop of Ypres in 1636, defended a strict Augustinian theory of the radical concupiscence of humanity after the fall (the incapacity of humans to choose anything but evil through their own power), the complete dependence upon grace for salvation, and the small number of the elect. His posthumous work *Augustinus* (1640) and its condemnation by the Sorbonne and by the papacy launched a bitter controversy between Jansenists and their critics over the nature of grace. His political pamphlet *Mars Gallicus*, which criticized Richelieu's policy of alliances with Protestant powers against Catholic Spain, rendered the Jansenists suspect as political as well as religious dissidents.

10. Jean du Vergier de Hauranne, abbé de Saint-Cyran (1581–1643), was a close associate of Jansenius at Louvain and a defender of the Jansenist theology of grace. An ally of Mère Angélique starting in 1633, he became confessor of Port-Royal in 1636 and was imprisoned by Richelieu in 1638. He was the author of numerous treatises and letters on theological topics.

11. Antoine Arnauld (1612–94), the leading theologian of Jansenist movement, was also celebrated for philosophical controversies with Descartes and Malebranche. He was a critic of Jesuit moral casuistry. His early work *De la fréquente communion* (1643) established his rigorist position on the desirability of delaying sacramental absolution and the reception of communion until the soul has undergone a radical conversion.

tice, all the members of the Pascal family gradually adhered to the austere moral and theological tenets of the Jansenist circle.

In 1647 Jacqueline and Blaise returned to Paris. Blaise pursued his groundbreaking experiments on the vacuum. Descartes visited the Pascal household to honor the new scientific celebrity, now his rival.[12] Jacqueline nursed the sickly Blaise, afflicted by a rare form of tuberculosis, as she intensified her religious study and devotional life. Both became ardent members of the lay circle that attended services at the convent of Port-Royal de Paris. Under the influence of the convent's confessor, Abbé Singlin,[13] and the abbess, Mère Angélique,[14] Jacqueline decided she had a vocation to become a nun at Port-Royal.

Étienne Pascal did not share Jacqueline's enthusiasm for her religious vocation. To resolve the conflict, father and daughter agreed that Jacqueline' would remain with her father until his death and that Étienne' would permit his daughter to live a secluded home life as a de facto nun.

Jacqueline remained under the direction of Port-Royal, composing her devotional treatise *On the Mystery of the Death of Our Lord Jesus Christ*[15] shortly before she entered the convent. The work elaborates a one-to-one correspondence between attributes of Christ's suffering in his Passion and the analogous virtues that a female disciple of Christ should cultivate. Clearly shaped by Jansenist theology, the treatise dwells on the passivity and abandonment of Christ in the Passion rather than on the physical and emotional dimensions of his suffering on the cross.

After her father died on September 24, 1651, Jacqueline prepared to enter the convent. It was Blaise, grown cool to religious concerns, who now begged her to remain at home. Defying her brother, however, Jacqueline entered Port-Royal on January 4, 1652.

12. For a description of Descartes's visit, see Jacqueline Pascal, "Lettre de Jacqueline Pascal à Madame Périer (25 Septembre 1647)," *LOM,* 509–12.

13. Abbé Antoine Singlin (1607–64), a protégé of Saint-Cyran, began his association with Port-Royal (1637) as a teacher of the boys in the *petites écoles.* The spiritual director of Jacqueline Pascal as a laywoman and as a nun, he became the chaplain of the convent until 1661, when he was forced to go into hiding as the anti-Jansenist persecution intensified. Throughout the "crisis of the signature," he counseled the nuns to sign the formulary without reservation.

14. Jacqueline Arnauld, Mère Angélique (1591–1661), was appointed abbess of Port-Royal as an adolescent and began the reform of the convent in 1608. Her support for Saint-Cyran in the 1630s turned the convent into a center of Jansenism. Her numerous letters and addresses, widely published by the Jansenist press, her revival of the convent school, and her alliance with powerful aristocrats (Madame de Longueville, Madame de Sablé) gave her a prominence well beyond the confines of the order.

15. See Jacqueline Pascal, *Écrit de Mademoiselle Jacqueline Pascal sur le mystère de la mort de Notre-Seigneur J.-C., LOM,* 157–76.

Under the direction of Mère Agnès,[16] the sister of Mère Angélique, Jacqueline pursued an abbreviated postulancy, given the reclusive years she had already spent in service to her father.

Still opposed to her vocation, Blaise communicated with his sister through letters and visits. The conflict between Jacqueline and Blaise became especially bitter over the question of the dowry. As was customary in monastic houses, Jacqueline expected her family to provide her convent with a substantial dowry at the moment she professed her vows. Since her father had left a large bequest to his three children, she assumed that her share of the inheritance would constitute this dowry. Unexpectedly Blaise and Gilberte, now married to Florin Périer, opposed the project and threatened legal action to keep the money in the family.

In her subsequent *Report of Soeur Jacqueline de Sainte Euphémie to the Mother Prioress of Port-Royal des Champs,*[17] Soeur Jacqueline recounts her struggle to accept the advice of her superiors to enter the convent without a dowry and to overcome her repugnance at the humiliation of an undowered vocation. Breaking the link between a dowry and the right to pursue a religious vocation constituted one of the axes of Port-Royal's reform of monastic life. In her later practice as novice mistress, Soeur Jacqueline would stress the freedom of the religious vocation and its independence from financial considerations. At the end of the dispute, however, Blaise Pascal relented and made a substantial contribution to the convent. Jacqueline was clothed in the religious habit on May 26, 1652, and solemnly professed vows on June 5, 1653.

The convent Jacqueline Pascal entered was already riven by controversy. Founded in 1204, the original Port-Royal (Port-Royal des Champs) was in a valley twenty miles south of Paris. By the beginning of the seventeenth century, the convent had declined to a dozen nonobservant nuns living in a dilapidated building. In 1608 the young abbess, Mère Angélique, began a vigorous reform that made the convent a model of asceticism. Flush with new vocations, in 1630 the community moved to a larger building in the Faubourg Saint-Jacques: Port-Royal de Paris. In 1638 a group of laymen (*les solitaires*) occupied the old buildings at Port-Royal des Champs and began their *petites écoles* for boys, complementing the work of the con-vent school for girls revived by Mère Angélique. In 1649 the bourgeoning community sent some of the nuns to reoccupy the Port-Royal des Champs cloister, thus establishing two con-

16. Jeanne Arnauld, Mère Agnès (1593–1671), was appointed successor to Mère Angélique as abbess of Port-Royal in 1636 and in 1658. She was mistress of novices during Jacqueline Pascal's novitiate and was the primary author of the Constitutions of Port-Royal (1665).

17. See Jacqueline Pascal, *Relation de la Soeur Jacqueline de Sainte Euphémie, adressée par elle à la mère prieure de Port-Royal des Champs, LOM,* 177–222.

vent locations. Throughout its reformed period, Port-Royal was largely an enterprise of the Arnauld family, another dynasty of the *noblesse de robe*. Sisters Jeanne Arnauld (Mère Angélique) and Agnès Arnauld (Mère Agnès) were its major superiors. Their brother Antoine Arnauld was its leading theologian, brother Henri (bishop of Angers) its chief episcopal defender, and nephew Antoine Le Maître a preeminent teacher and writer in the *petites écoles*.

From its inception, the reformed Port-Royal aroused opposition. Jesuit theologians attacked its moral rigorism and its theology of radical human depravity as suspiciously Calvinist. Political authorities, starting with Richelieu, criticized the democratic tendencies of the convent's theology and noted the attraction of the convent church for prominent aristocrats opposed to royal absolutism. With the appointment of Saint-Cyran as convent chaplain in 1636, the Augustinianism of Port-Royal became a militant Jansenism.

Soon after profession, Soeur Jacqueline assumed several positions of authority in the community: schoolmistress in the convent school, novice mistress, and subprioress. In her role as schoolmistress, Soeur Jacqueline composed her most influential work, *A Rule for Children*.[18] Written in 1657 at the request of her spiritual director, Abbé Singlin, the treatise details the spirit and method of education she employed with the boarding students at the convent.

On several particulars, the *Rule* reflects the pedagogical principles of the Jansenist *messieurs* who directed the *petites écoles* for boys. Like the *messieurs*, Soeur Jacqueline insists that pupils' successful moral and religious education demands that the teacher develop a personal, comprehensive knowledge of the moral character of each one.' Humility is the key virtue to be cultivated; dishonesty is the vice to be extirpated. Their salvation requires strict surveillance at all times, but she eschews violent measures such as corporal punishment, which only alienate children. Soeur Jacqueline's methods incorporate several of the pedagogical innovations of the *petites écoles*. She introduces the phonetic method of learning French and tutorial methods of instruction. Nonetheless, the curriculum is much less ambitious than that proposed in the *petites écoles*.

Even though influenced by the pedagogy of the male Jansenists, the educational theory and practice of Soeur Jacqueline differ substantially from that championed by the *messieurs*. This difference reflects a clear concern to offer an education proper to a school with a female faculty and student body.

First, the model of education she proposes integrates the students into

18. See Jacqueline Pascal, *Règlement pour les enfants*, LOM, 228–300.

the liturgical life of the convent. The typical school day begins as follows: rising between 4:00 a.m. and 5:00 a.m.; rising prayer; dressing in silence; silent kneeling prayer of adoration; recitation of liturgical offices of prime and compline; examination of conscience; silent breakfast at 7:00 a.m., during which the martyrology is read aloud. The entire day follows such a religiously charged pattern, modeled after the strictest monastic tradition.

If this approach to education reflects Port-Royal's effort to renew the ascetic fervor of the primitive church, it also contains its own subversion of the religious and the social orders. By insisting that pupils participate in the monastic office rather than confining their piety to popular devotions, the Port-Royal school subtly undermined the distinction between the laity and the vowed religious. The only book each pupil was to own, a Latin/French psalter, was not an uncontroversial choice in a period when the church frowned on vernacular translations of the Bible and the psalter was considered the exclusive prayer book of priests and religious. The catechism recommended by Soeur Jacqueline, the *Théologie familière* of Saint-Cyran, had been censured by the archdiocese of Paris in 1643. The *Rule's* instructions for preparing students for confession and Holy Communion, which stress the danger of sacrilege and discourage frequent reception of the sacraments, trumpeted the school's Jansenist ethos.

Even more subversive is the spiritual authority the *Rule* gives to women. If the priest is the sole confessor, the nun-teacher is now spiritual director, preparing the pupils for confession, knowing their moral struggles, monitoring their conduct after confession, and advising the confessor on the general moral state of the class. The chapter on instruction condemns rote catechesis. The nun-teacher is to explain religious doctrine at length, find appropriate applications for female students, field their questions, and encourage reflection on religious truths rather than simple memorization. This insistence on young laywomen's critical acquisition of a theological culture usually reserved to priests fueled the suspicion that Port-Royal was subtly eroding the hierarchical structure of the church.

During Soeur Jacqueline's decade at Port-Royal, the opposition to the Jansenists intensified. In 1653 Pope Innocent X issued the bull *Cum occasione*, which condemned as heretical five propositions concerning grace and freedom. It further argued that Cornelius Jansenius had defended these propositions in his controversial *Augustinus* (1640). In 1656 Pope Alexander VII reiterated this condemnation in *Ad sanctam beati Petri sedem* and insisted that the church was condemning these propositions precisely in the way that Jansenius had held them.

Reinforced by similar condemnations by the Sorbonne theology faculty and by the Assembly of the Clergy, the papal censures seemed to mark the end of Jansenism as a Catholic movement. Antoine Arnauld, however, devised a clever theological distinction to defend the Jansenist viewpoint. Arnauld argued that the church enjoyed divine assistance only in judgments concerning matters of faith and morals (*droit*), since these truths are central to salvation itself. However, when the church made judgments on matters of fact (*fait*), such as whether a given book was indeed heretical, its judgments were fallible, hence vulnerable to subsequent revision or even reversal. The application to the Jansenist case was clear. The Jansenists accepted the church's judgment of *droit* that the five propositions were heretical. But they rejected the judgment of *fait* that Jansenius and his disciples had endorsed such theories. The *droit/fait* distinction enraged the critics of the Jansenists, who argued that it destroyed church authority, and it disturbed a minority of Jansenists (especially the Port-Royal nuns) as disingenuous. However, it quickly gained support among the Jansenist clergy and among the Jansenist sympathizers in the aristocracy.

As the persecution against Port-Royal intensified, the unexpected occurred: a miracle. On Good Friday, March 24, 1656, the nuns and pupils in the convent boarding school went to the chapel to venerate a relic of the crown of thorns. Marguerite Périer, the niece of Soeur Jacqueline and a pupil at the school, had been suffering from a large abscess beneath her eye. The bone under the abscess was diseased, the wound had repeatedly hemorrhaged, and her eyesight had seriously deteriorated. Several doctors had recently examined Marguerite and had scheduled an operation. Shortly after she touched the relic to her eye, however, the abscess disappeared and she totally regained her vision.

Despite the allegations of fraud by Jesuit pamphleteers, a series of medical and legal inquests led the archdiocese of Paris to declare the authenticity of the miracle on October 22, 1656. An exultant Blaise Pascal, who was periodically publishing his Provincial Letters against Jesuit moral laxness the same year, celebrated the miracle as a sign of divine favor for the Jansenists against their enemies.

As soon as Louis XIV assumed personal government of the realm in 1661, the persecution quickened. On February 1, 1661, the Assembly of the Clergy drew up a formulary (*formulaire*) to be signed by all priests, nuns, and teachers. In the formulary the signatory submitted to the popes' earlier condemnations of Jansenius and the five propositions. On April 13 the king's council ratified the formulary and planned specific moves against Port-Royal, the center of Jansenist resistance. On April 20 the confessors and spiritual directors of the convent were dispersed. On April 23 and 24 the boarding students were dismissed and the convent school was closed. On May 31 the postulants and novices were expelled.

On June 8 the vicars general of the archdiocese of Paris officially presented the formulary for signature by subjects of the archdiocese. The Port-Royal nuns were singled out for signature. The vicars, however, softened the formulary by their introductory pastoral instruction (*mandement*), which explicitly recognized the validity of the *droit/fait* distinction in interpreting the condemnation of Jansenius.

Although Antoine Arnauld had urged the nuns to sign this irenic document, Jacqueline Pascal refused. In her letter of June 23, 1661, Soeur Jacqueline insisted that signing would be duplicitous, seeming to assent to a condemnation she knew to be wrong. She insisted that women, despite their lack of formal theological education, had a right to make a conscientious decision on this matter. She argued that martyrdom would be preferable to the violation of conscience that the diplomatic Jansenist clergy were tempting the nuns to accept: "What are we afraid of? Exile and dispersion for the nuns, confiscation of our temporal goods, prison and death, if you will? But isn't this our glory and shouldn't this be our joy?"[19] Despite her objections, Soeur Jacqueline signed the formulary with the other nuns on June 24–25. In violation of Arnauld's counsel, however, they added written codicils to their signatures specifying the heavily conditional nature of their assent to the church's condemnations.

Simultaneous with the "crisis of the signature," Port-Royal underwent several ecclesiastical inquests. The first series, conducted by the newly imposed overseer of the convent, Monsieur Bail, occurred on June 26–29. The second series, conducted by Monsieur Bail and Monsieur de Contes, grand vicar of Paris, took place on July 11–26.

The interrogation of Soeur Jacqueline tried to unearth possibly heretical beliefs that the nun might have communicated to her charges in her roles as novice mistress and teacher. Avoiding entrapment on the more controversial Jansenist doctrines, Soeur Jacqueline gave a number of equivocal responses. On the disputed issue of the small number of the saved, for example, she artfully transformed a controverted point of grace and freedom into a question of piety: "Usually, when I am praying, especially when I am before a crucifix, that question comes to mind. Then I say to the Lord: 'My God, how is it possible, after everything you have done for us, that so many people perish in misery?' But when these thoughts haunt me, I reject them, because I don't

[margin note: J. refused to sign the letter bk of her conscience]

---

19. See Jacqueline Pascal, "Lettre de la Soeur Jacqueline de Sainte Euphémie Pascal à la Soeur Angélique (23 juin 1661)," *LOM*, 402–14.

think I have the right to sound out the secrets of God."[20] If Soeur Jacqueline opposed Arnauld's casuistry on the question of the signature, she was more than capable of devising her own subtle theological distinctions to defend the orthodoxy of Port-Royal in the moment of its virtual dissolution.

On October 4, 1661, Jacqueline Pascal died. The physical cause of her death remains obscure. But the chroniclers of Port-Royal immediately proclaimed her the proto-martyr of the movement. In the space of several months she had witnessed the destruction of her life's work (the school and the novitiate) and had been subjected to a harrowing interrogation. Above all, by a bitterly regretted signature she had compromised the rights of conscience she had so stoutly defended.

THE WORKS OF JACQUELINE PASCAL

Jacqueline Pascal's works cover a wide variety of genres: poetry, letters, biography, autobiography, devotional treatise, educational treatise, judicial transcript. The only work published in her lifetime, *Vers de la petite Pascal* (1637), has long since disappeared. The posthumous emergence of the canon of Jacqueline Pascal, a process requiring two centuries, rests primarily on two sources for documentation.

The first source derives from the Périer family. Shortly after Jacqueline's death, Gilberte Pascal Périer used a prolonged stay in Paris to collect her sister's extant papers. These papers then became a part of the Périer family archives in Clermont. Gilberte's daughter, Marguerite Périer, entrusted this collection of Jacqueline Pascal's papers to the Oratorian community in Clermont when renewed anti-Jansenist persecution forced her to flee to the Netherlands. A scholarly Oratorian, Père Pierre Guerrier, copied the documents and produced a multivolume manuscript collection of Jacqueline Pascal's writings.

The second source derives from the publications of Port-Royal itself. From the beginning of the persecution, a group of nuns led by Mère Angélique de Saint Jean carefully conserved key documents to prove the orthodoxy of the convent and to chronicle its struggle against its tormentors. Sympathetic Jansenist printers, often working from clandestine presses in France and abroad, published this abundant literature. The 1665 edition of the Constitutions of Port-Royal added Jacqueline Pascal's *Rule for Children* as an appendix. The *History of the Persecutions of the Nuns of Port-Royal* (1733) published the transcript of the 1661 interrogation of Soeur Jacqueline.

20. Jacqueline Pascal, *Interrogatoire de Soeur Jacqueline de Sainte Euphémie (Pascal), sous-prieure et maîtresse des novices*, LOM, 302.

Certain works of Jacqueline Pascal have survived in only one source. A number of the poems and letters are present only in the Guerrier manuscript. The biographical sketch of Mère Angélique survived only in the published Port-Royal chronicles. Several works, however, are in both sources, often with variations in the text. As Pascal editors Faugère and Mesnard have argued, the Guerrier manuscript, closer to the original autograph, usually provides the more reliable version.

In 1845 two scholars independently produced published editions of the collected works of Jacqueline Pascal. Victor Cousin, a philosopher who devoted the later part of his life to books on seventeenth-century women, produced a biography of Jacqueline Pascal and a collection of her writings.[21] Pascal scholar Armand Prosper Faugère published the complete edition of the works of Jacqueline Pascal, Gilberte Pascal Périer, and Marguerite Périer.[22] Based on a wider collection of manuscripts and a more critical use of sources, the Faugère edition is the more reliable. In the latter half of the twentieth century, Jean Mesnard's critical edition of the works of Blaise Pascal included an annotated version of the writings of other members of the Pascal family, including Jacqueline.[23]

For this translation I used the Faugère edition as the major source, taking account of variants in the Cousin and the Mesnard editions. I also consulted the Faugère archives in the Bibliothèque Mazarine[24] to illuminate Faugère's editorial decisions. The Faugère edition of Jacqueline Pascal's works commends itself on several counts. Since its appearance in 1845, it has proved remarkably accurate and durable. The discovery of numerous Jansenist manuscripts and printed works since then has not altered the canon of Jacqueline Pascal as fixed by Faugère. The recent Mesnard edition (1964–91) of the works of the Pascal family largely confirms the accuracy of his editorial work. The availability of Faugère's edition on the Internet via the Gallica Project of the Bibliothèque nationale de France provides easy access for readers who wish to compare this translation with the French original. My translation of Pascal's *Rule for Children*, however, synthesizes the Faugère and Cousin versions, for reasons I explain in my introduction to that work.

21. Victor Cousin, ed., *Jacqueline Pascal: Premières études sur les femmes illustres et la société du XVIIe siècle*, 8th ed. (Paris: Didier, 1877). The original edition was published in 1845.

22. Jacqueline Pascal, Gilberte Pascal Périer, and Marguerite Périer, *Lettres, opuscules et mémoires de Madame Périer et de Jacqueline, soeurs de Pascal, et de Marguerite Périer, sa nièce, publiés sur les manuscrits originaux par M. P. Faugère*, ed. Armand Prosper Faugère (Paris: Auguste Vaton, 1845). Cited throughout as *LOM*.

23. Blaise Pascal, *Oeuvres complètes avec tous les documents biographiques et critiques; les oeuvres d'Étienne, de Gilberte et de Jacqueline Pascal et celles de Marguerite Périer; la correspondance des Pascal et des Périer*, 4 vols., ed. Jean Mesnard (Paris: Desclée de Brouwer, 1964–91).

24. Bibliothèque Mazarine: Fonds Faugère (1810–87).

This book includes the following works by Jacqueline Pascal:

Poems

Poetry (1638–43): This section presents the major poems Jacqueline Pascal wrote during her adolescence. The selection privileges poetry using feminine images of God and defending 'her writing as a divine vocation.

Virtue

On the Mystery of the Death of Our Lord Jesus Christ (1651): Written shortly before she entered Port-Royal, this devotional treatise matches each moment in the Passion of Christ with a particular virtue that the female disciple of Christ should cultivate.

Vocation

Report of Soeur Jacqueline de Sainte Euphémie to the Mother Prioress of Port-Royal des Champs (1653): This autobiographical narrative recounts "the crisis of the dowry" and Jacqueline Pascal's long-standing effort to maintain her vocation against family opposition.

Running a School

A Rule for Children (1657): Based on her work at the convent school, this treatise presents Jacqueline Pascal's philosophy of education for women. The first part details the daily order of the school. The second part studies the spirit and the virtues that should animate this education.

Defense vs. charges of heresy

Interrogation of Soeur Jacqueline de Sainte Euphémie (Pascal) (June 1661): A transcript of Jacqueline Pascal's interrogation by church authorities during the "crisis of the signature," the text presents her defense of Port-Royal against charges of heresy.

Ideal Nun

A Memoir of Mère Marie Angélique by Soeur Jacqueline de Sainte Euphémie Pascal (August 1661): A biographical sketch of the Port-Royal abbess, the text offers a portrait of the ideal nun. The moral rigorism, the critique of superstition, and the stress on the fear of God carry a Jansenist stamp.

Contesting of male authority

Letters (1647–61): This selection of letters privileges those in which Jacqueline Pascal contests male authority on behalf of conscience. Of special interest are the letters to her father Étienne (1648) and her brother Blaise (1652) defending her right to pursue a religious vocation and the letter on "the crisis of the signature" (1661) defending the right to dissent from the church's condemnation of Jansenius.

INFLUENCES ON HER AND HER INFLUENCE

The sources of Jacqueline Pascal's thought are almost entirely theological. References to the Bible and to the Catholic liturgy, especially the Divine Office, permeate all her works of maturity. She has a substantial patristic culture, manifested by her allusions to the works of Gregory the Great, Jerome, John Climacus, and the desert fathers. As with other Jansenists, her interest in the patristic heritage is primarily moral. It is the ascetic message, the rigorist stress on the cultivation of virtue, that draws her. From the time of her conversion to the Jansenist cause in 1646, the works of Saint Augustine shaped her theology of grace.

[margin note: Theology of grace]

Among contemporary Catholic authors, Jansenist theologians are primary. The works of Saint-Cyran and Antoine Arnauld dominate. Jacqueline Pascal frequently cites their rigorist views on the reception of the sacraments. Saint-Cyran in particular is held in highest esteem as the definitive authority in religious disputes. She also cites the letters and speeches of Mère Angélique and Mère Agnès as models of theological wisdom.

If the content of Soeur Jacqueline's writings draws almost exclusively from the narrow world of Jansenist theology, their style employs certain of the literary techniques favored in the salons of her adolescence. Many of the epigrammatic passages in *On the Mystery of the Death of Our Lord Jesus Christ* and in the letters echo the *maximes* of the period. Her biographical and autobiographical pieces often use the technique of the *portrait moral* to describe the temperament of someone in the narrative. This confluence of witty *salonnière* style with the somewhat dour theology of Jansenism lends a distinctive voice to her argument.

[margin note: Writing draws from Jansenism but uses salon techniques]

Shortly after her death Jacqueline Pascal's works began to influence the Jansenist movement and the broader Catholic community. The publication of *A Rule for Children* in 1665 established her as the preeminent female voice in Jansenist education. Her pedagogical theories influenced neo-Jansenist experiments in education for girls. Numerous commentators in the late nineteenth century, both Catholic and secular, studied her treatise and her educational initiatives at Port-Royal as pioneering experiments in the education of women. The comprehensive study of Jansenist pedagogy by Frédéric Delforge (1985) is a recent example of the long-standing interest accorded her as an educational philosopher.

[margin note: Female voice in Jansenist education]

Jacqueline Pascal also influenced the popular perception of the Port-Royal nuns as martyrs to a persecuting throne and altar. Her letter of June 23, 1661, on the crisis of the signature and the transcript of her interrogation by church authorities in 1661 became literary monuments to the Jansenist defense of conscience.

Her own untimely death seemed to seal in blood the plea for women's religious and cultural rights that she had crafted in her works on the dowry, on education, and on the limits of ecclesiastical and political authority.

NOTE ON THE TRANSLATION

In this translation of the works of Jacqueline Pascal I have attempted to privilege accuracy and clarity. The concern for accuracy required certain sacri-

[margin note: Concern for exactitude in the translation]

fices in translating' the poetry. I made no effort to reproduce the intricate rhyme schemes of the French originals. This freer translation permitted Pascal's positions on religious, political, and sentimental matters to emerge with greater exactitude. The concern for clarity governed the translation of Pascal's prose narratives and letters. A literal translation of the lengthy paragraphs and elliptical sentences of the French originals would have produced extremely dense English prose. Subdividing the paragraphs and sentences permitted greater clarity in the translation, although it weakened the informal, conversational tone of the originals.

[margin note: Gender translated so as not to distort JP's theology]

I used inclusive language in translating anthropological terms. *L'homme*, for example, is rendered as "humanity" or as "the human being." In translating theological terms, however, I respected the gender differentiation of the originals. Jacqueline Pascal's theological argument repeatedly appeals to God the Father and to God the Son, as it does to Mother Church. Substituting a neutered "God" for the gendered religious references would have led to inaccurate translation and to a serious distortion of the Trinitarian theology of Jacqueline Pascal.

SUGGESTIONS FOR FURTHER READING

Study of the original texts of Jacqueline Pascal is essential for those who read French. Once rare, the Faugère edition is now available on the Internet via the Bibliothèque nationale de France: http://gallica.bnf.fr/Fonds_Tables/002/M0029447.htm. Although dated, the Cousin edition offers a neoromantic portrait of the "character" of Jacqueline Pascal. The Mesnard edition of Blaise Pascal lets readers place Jacqueline's works in the broader framework of the canon of the Pascal and Périer families.

The biographical sketches of Jacqueline Pascal by Gilberte Pascal Périer[25] and Marguerite Périer[26] still provide striking details on the emergence and testing of Jacqueline's religious vocation. They are also specimens of Jansenist hagiography, transforming her trials into the heroic narrative of the Jansenist circle's proto-martyr.

Several secondary works study Jacqueline Pascal's educational philosophy. Frédéric Delforge's *Les petites écoles de Port-Royal* (1985) is a magisterial study of the educational theory of the early Jansenists, with several sections

---

25. See Gilberte Pascal Périer, *Mémoire composé et écrit de la main de Madame Périer, touchant la vie de la Soeur Jacqueline de Sainte Euphémie Pascal sa soeur*, LOM, 54–77.

26. See Marguerite Périer, *Copie d'un mémoire écrit de la main de Mademoiselle Marguerite Périer*, LOM, 418–46.

devoted to Jacqueline Pascal. In their earlier studies of education at Port-Royal, Charles-Augustin Sainte-Beuve (1859), Antoine Ricard (1883), and Félix Cadet (1887) devote considerable attention to Jacqueline Pascal and the convent school. These pedagogical studies, however, tend to assimilate her approach to the concerns of the *messieurs* and their schools for boys. The originality of Jacqueline Pascal's model of education, especially its simultaneous retrieval of the monastic office and its expansion of women's spiritual authority, is often obscured.

Numerous works have dwelled on Jacqueline Pascal's relationship with her brother Blaise. François Mauriac (1931), Mildred V. Woodgate (1944), and Marguerite Perroy (1959) have written durable studies in the genre. The problem is that such works habitually cast Blaise as the thinker and Jacqueline as the inspirational mystic. The role of Jacqueline Pascal as a theorist in her own right is often suppressed in the story of the great man's path to conversion.

If this book serves no other purpose, it lets Jacqueline Pascal speak in her own analytical voice. It invites readers to discover a philosopher and theologian with her own sophisticated argument on conscience, the cross, and education. Critical of paternal authority in the family and in the church, Jacqueline Pascal emerges as one of early modernity's apologists for the spiritual rights of women.

BIBLIOGRAPHY ON JACQUELINE PASCAL

Primary Sources

Cousin, Victor, ed. *Jacqueline Pascal: Premières études sur les femmes illustres et la société du XVIIe siècle.* 8th ed. Paris: Didier, 1877. Originally published in 1845.

Pascal, Blaise (1623–1662). *Oeuvres complètes avec tous les documents biographiques et critiques; les oeuvres d'Étienne, de Gilberte et de Jacqueline Pascal et celles de Marguerite Périer; la correspondance des Pascal et des Périer.* 4 vols., ed. Jean Mesnard. Paris: Desclée de Brouwer, 1964–91.

Pascal, Jacqueline, Gilberte Pascal Périer, , and Marguerite Périer. *Lettres, opuscules et mémoires de Madame Périer et de Jacqueline, soeurs de Pascal, et de Marguerite Périer, sa nièce, publiés sur les manuscrits orginaux par M. P. Faugère,* ed. Armand Prosper Faugère. Paris: Auguste Vaton, 1845.

Secondary Sources

Beaunier, André. *Visages de femmes.* 4th ed. Paris: Plon-Nourit, 1913.

Cadet, Félix. *L'éducation à Port-Royal: Saint-Cyran; Arnauld; Lancelot; Nicole; De Saci; Guyot; Coustel; Fontaine; Jacqueline Pascal.* Paris: Hachette, 1887.

Cahné, Pierre. "Une école de la 'modestie': Le 'Règlement pour les enfants.'" *Chroniques de Port-Royal*, no. 31 (1982): 121–26.

Carré, Irénée. *Les pédagogues de Port-Royal: Saint-Cyran, De Saci, Lancelot, Guyot, Coustel, Le Maître, Nicole, Arnauld, etc. Jacqueline Pascal; Histoire des petites écoles, notices; extraits et analyses avec des notes.* Paris: C. Delagrave, 1887.

Delforge, Frédéric. "Le ministère pédagogique de Jacqueline." *Chroniques de Port-Royal*, no. 31 (1982): 107–19.

———. *Les petites écoles de Port-Royal: 1637–1660.* Paris: Editions du Cerf, 1985.

Delplanque, Albert. *Les femmes de Port-Royal.* 2 vols. Paris: P. Lethielleux, 1912, 1921.

Descamps, Geneviève. "Jacqueline et Gilberte Pascal, témoins de la conversion de Blaise." *Chroniques de Port-Royal*, no. 31 (1982): 31–47.

Descotes, Dominique. *Blaise Pascal "auvergnat," la famille à l'oeuvre: Exposition réalisée à l'occasion des Journées de Port-Royal; deux grandes figures d'Auvergne, Gilberte et Jacqueline Pascal, Clermont-Ferrand, 9–11 octobre 1981.* Clermont-Ferrand: Amis CIBP, Bibliothèque municipale et interuniversitaire, 1981.

Dutoit, Marie. *Jacqueline Pascal.* Paris: Librairie Fischbacher, 1897.

Féret, Charles Théophile. *Les amours de Jacqueline Pascal.* Paris: Fayard, 1928.

Giraud, Victor. *Soeurs de grands hommes: Jacqueline Pascal, Lucile de Chateaubriand, Henriette Renan.* Paris: G. Crés, 1926.

Goyet, Thérèse. "Une poétesse de douze ans: Jacqueline Pascal." *Chroniques de Port-Royal*, no. 31 (1982): 127–36.

Lagarde, François. "Instruction et conversion: Le *Règlement pour les enfants* de Port-Royal." *Travaux-de-Litterature* 2 (1989): 125–35.

Magnard, Pierre. "La spiritualité de Jacqueline Pascal." *Chroniques de Port-Royal*, no. 31 (1982): 137–52.

Mauriac, François. *Blaise Pascal et sa soeur Jacqueline.* Paris: Hachette, 1931.

Mesnard, Jean. "Blaise Pascal et la vocation de sa soeur Jacqueline." *XVIIe Siècle* 11 (1951): 69–92; 15 (1952): 373–96.

———. "Gilberte et Jacqueline au pays d'Auvergne." *Chroniques de Port-Royal*, no. 31 (1982): 11–29.

N. H. *Jacqueline Pascal, or A Glimpse of Convent Life at Port Royal. From the French of Victor Cousin, Prosper Faugère, Vinet, and Other Sources.* Trans. N. H. and introd. W. R. Williams. New York: R. Carter, 1860.

Pascal Périer, Gilberte. *La vie de Monsieur Pascal; suivi de La vie de Jacqueline Pascal.* Paris: Table Ronde, 1994.

Perroy, Marguerite. *Les Pascal: Un trio fraternel.* Paris: Letouzey et Ané, 1959.

Picquenard, Thérèse. "Portrait dit de Jacqueline Pascal." *Chroniques de Port-Royal*, no. 31 (1982): 104–6.

Rennes, Jacques. *Vie de Jacqueline Pascal.* Geneva: Roulet, 1948.

Ricard, Antoine. *Les premiers Jansénistes et Port-Royal.* Paris: E. Plon, 1883.

Sainte-Beuve, Charles-Augustin. *Port-Royal.* 1859. Ed. Maxime Leroy. 3 vols. Paris: Gallimard; Bibliothèque de la Pléiade, 1952, 1954, 1955. A detailed study of education at Port-Royal is found in 2:417–603.

Société des amis de Port-Royal, *Deux grandes figures d'Auvergne: Gilberte et Jacqueline Pascal; Colloque organisé par le Centre International Blaise Pascal; Actes. Chroniques de Port-Royal*, no. 31 (1982). The entire issue is devoted to the proceedings of the colloquium.

Vircondelet, Alain. *Le roman de Jacqueline et Blaise Pascal: La nuit de feu.* Paris: Flammarion, 1989.

Weitzel, Sophie Winthrop. *Sister and Saint. A Sketch of the Life of Jacqueline Pascal.* New York: Anson D. F. Randolph, 1880.

Woodgate, Mildred Violet. *Jacqueline Pascal and Her Brother.* Dublin: Browne and Nolan, 1944.

POETRY OF JACQUELINE PASCAL

INTRODUCTION

This selection of poetry features the works that established Jacqueline Pascal's reputation as a poet in her adolescence. They belong to the favored genres of the period: sonnet, rondeau, epigram, pastoral, encomium. The early poems show the influence of the salon lyricist Benserade, while the later works bear the more heroic stamp of Corneille. In content the poems alternate among political, religious, and sentimental concerns. The political poems celebrating the personages of the French court first brought Jacqueline Pascal to the attention of the literary public. "On the Conception of the Virgin," winner of Rouen's Prix de la Tour, confirmed her eminence as a poet prodigy.

In both theme and style the poetry of Jacqueline Pascal manifests a clear evolution. The political and romantic interests of the early works gradually yield to the religious preoccupations of the later poems. The subtle, meditative reflection of the mature works replaces the bombastic exercises in rhyme and rhythm of the first poems.

From the perspective of gender, the poetry possesses additional interest. In several poems ("Epigram to Thank God for the Gift of Poetry," "Stanzas on the same Subject") Jacqueline Pascal insists that her vocation as a writer is a gift from God. Society can neither create nor abolish her sacred right to express her beliefs in writing. Her poetry also privileges feminine images of divine power (the Blessed Virgin Mary, Saint Cecilia) and of political power (Queen Anne of Austria, Mademoiselle de Montpensier, the Duchesse d'Aiguillon). In "To the Queen, on the Regency," celebrating the inauguration of Queen Anne's rule as regent of France, Jacqueline Pascal defends the value of a female political ruler against misogynist critics.

This translation of selected poetry is based on Jacqueline Pascal, *Vers de*

Mlle Jacqueline Pascal, in the Faugère edition, *LOM,* 116–56. The Faugère edition is based on the Guerrier manuscript, Père Guerrier, Ms. 1er recueil, 240ff.

SONNET TO THE QUEEN[1]
(ON THE SUBJECT OF HER PREGNANCY;
PRESENTED TO HER MAJESTY)

Let us rejoice, since our princess
Fulfills our hopes after such a long time.
By this pregnancy we know
That our anguish has died and that our sorrow has ceased.
    May our hearts in this moment be full of joy,
Since our enemies will be routed from their thrones.
A dauphin will plunge them into confusion.
All their plots will collapse.
    French people, offer your prayers to God.
This dear dauphin, whom you so long wanted,
Will soon fulfill your every hope.
    Great God, I passionately beg you
To take our queen under your protection.
If you save her, you save France!

(May 1638)

EPIGRAM ON THE QUICKENING OF THE QUEEN'S CHILD[2]
(ALSO PRESENTED TO HER MAJESTY)

This invincible child of an invincible father
    Already makes us hope without limit.
Although he is still in the womb of his mother,
    He makes himself both feared and desired.
He will be more valiant than the god of war
Before he has even glimpsed the heavens.
    When he moved only slightly,
It was an earthquake for our enemies.

(May 1638)

1. Jacqueline Pascal, "Sonnet à la Reine, sur le sujet de sa grossesse, présenté à S.M.," *LOM,* 121. The addressee is Queen Anne of Austria, wife of Louis XIII. The dauphin is Louis XIV.

2. Jacqueline Pascal, "Épigramme sur le mouvement que la reine a senti de son enfant, présentée aussi à Sa Majesté," *LOM,* 121–22.

STANZAS FOR THE QUEEN[3]
(TO THANK HER MAJESTY FOR THE KIND RECEPTION
SHE DEIGNED TO GIVE THE PREVIOUS POEMS,
ALSO PRESENTED TO HER MAJESTY)

My dear children, my little poems;
In the whole world is it possible to find
A greater good than the one you possess?
    You are filled with happiness.
    The queen grants you a signal honor.
Her Majesty gives you a warm welcome.

Her hand deigned to receive you.
Her sweet eye fell to gaze upon you.
Silently her ears listened to you.
    By an excess of goodness,
    Without any merit on your part,
Her mouth called you small marvels.

But despite my glorious state,
The great sadness of no longer seeing her eyes
Opens my soul to a lingering ennui.
    One moment of pleasure
    Only deepens my desire
And leaves me with an endless regret for its loss.

(May 1638)

EPIGRAM FOR MADEMOISELLE[4]
(WRITTEN SPONTANEOUSLY UPON HER COMMAND)

Muse, our great princess
Commands you today to exercise your skill
To praise her beauty. But we must admit
    That no one could satisfy this request.
The only way that we could praise her
Is to say, in a word, we cannot do it.

(May 1638)

---

3. Jacqueline Pascal, "Stances à la Reine, pour remercier S.M. du bon accueil qu'elle a daigné faire aux vers précédents, présentées de même à S.M.," *LOM*, 122.

4. Jacqueline Pascal, "Épigramme à Mademoiselle, faite sur-le-champ par son commandement," *LOM*, 123. The addressee is Mademoiselle de Montpensier (called la grande Mademoiselle), cousin of Louis XIV. She headed a literary salon noted for its production of *portraits moraux*.

ANOTHER EPIGRAM, TO MADAME D'HAUTEFORT[5]
(ALSO WRITTEN SPONTANEOUSLY;
ALSO WRITTEN BY COMMAND OF MADEMOISELLE)

Beautiful masterpiece of the universe,
Adorable object of my verse,
Do not admire my impromptu poetry.
Your eye, which has conquered the universe,
Suddenly captured my heart and
In the same blow captured my imagination.

(May 1638)

[SONNET] TO MADAME DE MORANGIS[6]

It is hard to paint Phyllis, truly a miracle of heaven!
Her divine virtues are without equal:
The allure of her body, which captures our eyes;
That of her mind, which charms our ears.
I would say that her looks, always victorious,
Make mortals everywhere devote their vigils to her,
That her charms are such as capture the gods
And make them take note of her own wonders.
But to express truly her rare qualities,
My painting is just not beautiful enough.
One or another of my colors does not ring true.
So let us leave this rash project.
To paint a divinity, I clearly feel
That my brush is too clumsy, my hand too dull.

(July 1638)

STANZAS WRITTEN SPONTANEOUSLY[7]

One day, in the deep woods,
I was surprised by a voice.

5. Jacqueline Pascal, "Autre Épigramme à Madame D'Autefort, faite le même jour sur-le-champ, par le commandement aussi de Mademoiselle," *LOM,* 123. The addressee is Marie de Hautefort, a close friend of Mademoiselle de Montpensier, a frequent participant in the salon discussions of Montpensier at the Palais du Luxembourg and a partisan of the Fronde.

6. Jacqueline Pascal, "À Madame de Morangis, Sonnet," in *LOM,* 124. Madame de Morangis was a Parisian neighbor and friend of the Pascal family. She introduced Jacqueline Pascal to Queen Anne and her entourage at the court at Saint-Germain-en-Laye.

7. Jacqueline Pascal, "Stances faites sur-le-champ," *LOM,* 125.

It was the shepherdess Sylvia
Who spoke to her dear lover
And paid him this compliment:
"Without a doubt, I love you more than my own life!"

Then I heard this fine lover
Amorously respond to her:
"My soul is delighted by this.
I'm dying, come help me.
To heal me, always say,
'Without a doubt, I love you more than my own life!'"

O blessed lovers, live
In this perfect happiness,
Against all fury of jealousy.
And may each of you say
In the daily train of your love:
"Without a doubt, I love you more than my own life!"

(July 1638)

EPIGRAM TO THANK GOD FOR THE GIFT OF POETRY[8]

I am not so taken
By the charms of poetry
That I cannot recognize in front of everyone,
Great God! that it's not study
That has given me this skill,
But that, not meriting it, I hold this power from you.

(August 1638)

STANZAS ON THE SAME SUBJECT[9]

Father of this vast universe,
If the zeal to write poetry
Has deeply enchanted my soul,
I humbly admit before everyone
That I received this zeal from you!
From you, I say, O great God! without meriting it.

8. Jacqueline Pascal, "Épigramme pour remercier Dieu du don de la poésie," *LOM,* 126.
9. Jacqueline Pascal, "Stances sur le même sujet," *LOM,* 126–27.

Yes, I received from your goodness
This fine gift so long desired
By the ardent wishes of so many great souls.
By some secret decision,
My young and weak understanding
Is enlightened by you through these divine flames.

Lord, an ungrateful heart
Cannot appear innocent
Before your holy face. So is it not just
That, smitten by a divine torch,
I use your very gift
To praise your august name?

As the streams, the brooks,
The rivers and all the waters
Return to the sea, place of their origin,
So my tiny poems, great God!
Without concern for the world,
Will return to you, their divine source.

(August 1638)

STANZAS TO THANK GOD
FOR HER RECOVERY FROM SMALLPOX [10]

Mover of this great universe,
Inspire me to write powerful poetry.
Send me the voice of angels,
Not to praise mortals,
But to intone your praises
And to thank you at the foot of your altars.

Your sovereign goodness
From the height of heaven has visited
The poorest worm on earth,
And saved from a fatal blow
A body more fragile than glass,
During all the violence of an illness beyond bearing.

So we see that in truth,
Great God! your goodness

10. Jacqueline Pascal, "Stances pour remercier Dieu, au sortir de la petite vérole," *LOM,* 127–28.

Toward me was limitless,
Saving me from a peril
That, without your supreme mercy,
Would have killed me in the springtime of life.

Oh! My heart is so happy
When I see in the mirror the scars
And the marks of my smallpox.
I consider them sacred witnesses
That according to your holy word,
I am not among those whom you love the least.

I say that I consider them, O sovereign God!
As a seal with which your hand
Wanted to stamp my innocence.
This consoling thought
Makes me realize
That I should not lament this affliction.

But, great God, my work is futile.
A mind more than human is necessary
To narrate accurately all your marvels.
Portraying this superabundant goodness—
Capturing the eyes and the ears of others—
Exceeds my power, but not my will.

(November 1638)

TO HIS EMINENCE THE CARDINAL, DUC DE RICHELIEU[11] (EPIGRAM)

O incomparable Duke, I complained about my fate,
Which seemed to forbid my eyes from ever seeing you,
And which made my luck doubly unfortunate,
By giving me a hope I did' not seem able to fulfill.
But on that marvelous day—in that moment
When I saw you and when you fulfilled my wish—
My soul tasted greater happiness than one could ever desire.
Since that time, I venerate your kindness toward me.

11. Jacqueline Pascal, "A Monseigneur L'Eminentissime Cardinal duc de Richelieu, Epigramme," *LOM*, 128–29. The addressee is Cardinal Richelieu, the prime minister of Louis XIII. The poem recalls the pardon of her father Étienne Pascal accorded to Jacqueline Pascal by the cardinal.

You had saved for just one day
All the blessings that I could ever have desired.

(May 1639)

[SONNET] TO MADAME THE DUCHESSE D'AIGUILLON[12]

You, divine Apollo, whose admirable skill
Surpasses the human mind, give me the capacity
To praise the virtues we cannot even conceive.
Such we find in this incomparable duchess,
But I invoke you in vain. You are pitiless.
You steal away any hope I ever had
Of satisfying this pressing duty.
Its fulfillment demands the greatest of luck.
But no, wise Apollo, I no longer blame you
For making my work and desires fail
By refusing me this extraordinary boon.
I recognize my fault. I see now
That you are not unjust in refusing me,
Because this is a power that even you do not possess.

(January 1640)

SONNET OF DEVOTION[13]

Great and perfect author of earth and wave,
Creator and sustainer of the least mortal,
I come with reverence to the foot of your altar,
To beg your goodness, which supports us all.
 There my hope rightly rests.
 There, awaiting your eternal decrees,
I defy the demons and their brutal plans.
There I hear without fear the roar of thunder.
 But the powerful evil assaulting my senses
Beats down my heart and weakens my best intentions.
It lowers the flame stirring up my zeal.
 Great God! If I end in this cool apathy,

---

12. Jacqueline Pascal, "À Madame la Duchesse d'Éguillon, Sonnet," *LOM,* 129. Madame d'Aiguillon, the niece of Cardinal Richelieu, was a prominent salon hostess and benefactress of religious charities.
13. Jacqueline Pascal, "Sonnet de dévotion," *LOM,* 129–30.

At least preserve my sincere faith
And protect my love from becoming deadly!

(February 1640)

[EPIGRAM] TO SAINT CECILIA[14]

Noble daughter of heaven, your generous heart,
Having cleared a thousand dangerous hurdles,
Felt itself consumed by a divine flame.
Your inflamed soul found the fire so sweet
That you immediately wanted it to inflame your spouse.
You shared with him the passion of your soul
And your zeal only became more ardent.
But let us stop just gazing at this blessed enterprise.
The fire that inflamed you is such
That the more you share it, the more we feel it.

(November 1640)

ON THE CONCEPTION OF THE VIRGIN[15]
(FOR THE POETRY CONTEST OF 1640;
WINNER OF THE PRIX DE LA TOUR)

Abominable authors of a false belief,
Your hypocritical bosom encloses a rancorous heart.
Cast your weak eyes upon the ark of the covenant.
You will see how similar it is to the queen of heaven.

Compare their extraordinary beauties and effects,
And then confess reverently
That the Mother of God, this queen of angels,
Could only have been pure at her conception.

One contains in its womb the happiness of our fathers,
The other contains in hers our dearest hope.
One by its power turns aside their miseries,
The other by hers keeps us from sin.

---

14. Jacqueline Pascal, "À Sainte Cécile, Épigramme," *LOM,* 130. An early Christian martyr, Saint Cecila is the patroness of music.

15. Jacqueline Pascal, "Sur la conception de la Vierge, pour les palinods de l'année 1640, qui emportèrent le Prix de la Tour, Stances," *LOM,* 130–31.

If one has won numerous battles,
Because a treasure is hidden in its womb,
The other has done no less, since she has in her entrails
What is necessary for us to conquer and to master sin.

The sacred ark was taken to a place full of vice.
As soon as it went there, it cast down false gods.
She also fled her abode and painfully accepted
To live in a place so little beloved of the heavens.

Therefore, if a simple and much less necessary ark
Could not inhabit a profane place,
How could you think that this blessed Mother,
Who was the very temple of God, could have been an impure
    temple?

(December 1640)

[STANZAS] AGAINST LOVE [16]

Foolhardy enemy, conqueror of weak souls,
You have only illusory flames to overcome us.
You are a god with neither power nor judgment.
Love, throw away the bow with which you want to overcome
    us.
In your blindness, its vain use
Can blind only those who let themselves be targets.

Your fires are without effect and your arrows without force,
When the heart has tasted a sweeter love,
And when virtue has subdued it.
That is the greatest bulwark the soul must keep.
It is the only method we must use
To protect ourselves from the venom of your flame.

This is the fine enemy whose power overwhelms you,
Whose unvarnished beauty haunts and shames you.
From the first moment virtue captures a heart.
It is the only bond that keeps my feelings
Free from your slavery and from your severity.
It makes reason flee you and despise you.

16. Jacqueline Pascal, "Contre l'amour, stances," *LOM*, 132–33.

The least subtle mind is a victor over your claims.
It mocks your flames without fearing your arms,
Because reason dulls your false allure.
Whoever wants to resist you is immediately the master.
So little power accompanies your arrows
That whoever fails to conquer you did not want the conquest
    after all.

(February 1642)

[SONNET] ON THE APPARENT HEALING OF THE KING[17]

Vain great ones, finally you are powerless.
This infinite crowd of courtiers
Could not prevent death triumphant
From taking the pride of my life to the tomb.
    These tiny scions, whose only virtue
Was to bring dismay to the highest places,
Could only mourn this apparent death
And end up making my pain all the sharper.
    Although my soul was ravished in this suffering,
I asked for your life for the good of the state.
Then heaven heard this just intention.
    To lessen my plight, miracles had to be performed.
If I was healed despite all these obstacles,
It is my virtue alone that played my doctor.

(April 1643)

[SONNET] TO THE QUEEN, ON THE REGENCY[18]

Great queen, begin a reign of wonders.
Since our happiness depends on you alone,
Sow your unparalleled virtues throughout the earth.
Make the greatest kings jealous of your great deeds.
    Continue the cares of your divine vigils.
May your goodness let everyone know

17. Jacqueline Pascal, "Sur la guérison apparente du roi, Sonnet," *LOM,* 134–35. The subject of the poem is the illness and recovery of Louis XIII in early 1643.

18. Jacqueline Pascal, "À la reine, sur la régence, sonnet," *LOM,* 135. The addressee of the poem is Queen Anne of Austria, who served as regent of France from 1643 to 1661, during the minority of her son, Louis XIV.

That a thousand terrors vainly strike our attention
When we have a government you have made so kind.
    Indiscreet politicians, speak without violence.
Don't trouble our joy at the birth of her reign
By saying that the kindness of a woman is a weak foundation.
    Learn to support your illustrious princess,
Whose divine spirit knows how to mix skillfully
The kindness of her sex with the strength of yours.

(May 1643)

ON THE MYSTERY OF THE DEATH
OF OUR LORD JESUS CHRIST

INTRODUCTION

Written shortly before Jacqueline Pascal's entry into the convent, *On the Mystery of the Death of Our Lord Jesus Christ* is a devotional treatise on the Crucifixion. She wrote this meditation in response to a spiritual note sent to her from Port-Royal by Mère Agnès. Following the custom of the convent, Mère Agnès sent a monthly note to lay friends of the convent recommending meditation on a particular theme (in this case, the Passion of Christ). Jacqueline Pascal composed this work in May–June 1651.

In the work Pascal establishes a parallel between a particular attribute of Christ during the Passion and a specific virtue that his disciples should develop. In meditation XVI, for example, the nudity of Christ on the cross teaches the meditant how absolute is the material and spiritual poverty she must embrace.

On the Mystery follows a distinctively Jansenist theology in its treatment of the Passion. Unlike many other devotional pieces on the cross written during the Counter-Reformation, the treatise devotes little attention to the physical and emotional suffering of Christ. Its somber depiction of the Passion stresses two motifs: the world's radical opposition to Christ and the absolute passivity of Christ in his suffering and death.

Many meditations trace the contempt of the world provoked by the cross: the blasphemies surrounding Christ's death as a criminal (XVIII), the rejection of Christ because of his manner of death (XIX), and the jealous hatred of political authorities (XLIX). As an increasingly persecuted religious minority, the Jansenists conceived their own lot as a participation in Christ's rejection by the world. Many passages evoke the utter passivity of Christ in the Passion: his insensibility to pain and pleasure (XX, XXI, XXII, XXIII) and the absolute poverty of his death (XVI, XVII). Like other spiritual currents in the French Counter-Reformation, the Jansenists stressed complete abandonment to God's will as the apex of discipleship. The treatise ends in a depiction of the annihilation of the personal will of the disciple totally abandoned to divine initiative (LI).

This translation is based on Jacqueline Pascal, *Écrit de Mademoiselle Jacqueline Pascal sur le mystère de la mort de Notre-Seigneur J.-C.*, in the Faugère edition, *LOM*, 157–76. The Faugère edition is based on the Guerrier manuscript, Père Guerrier, Ms. 2e recueil, 265ff.

I. Jesus died out of love toward his eternal Father. He died, through an infinite offering, as reparation for the infinite offense committed against God. He also died out of love for us, because he satisfied our debts by his death. As a result, the little we can do—and we can do nothing without him—suffices to pay all the debts.

From this I learn that I must die to the world out of love for God. I must return to him everything that I owe him by giving him my undivided heart and by doing penance as satisfaction for my sins. This death requires such penance, as does a proper love for myself.

II. Jesus did not die in order to live no longer. He died in order to exist no longer in the suffering, the weakness, and the other infirmities of this human life. He died to live eternally a life free of all these miseries—a life completely spiritual, completely heavenly, completely divine.

From that I learn that after my death to the world separates me from clinging to the corruption of nature, I must live in God alone. I must no longer live in anything that belongs to the previous life.

III. Jesus truly died. His death was not simply symbolic or a matter of desire.

That teaches me that I must truly die to the world. I should not content myself with some vague desires or with some abstract theory.

IV. The death of Jesus had nothing extraordinary about it. His body was deprived of life, just like anyone else's. He remained dead in the posture and in the way that is proper to this state.

This teaches me that although I must truly put to death the flesh and all its desires, I must avoid anything extraordinary or idiosyncratic in my actions. I must do only those things that are proper for my state in life and for my present condition.

V. Jesus died a true interior death. His holy soul and his body were truly separated. Afterward he underwent all the privations caused by death: the loss of sight, of hearing, of understanding, of all movement. They had to carry him to the sepulcher. He did not take himself there. He clearly wanted to deprive himself of all these things, although they were holy in him.

This teaches me to die to myself in all things, even the most innocent. I should no longer bring about anything by my own action. Rather, I should so want everything to come about by obedience to the counsels of Christianity and to the superiors God has given me that one could truly say that my soul is no longer in me, that it is so separated from my body that it is no longer my own soul that makes it act.

VI. Jesus died not only from his own sight, but also from the sight of his holy mother, of his relatives and his friends. His death deprived them of the consolation of his presence and deprived him of the consolation of theirs.

This teaches me to die not only to what concerns my own person, but to all concerns of flesh and blood, and to all concerns of friendship. In other words, I must forget everything that does not clearly concern the salvation of my friends. I must not involve myself in temporal matters.

VII. Jesus died in the sight of the whole world. The world was thus deprived of his presence and the fruit of his exhortation. He left behind only the disciples, who were copies of the holy life they imitated.

That teaches me that when we die to the world, we must no longer socialize and that we must be content with simply letting this living death influence others by its good example and by its pleasant fragrance.

VIII. Jesus did not want to die from old age. He anticipated death by dying in the strength of youth.

That teaches me not to wait until my body declines before I die to the world. A mystical death must anticipate a physical one.

IX. Jesus died a violent death, not a natural one.

I learn from this that although nature finds this violent death repugnant and although everything human within me pushes me to flee it, I must do violence to these urges if I am truly to die to the world.

X. Jesus died on the cross, elevated above the entire world. Everything, even his holy mother, stood beneath his feet.

I learn from this that my heart must be above all the things of the world. By this elevation of the soul, which is not vain but heavenly, I must consider as beneath me everything great and admired. Since I must glory only in the cross of my Savior, I must esteem nothing as much as I do it.

XI. Jesus so wanted to be separated from earth when he died that he touched it only by the instrument of his torture, where it necessarily had to be joined to the earth.

This teaches me to consider everything that forces me to participate in the things of this world as a torture. I must maintain a real hatred in my heart for these things. Still, I must submit to them, on condition that they constitute a hard cross for me. By dying to the world, I no longer touch the earth, just as my tortured Savior no longer did.

XII. Jesus died covered with horrible wounds and racked by pain. Nonetheless, some people think it is not the pain that made him die, since it was not able to do so earlier.

This teaches me that although I am surrounded and disturbed by the evils in the world, they must not be the reason for my death to the world. Just as I am not obliged to live with them so that I might suffer more, I am not permitted to die to them simply to avoid them.

XIII. Jesus died outside the city.

That teaches me that the first thing we must do is to leave the centers of the world, in order to die to the world.

XIV. Although Jesus died outside the city, he was still accompanied by many people.

That teaches me that although I can neither leave the world completely nor totally desert the places where I live, I should not put any limits on my generosity in dying to the world.

XV. He died publicly in front of all of those who wanted to see him.

I learn from this that although my condition exposes me to the gaze of the entire world, that must not prevent me from dying to it.

XVI. Jesus died completely naked.

That teaches me to strip myself of all things.

XVII. Although Jesus clearly consented to undergo this stripping, he still did not strip himself.

That teaches me not only to strip myself of everything, but to accept that God will strip me in whatever manner he chooses.

XVIII. The death of Jesus made him contemptible to the evil. For them it acted as a veil that hid his divinity from their eyes. It provided them with an occasion for the worst blasphemy. But for the good it was an occasion to recognize and to confess him publicly. An object of scandal for one group, it was an object of consolation for another.

That teaches me to prepare myself for this shame. Undoubtedly the carnal will despise me. They will attribute to weakness, to stupidity, and to madness my renunciation of the world. But the more spiritual will attribute it to the movement of God's spirit. They will be moved by it and will glorify it.

XIX. As the prophet foretold, Jesus Christ was despised by humanity and became an object of contempt for his people.

Since his death was considered shameful by the world, I learn to accept joyfully the contempt with which the world will greet me.

XX. Jesus died in insensibility to all evils, although his body was covered completely with sores.

That teaches me to be insensible to all disturbing events.

XXI. Jesus is insensible to all events, good or evil. Thus he is in perfect tranquillity.

That teaches the equanimity with which I must accept all the commotion of the world, good or bad, in order to live in perfect rest.

XXII. Jesus died not only in insensibility, but also in the privation of all the pleasures of life.

That teaches me that I must not only maintain true indifference but also positively deprive myself of all the pleasures of life.

XXIII. Being dead, Jesus is actually in a perfect insensibility concerning the things of the world, of its goods, and of its evils. But the divinity remains united to this insensible body. The Holy Spirit remaining within the body has its desires, its feelings, and its passions—so to speak—with the result that this insensible body, wholly penetrated by the divinity, and nothing but the divinity, no long has any sentiments concerning the things of the earth. Everything sensible in it exists only by the sentiment of the spirit of God, since it is nothing else but he.

I learn from this that insensibility must make me unmoved by the various events in the world. But it must not make me incapable of feeling joy or sadness any longer. It is only the joy and sorrow of the world that I should no longer feel. Being freed from concern for the things of the world, I should focus only on the things that concern God. Having made a complete abnegation of my own soul, from now on I must act only by the movement of the spirit of God.

XXIV. Jesus had no life whatever during the entire time of his death. Nonetheless, his hands and feet by their wounds, his mouth and tongue by their encounter with gall, and the wounds of his body acted as so many tongues and voices. By a clearly intelligible language proper to their own condition, they proclaimed the greatness of God, who had demanded such a satisfaction. They reproached humanity for the sins that had required such a reparation and preached incessantly to Christians about the greatness of their duties. Throughout all this, his tongue maintained perfect silence.

That teaches me that although I should not be silent on all these things, according to the state of life in which God has placed me, I still must try to witness them more by my actions than by my words. When my words and my voice fall silent, my actions must not fail me.

XXV. Although without movement, Jesus in death is still moved when it is necessary. He is taken down from the cross and carried to the tomb. But he has nothing to do with all that, since he does not do it by himself.

This teaches me that I must act whenever it is necessary, but that I must never perform any action by the power of my own will.

XXVI. Jesus is still bound to the cross for a while after his death. Even when he is taken down from it, his body is still covered with all his sores. He is still in poverty and in obloquy. As a result, he is still deprived of the goods that are the opposites of these evils. If by a miracle, which he did not want to do, his soul had returned to the body to make it passible once again, he would have immediately felt all the pangs of the universal pain that he felt during the Passion.

This teaches me that the possession of all the goods of the world and the endurance of everything that he carefully avoided should not have the power to affect me. Being dead to the world, I have become indifferent to all that the world has and to all that the world is. I must not cease to flee certain things and ardently to seek others. If God, by a punishment that would be only too just, permitted this spirit of the world to revive within me—where I would see myself surrounded by everything he calls evils and by everything he calls goods—I would begin to feel the suffering that such a state causes in people who are affected by these events. This suffering, which I would voluntarily procure, would act as a kind of satisfactory punishment for my sins. I would be saved as if by fire. My hope is that just as my Savior no longer wanted to be passible in the state of death, his all-powerful grace will prevent those who have spiritually imitated his death from returning to commerce with the things of the world.

XXVII. After his death Jesus had his side pierced by the thrust of a lance. Blood and water flowed out of it. By a miracle they remained in a liquid state. This wound remained open even after his resurrection.

I learn from this that after killing the effects of the flesh—and with it all the passions that give it life, just as charity gives life to the soul—I must attack the principle of the flesh itself. I must do this, even though I feel that it 'has no life left. I must do this by constant mortifications that try to suffocate this power, if it is not already completely dead. By practicing everything that is contrary to it, I develop with God's grace the habitual power to accept peacefully either my own physical death or the wound of my Savior, after which he could no longer live according to nature. By this wound all the remains of human weakness and strength leave the body. They served only to make me incapable of doing good and capable of doing evil, which lived in our heart and which, by a tragic marvel, manages to remain in us after having died to the world. Ceaselessly we must reopen this wound, so that it never closes completely.

XXVIII. I see Jesus dead in three different places: on the cross, in the sight of everyone; at the foot of the cross, surrounded by his friends; in the tomb, in total solitude. In these three places he is equally dead.

This teaches me that in whatever state I may find myself, whether in conversation or in solitude, I must remain dead to the world. This rule applies to the one as much as to the other.

XXIX. When Jesus is on the cross surrounded by people, I see that his hands are filled by the nails that attach him to the cross. Then his hands are empty when his disciples take him down from the cross and also when he is alone in the sepulcher.

This teaches me that if divine providence gives me some temporal things to administer, I must submit myself to these tasks, although these obligations keep me tied to the things of the world. At the same time, the aversion I would experience for all these offices would act like the nails of my Savior, which gave him such terrible sores as they fastened his body to the cross and, through the cross, to the earth.

I learn from the time of his empty hands that in whatever state I find myself, whether busy with human affairs or in retreat, I can still keep my hands free of worry about business or work, if God pleases to so free me.

XXX. After his death, they clothed Jesus Christ in the vestments proper to the dead.

I learn from that to witness even by my clothing that I am dead to the world.

XXXI. Although Jesus was clothed with funeral garments, they were proper to his state, because he was truly dead.

That teaches me that although I must witness by my clothing that I am dead to the world, I must not do anything extraordinary or eccentric. I should just wear what is proper to my state in life.

XXXII. The sheet they wrapped Jesus in did not belong to him.

I learn from that not to attach myself to those things that are closest to me and that are most useful. I learn not to consider them as my own, but to consider them as belonging to someone else.

XXXIII. Jesus manifests that he has died not only by his clothing, which is that of the dead, and by his new home, which is the sepulcher, but also by the very position of his body.

This teaches me that I must witness to the world that I am dead to it, not only by my clothing and by my house, but also by all my actions.

XXXIV. Immediately after the death of Jesus, his body was taken away from human eyes to be enclosed in the sepulcher. From that moment on, no one any longer saw him, even after his resurrection. He appeared only to certain disciples.

That teaches me that after dying to the world, I must hide myself from it so that it no longer sees me. If I cannot make myself completely invisible and charity obliges me to reveal myself to someone, it should be only to true disciples of Jesus Christ. That is what Saint Paul teaches me when he says to Christians "you are dead and your life is hidden."[1] He does not say "may your life be hidden," which could be interpreted as a counsel of perfection. Rather, he says "your life *is* hidden." He means that this is the natural state of Christians.

XXXV. Jesus wanted to be embalmed shortly after his death, although he did not need it to prevent the corruption of his holy body.

I learn from this to desire more than dying to the world. Whatever virtue I may have received by God's grace, I want to use every possible precaution to prevent any corruption. I can achieve this easily enough if I am always fortified with myrrh and aloes, that is to say, mortification and prayer.

XXXVI. After his death, Jesus was enclosed in the stone sepulcher, as in a place of retreat. There he removed from his eyes the means to see naturally everything outside. Moreover, he wanted death to close his eyes. Thus he was deprived even of the sight of the place where he was enclosed.

That teaches me that in order to imitate my Savior on this point, it is not enough to remove myself by desire or even by effort from the business and the sight of the world. I must also disengage myself from the closest and the most intimate domestic concerns, without finding delight in the sight and in the use of these things.

XXXVII. Jesus is enclosed alone in this sepulcher. He was thus separated from those who died with him—the good thief as well as the bad. The good thief, however, was united to the soul of Jesus Christ at the moment of his death.

That teaches me to separate myself, as much as I can, from those people who have renounced the world as I have, even from the perfect, in order to settle into a true and effective solitude. At the same time, however, I must remain united with others through a purely spiritual affection in order to enjoy together a happiness as perfect as any that can be experienced in this life. This affection consists in a perfect union of hearts formed by charity.

XXXVIII. Jesus is enclosed in the sepulcher only after he is completely dead and the authorities have confirmed it.

1. Col. 3:3.

That teaches me not to leave the world completely until I am certain of being truly dead to the world.

XXXIX. In this state Jesus was deprived of access to all the objects that strike the senses. Not only was he wrapped in a sheet and in a shroud in an impenetrable cave, he was removed from all sensible things. In addition, because he no longer had any life, he no longer had any emotions. If he had' not had the faculty of feeling removed, he would still have been exposed to all kinds of things.

That teaches me that in order to perfectly imitate my Savior on this point, it is not enough to enclose myself within thick walls and to bury myself beneath veils. It is necessary to make unbreakable resolutions or even solemn vows that take away the power of all the things of the world. The vows make the use of these things impossible and preserve us against them, even when we are exposed to them.

XL. Jesus was enclosed in a place of retreat, but he did not want it to be his own.

That teaches me that it is not enough to separate myself forcibly from the world and even to hide myself from its gaze. I must also free myself from affection for my place of retreat, and I must treat it as a borrowed room.

XLI. As long as Jesus is in the tomb, he remains there peacefully. Nonetheless, he leaves it at the proper time.

I learn from that to have neither love nor attachment for the place of my retreat.

XLII. Jesus died in a perfect solitude from the perspective of all created things. But he was always accompanied by his divinity.

That teaches me the necessity of complete detachment, at least in my heart, in order to place myself in true solitude. At the same time I must be filled with the spirit of God.

XLIII. The death of Jesus did not separate either his body or his soul from his divinity. On the contrary, it cut away everything except the divinity. The body and soul were now united to the divinity in a far more astonishing way, inasmuch as it is much more difficult to imagine how a dead body is united to the living God and how the same divinity is united personally to two things, body and soul, now completely separate.

I learn from this that my death to the world must grow and must increase my union with God. It must fill me with a greater charity for him and for my neighbor.

XLIV. The death of Jesus did not destroy his body, which remained intact in the sepulcher. God did not permit his holy body to undergo corruption. The only new thing brought about by death was repose rather than movement or agitation.

This teaches me to die to the world. It is not a question of destroying or of ruining one's body. Rather, it is simply a question of stopping the disturbances and the commotion of the heart by a holy repose that destroys the source of this commotion, which is nothing other than the passions.

XLV. As long as Jesus remained dead, his holy body remained always in the ground. In such a way he remained separated from all the business of humanity.

This teaches me that although I am dead to the world, I must not cease to remain on the earth. I must live in exile from all the business of the world.

XLVI. Jesus is not inactive in death, because he goes to deliver the souls of the holy patriarchs.

That teaches me that it is not necessary that my death to the world make me live a lazy life. I must work incessantly in the works of charity, especially the spiritual works. These should be directed toward myself as much as toward my neighbor, since I must work to liberate all my good desires.

XLVII. Jesus did not enter triumphantly into heaven at the moment when death separated him from the world. He waited until several days afterward.

This teaches me to suffer in patience the privation of celestial consolations that even people dead to the world often experience. I learn to await peacefully the time ordained by God to make me enter into the sensible possession of grace, which is the foretaste of glory, and then the unending moment of eternity itself, which will plunge me into perfect glory.

XLVIII. When Jesus died, he did not leave his children orphans. To assist them he sent the Holy Spirit, which is his divine love. He himself remains invisible until the end of time.

I learn from this to separate myself from my relatives and friends in whatever way I can. Nonetheless, I must always remain united to them by an affection born purely from God, and I must assist them with my prayers.

XLIX. After his death, Jesus was surrounded by his enemies more than by his friends. They gladly would have prevented the marvels of his new life, as they tried to suppress the truth about it. But they did not succeed in either project.

This teaches me that although my enemies are more numerous than my friends and that enemies constantly surround me after my death to the world, I must not stop prolonging this death by the new life that I must live. I must resist all their efforts to defeat me.

L. By the death of his natural body, Jesus gave life to his angelic body, which is the church.

That teaches me that my death to the world must be the guiding principle of my life in God.

LI. The mystery of the death of Jesus contains all the other mysteries that precede it. They all led up to this death, which alone brought about the redemption of the world.

This teaches us something essential about the soul. All a soul's good movements, all its good desires, all the good actions God has it perform are perfect and salvific only when they reach the point where the will dies by annihilating itself into the very will of God. After this, the resurrection cannot fail to follow. It will give a new life to those souls who have renounced the very principle of spiritual death: self-will.

Amen

REPORT OF SOEUR JACQUELINE
DE SAINTE EUPHÉMIE TO THE MOTHER
PRIORESS OF PORT-ROYAL DES CHAMPS

INTRODUCTION

An autobiographical narrative, the *Report of Soeur Jacqueline* recounts the "crisis of the dowry" that shook Jacqueline Pascal shortly before she professed vows as a nun. According to the custom of the period, families were expected to provide the convent with a dowry at the moment their daughters professed vows. Jacqueline Pascal expected to use her share of the inheritance from her father Étienne as her dowry. Her brother Blaise and her sister Gilberte, however, opposed this project and threatened legal action to keep the money in the family. The *Report* recounts the bitter dispute between Jacqueline and Blaise over the proposed dowry. It dwells on the repeated efforts of the superiors of Port-Royal (Abbé Singlin, Mère Agnès, Mère Angélique) to counsel Jacqueline to pronounce her vows without a dowry.

More than a narrative of events, the *Report* uses the technique of the *portrait moral* to present the salient virtues and vices of the major actors in the crisis. Abbé Singlin's prudence and discretion are depicted. The compassion and patience of the novice mistress Mère Agnès emerge. The wisdom, courage, and shrewdness of abbess Mère Angélique are highlighted. The *Report* evokes the bitterness of Blaise Pascal, firmly opposed to his sister's vocation and momentarily alienated from the Jansenist movement. It also candidly presents the dominant vices of Jacqueline herself, especially her pride and her obstinacy. Her struggle to accept the counsel of her superiors and pronounce her vows undowered clearly flows from her personal sense of honor and her aristocratic sense of class pride.

The *Report* provides more than the chronicle of Jacqueline Pascal's struggle against the humiliation of an undowered vocation. It reflects the broader effort of Port-Royal to break the link between the right to pursue a religious vocation and the wealth of a candidate's family. The superiors insist on a

41

woman's right to follow a religious vocation independent of her family's de-sire or resources. This dismissal of the dowry and weakening of parental pre-rogatives on the question of vocation parallels the policy at the Port-Royal convent school. Mère Angélique insisted that the school admit only pupils whose parents had not already designated them for marriage or for the con-vent. The personal discovery of one's God-given vocation, free from parental pressure, was one of the goals of education at Port-Royal. In undercutting the practice of the dowry and in insisting on the individual's right to pursue her own vocation, Port-Royal defended women's personal freedom to determine their own state in life.

This translation is based on Jacqueline Pascal, *Relation de la Soeur Jacqueline de Sainte Euphémie, adressée par elle à la mère prieure de Port-Royal des Champs,* in the Faugère edition, *LOM,* 177–222. The Faugère edition is based on the follow-ing manuscript: *Relations concernant la vie de Mère Angélique et de plusieurs de ses religieuses* (BNF fr. 1389). In 1652–53 Mère Angélique de Saint-Jean and Antoine Le Maître began to collect memoirs attesting to the sanctity of Port-Royal, especially of its reforming abbess Mère Angélique. Composed in 1653, the *Report of Soeur Jacqueline* follows the conventions of these apologetic memoirs.

Glory to Jesus, to the Most Blessed Sacrament
Port-Royal
June 10, 1653

Dearest Mother,[1]

I have no doubt that your charity led you to commiserate with me be-cause of the grave affliction God sent me at the moment of my religious pro-fession. Perhaps it was meant to serve as a counterweight to the extreme joy I experienced at that time. In recognition of your sympathy, I feel obligated to share with you the consolation I ultimately received in this crisis.

That is why I have undertaken the honor of writing to you. For you to understand this consolation, however, I need to explain the turn of events I've undergone. I thought I should give you a brief sketch of these events. This will enlighten you on my situation. It will also satisfy the obligation I have to publicize—at least among ourselves, since I've been forbidden to dis-cuss it further—what I know to be an extraordinary personal experience of the disinterestedness of this house, of the great charity of our mother superi-

---

1. The addressee is Mère Marie-Dorothée de l'Incarnation (née Dorothée Leconte), prioress of Port-Royal des Champs and a close associate of Mère Angélique and Mère Agnès in the reform program of the convent.

ors, and of the purity of their intentions and of their conduct. These qualities have been so obvious in my trial that we don't need any other proofs to recognize that our superiors consider only God in all the areas where they are obliged to act.

Dear Mother, my conscience urges me to publish this testimonial, even more worthy of faith since it is completely voluntary. I don't dare to make it public, because the modesty of our mother would never tolerate this. This modesty prevents me from daring to attempt what gratitude and justice ask of me. I fear that the vow of obedience would next forbid me from doing the little that is still permitted, because it is not forbidden: namely, leaving you a small memorial that will preserve, thanks to the silence and to the confidentiality that we will keep between us, the details of what has happened. Otherwise we would have to let it perish. It will be the monument of my gratitude and the faithful witness of the memory I maintain from the grace I have received. I can do nothing more than this.

You surely know, dear Mother, that as soon as I received approval for my profession of vows, I wrote to my family members in order to put the last touches on my worldly affairs and to give them my indications on how I wished to dispose of the bit of worldly goods God had given me. Freely and frankly, I told them I wanted to surrender everything I had to him, since I was renouncing all temporal goods. I had every reason to believe they would approve all my plans. Knowing the depth of my intentions and the disposition of my heart concerning them, I vainly presumed that nothing I did would ever disturb them. You know I had every reason for this confidence, given the union and the affection that always reigned among us.

However, they were bitterly offended by my plans. They thought I was clearly harming them by wanting to disinherit them in favor of some strangers I preferred. Although they weren't uncivil to me, this is what they thought.

To make a long story short, dear Mother, they considered everything from a totally secular viewpoint, as if they were completely worldly people who had never known even the name of charity. They saw only that I intended to make a gift to some other people—whose needs they didn't ignore—and that this project of benevolence toward these strangers seemed prejudicial to their own interests. They just did not want to know the motive that drove me to have this intention.

God permitted this conflict to occur, undoubtedly as a way to humble both sides and to make us recognize how vain it is to try to found anything on affection among creatures. If the respect I owe my relatives permits me to say so, I can attribute this blindness to no other cause than God's judgment on us. I was so certain they were enlightened on the things concerning God that I just didn't expect to find them so worldly on a question of piety that, moreover, was of so little consequence and had so little effect on their interests. I didn't think I needed to hesitate for a moment to propose this alleged disinheritance to them. I only wanted to do this for God. Not only did I think they would approve this plan, I thought they would be eager to participate in the small charitable contribution I had proposed by giving their enthusiastic consent. After all, they themselves had often made charitable gifts that anyone would call considerable.

But, dear Mother, you have nothing to do with all that. I need to tell you only that, in the next part of the story, this alleged lack of affection on my part gave them a field day to preach about the inconstancy of the human spirit and the instability of its attachments. If they had just limited themselves to such criticism, they would have given voice to their own spirit without disturbing mine. But they went further. Each one wrote to me in the same fashion and, without telling me they were offended, treated me as if they were deeply offended. In every response to my proposals, they made a caustic analysis of my affairs. They told me the nature of my inheritance was such that I could not dispose of it as I wanted, nor could I designate anyone I wanted to receive it.

The reason given was that keeping our possessions together would keep us and our inheritance safe from any possible want for a long time. They also gave other quibbling reasons. I won't bore you by reciting them. They wouldn't have come up with these reasons if they hadn't been in such a foul mood. I know that literally these reasons might make some sense, but these are not the sort of arguments we had ever used when we were together.

They added that if, notwithstanding all these objections, I tried to dispose of something, I would trigger legal proceedings by them against those to whom I had given something. They insisted this legal action would be inevitable because of some formality of justice that had to be respected. To avoid this evil, they were going to request a legal order that I be forbidden to dispose of my inheritance, since I didn't have the power to do so. They wanted to reduce me in this way to relying only on a tiny sum of money that I had brought here before my vesting as a nun. They didn't know that I had designated this modest sum in advance for several charities.

Dear Mother, I beg you to judge the state I was thrown into by these letters, so different in style from our ordinary manner of acting. They made it necessary for me to think about delaying my profession for four years in order to retrieve my inheritance from its status as equity for the other parts of our holdings. I didn't even know if it would be completely free for disposal after this long delay. I also considered the embarrassment of being received into the convent without a dowry and of having the dishonor of visiting this injustice on the convent. The anguish I experienced about this was so violent that I am amazed I didn't collapse under it.

As soon as Mère Agnès[2] knew I was afflicted, she sent for me. I explained to her that what disturbed me the most deeply was the terrible alternatives I faced: either to defer what I had desired for so many years with such passion or to undertake it in conditions that seemed so painful to me.

She told me several things to console me. She said that we should be concerned only about what is eternal. Everything that is only temporal is never irreparably broken and doesn't merit our crying about it. We should keep our tears for our sins, since they are the only true calamities. Everything else is nothing. When trouble comes, we should figure out the best means of resolving the problem rather than losing time by bemoaning our fate.

With her customary goodness she added that if we followed her advice on this issue, the problem would find a quick and easy solution. She wanted me to leave all my affairs as they were and to think no longer about anything except making my profession. I should worry about nothing else. She added several other fine considerations.

Next she spoke with a greater lightheartedness in order to omit nothing that could soften the bitter state in which I found myself. She said it would be shameful for the convent and unbelievable for those who know the convent to hear it said that a novice, ready to make her profession of vows, was capable of being upset by anything. This would be even more incomprehensible if they knew that the cause of this distress was seeing herself reduced to being received for free.

Next she tried to make me understand how this was the greatest benefit that could have come my way. Our mother said that she would have desired nothing so much as having been free at the moment of her profession to do what she really wanted: to give all her possessions to the poor and to be received out of charity into an obscure convent. To leave no possible pretext for my sadness, she tried to make me see that this was not only the most honorable, but also the most beneficial and useful course of action for the convent itself.

If the charity we owe our neighbor does not permit us to wish that he do us injustices, the charity we owe ourselves must give us joy when he does these injustices. There is no temporal benefit that can compare with this, because there is nothing more profitable to religion than true poverty. It is not

2. Mère Agnès was Jacqueline Pascal's novice mistress.

[Marginal annotations:]
JP worried about not bringing a dowry
Choice - defer or do painfully
Only be really concerned w/ eternal; work to resolve troubles
worry about nothing except making profession
Vocation should take supremacy
Must find joy in charity

always permitted to procure it, but it is good to desire it, to love it, and to re-joice over everything that can contribute to it. We should tremble and be very suspicious when we receive material wealth. We should consider it as a trap and as the enemy of the virtue and of the spirit of poverty. We should re-joice not only when we don't receive what we had expected, but also when someone has taken away what we already had. Then, at least, we are no longer responsible for it.

Finally, dear Mother, she used so many different methods to drive home her point that she practically managed to have me rejoice over everything that had so disturbed me. I no longer dared to have any sorrow except com-passion for those who had so disturbed me. If I had stayed in this calm state, I would have faced this problem exactly as she hoped I would. But I was too weak and too upset to be capable of such virtue. I must admit with embar-rassment that shortly after the interview I returned to my original weakness and to my original feelings.

Next she had me talk to Monsieur Singlin,[3] to whom I recounted every-thing that had happened. During that time she took the trouble of going to explain the situation to our mother.[4] Immediately returning, she said that our mother's opinion was that I should abandon all my wealth to my siblings, without meddling any further in what would no longer belong to me. I should let them determine the disposition of everything without bothering myself about it. I should think only about making my profession without having any other cares.

At first Monsieur Singlin didn't agree with this point of view. He feared there might be too much generosity, and not enough humility, in this action. He told us forcefully that after overcoming the lust for wealth, which reigns almost everywhere, we should fear falling into the other extreme, which is the lust for honor. This lust for honor flows from the vanity we derive from the actions we take after abandoning our greed. It manifests itself by con-tempt for those still attached to material gain and by the ostentatious display of our virtue. After establishing our honor as being superior to the love of riches—as others have staked their honor on possessing many of these riches—we need to be careful that we don't perform actions that are cer-tainly opposed to greed but that by the same principle and with the same ambition make some people proclaim their righteousness with too great a passion and make other people too easily concede this righteousness.

---

3. Abbé Singlin was the spiritual director of the Port-Royal convent and Jacqueline Pascal's per-sonal confessor..
4. Mère Angélique, the abbess of Port-Royal.

In everything we must make ourselves neutral by stripping ourselves of all particular interests. We should only consider what justice demands in each case. If the people we do business with wander from the right path and initiate some injustice against us, charity obliges us to use every means to help them recognize their duty toward us and return to it, just as we would deserve similar assistance if it were a question of someone else's interests. Of course this must be done on condition that we are not acting out of some hidden greed that is using charity as a pretext. Our action must be based on a completely impartial concern to see justice respected everywhere. Nonetheless, after he had reflected some more on this issue, he accepted our mother's judgment. He feared that this stiff opposition of my siblings indicated their deep attachment to this inheritance, which they perhaps had considered as something already acquired. If that was the case, it would only disturb them without profiting them if we demanded that they accept that things were going to turn out differently than they wanted. Instead of reminding them of their obligations, we would only embitter them.

Actions must be based on justice not individual interests

Seeing that I resisted this solution as strongly as I could, because I was unable to accept that we would let things slip away in this way, he told me that he knew all the parties to this action well. He was confident that they were reasonable and that undoubtedly there must have been some misunderstanding that made them so unreasonable in this matter. So we had to hope that when we saw them and informed them about everything, they would do justice for themselves and for me on their own initiative. If they did this, there would be nothing further to worry about. If, after we saw each other, they didn't do this, that would prove to me the error I would make in trying to force them to do this right now. I would only irritate and embitter them. In conclusion, he told me that I absolutely had to adhere to this solution. Of all the positions considered, this was the one closest to the charity and to the good example we should give them.

Explain situation to family

Dear Mother, I undertook this resolution with such firmness because it could be resisted so easily. I really don't know whether it gave me more a sense of grateful charity or of renewed joy because my profession would not be delayed. It seems to me that both sentiments were so powerful in me that I couldn't surrender uniquely to one or the other.

Nonetheless, I had to submit myself to what I had been ordered to do. The order so pleased my own desires that I don't think it would have been possible to refuse it. Still, I had difficulty in accepting this unexpected, overwhelming gesture of charity: the willingness to accept me freely into the order.

Difficulty in accepting the charity of being admitted freely

To console myself, I begged that the order accept me as a lay sister. This was the only rank in which I could imagine some solution to the distress I experienced. This thought did not arise at the first moment I saw myself reduced to choosing between delaying of my profession and being a ward of the convent. Because delay seemed impossible to my ardent desires, it seemed to me that I should commit my entire life to humble service to the sisters. This service would be a witness to the sisters of my gratitude for the double grace they would be granting me by receiving me without dowry. If their charity had the kindness to match my impatience, service as a lay sister seemed the proper response.

Recognizing how unworthy I was of such a favor, I couldn't accept that the sisters wouldn't see clearly enough the gratitude I maintained toward them. I would try to make up this debt by the little work that I would be capable of doing. Moreover, I already have serious deficiencies in the area of work. At first Monsieur Singlin did not disapprove this proposal. He agreed that there was nothing in the convent that could be more useful for me to do.

But God, who sounds the depths of the heart, knew I was not worthy of taking up a state of life so elevated in his sight and that my past and present pride merited a punishment rather than a reward. God removed Monsieur Singlin's original inclination to consent to this project. After more examination, he judged that I should not yield to this desire, because he didn't think I had the sufficient strength for this type of service. This being the case, I might end up spending more time taking care of myself than taking care of my companions. This in turn could disturb others by letting them think we were doing this for reasons other than service. It might seem that this was a concession to a particular person, a practice that is always odious because it offends charity and the religious spirit that tolerates no distinctions among the different sisters. So he decided to refuse absolutely the request I had made to him. I quickly retreated to letting things stand according to the exact terms that our mother had first proposed.

At that very hour I wrote to my siblings about my decision. I wrote at Monsieur Singlin's command and in the style he wanted me to use. He feared that I might prove too inflammatory in my letter. Still, he agreed that I could let them know quite clearly how unjust they had been and how they had distressed me. It was important to help them do justice by their own initiative and to challenge their belief that they had been offended. Their false belief made them think that they treated me properly if they simply avoided more explicit manifestations of anger and that they had no other obligations in this matter than to pardon me in their hearts.

At the same time he warned me to add many signs of my affection and concern for them, even signs of tenderness, and to avoid any sign of bitterness. God had given me the grace to avoid bitterness in this affair. If any embittered remarks filtered into my letter, they would surely notice it and would use this as a pretext to prolong the conflict.

He especially ordered me to let them know as discreetly as possible about the charity I had just received, about the convent's desire to have me profess my vows without any delay, with no concern about the state of my finances. I should tell them that this charity implied no animosity toward them at all. It was not inspired by any spite or by some gust of bravado. Nor was it a gimmick to prick their sense of honor. I just expressed as simply as I could the sentiments of the convent and of my companions on this question, which were just the opposite of the aforementioned sentiments. I simply tried to make them understand that we didn't think a small material gain in any way sufficient to delay something as important for a soul as the total and solemn consecration it wants to make of itself to God.

Since the letter could not be very short, I took until the evening to complete it. I couldn't see our mother that day. The next day, however, she had the whole novitiate assemble to see her. You know that she had the custom of doing so whenever she arrived from Port-Royal de Paris. I found myself with the other sisters.

When it was my turn to greet her, I couldn't prevent myself from telling her that I was the only sad nun among all those who had the joy of seeing her again. She said: "What! My daughter, is it possible that you are still distressed? Haven't you resigned yourself to everything that has happened? Haven't you known for a long time that you must never presume the friendship of creatures and that the world loves only its own? Aren't you happy that God has clearly let you know this in the person of those from whom you least expected it? This removed any possible doubt you might have about it before you left this illusion once and for all. This helped you to undertake this action with even greater courage, since it has now become a necessity for you. It should make you unshakable in the decision you have made, because in a certain sense you can say that you no longer have anyone left in the world."

Tearfully I responded by saying that it seemed I was already so detached from the world that I didn't need this experience. She told me: "God wants to make you see that you are quite mistaken in this belief. If you really had this indifference, you would consider everything that happens with true indifference rather than troubling yourself as you do. That is why you must realize what a great grace God is giving you and how you can profit from it."

She told me several other things on the vanity of all human affection. She hugged me with great tenderness until she had to leave me so that others could approach her.

The next day, having noticed an extraordinary sadness in my face during the office of prime, she left the choir stall before the beginning of Mass. Calling me over, she did everything she could to relieve my distress. But this time was too brief to satisfy her sense of charity. Immediately after Mass, she made a sign for me to follow her. She seated me next to her. For an entire hour she held me with my head upon her bosom, hugging me with the tenderness of a true mother. Alas! I can truly say that she neglected nothing in her power in her efforts to allay my chagrin.

Thanks be to God, dear Mother, that I have enough presence of mind and enough memory to lose nothing of the precious liquor with which she tried to soften the bitterness my heart tasted. I believe I gained a great deal by my ordeal. I dare say I could give you a rare present if I could describe all of it. But I do not have enough skill and art to preserve everything, as would be ideal. I was able only to prevent the loss of the memory. To preserve what little remains of this memory, I place this letter in your hands. Let it be treated as a relic, which remains of great worth even if it is only a tiny particle of a vast whole.

The letter is intended to preserve the memory/emotions of the event

With a severity full of kindness she first said to me: "My daughter, I cannot hide my astonishment to see you so overwhelmed by something that is really nothing at all. You surprised me yesterday when you told me you were distressed. I wasn't sure exactly what to say. I thought that you surely had forgotten everything that had happened. Since there had been no change in the decisions previously made, you had nothing further to worry about. I assure you that I had no idea what you wanted to say. It took me a little time to figure it out and to go back to this old business."

I felt crushed by this response, but the embarrassment was not sufficient to prevent my admiration for this power to forget quickly. My Mother, you surely remember that this problem was so recent that we had arrived at a solution to it only the day before. However, she didn't even think about it anymore. This showed how she considered all these things with true indifference and with what sincerity she wanted me to detach myself from all of them, considering this business as something definitively closed. There was no longer any reason even to think about it.

JP needed to detach herself

But I was far distant from such a rare virtue. I could only respond to her through my tears. Seeing this, she anticipated a possible excuse by saying: "Why do you cry like that? Why don't you cry as much for the sins of the world? You should consider only God and the interests of the conscience of your relatives in this affair. When you see people falling into faults and infidelities far graver in God's sight, why haven't you cried for them as intensely as you have when some people only failed to show some of the affection they owed you?" I responded with what I thought was a truthful answer. I said that I was bothered only by the injustice they had done to the convent. As for myself, I felt no personal bitterness or distress. In fact, I thought I was personally quite indifferent.

She told me: "You are mistaken, my daughter. Nothing outrages us more than friendship violated. You had a true affection for them and you saw that theirs was not equal to yours. Although it's obviously true that they still love you a great deal, they are still in the world. All the particular graces God has granted them, which permitted them to have more light about the things of God than most people do, cannot change the fact that when you are in the world, you act as the world acts. In other words, self-interest always takes first place. You are shocked by this fact, without even thinking about it. It's true that you haven't done the same. You are no longer in the world, but you still haven't completely left it. The proof is that your passionate focus on the injustice done to the convent by this affair (although I know very well that what really irks you the most is the injustice done to you personally, because self-love clearly flavors your entire reaction) is not matched by a similar inflamed reaction to all the other injustices visited on the convent."

On this point she had the kindness to tell me in some detail several stories of the same nature, without revealing the names of the persons involved. In my opinion she did this both to give me the consolation that derives from discovering others who face the same problems and to let me know that we always put more passion into our defense of some question of justice when we have a personal stake in the outcome than when we are truly disinterested.

After I confessed my personal hurt in this affair, she added the following out of the kindness of her heart: "This is one of the reasons I am glad this trial occurred. Even for the double of your inheritance, I would not have wanted you to miss this test before your profession. You weren't tested enough during your novitiate. Look, Sister, you renounced the world with great ease. God had given you the grace to realize the vanity and the fragility of all the diversions and of all the amusements of the world, which charm and captivate other girls. This doesn't mean you are better than they are. It is God who gave you this grace. Undoubtedly you are seriously detached from the world. But there are still two things you must strip away, and you haven't thought enough about them. First, although you do not have great wealth according to the world's standards, you do have substantial wealth according to the standards of religious life, where you should have next to nothing of value. Second, the principal wealth of your home was the intimate friendship and union that made you share everything and that was so pervasive that you

God wanted to make JP poor

God demands detachment from the material

could simply take it for granted. God wanted to strip both possessions away from you in order to make you truly poor in everything.

"The sacrifice of affection was even greater than that of material goods, since you had already offered the convent some alms that could have served as a small substitute for the greater donation you wanted to give it. You should be satisfied with the material side of the sacrifice. Your generosity did not become less simply because things didn't go as you had intended them to.

"But you didn't think about freeing yourself from the affection and the esteem that you had for your relatives, because it seemed completely innocent to you. And in fact, everything about this was completely legitimate and completely proper. Still, you understand that God wanted more detachment from you. That is why he wanted you to know the sentiments they held toward you.

Must abandon the secular to see God

"This is why I must tell you that I had such joy when this crisis erupted, because they didn't maintain the same attitude toward you. You wouldn't have learned anything, and you would have remained in the same flattering thought that they supported you as much as you supported them. And in effect, up until this point there was every reason to maintain this illusion. But believe me, this situation is rare. Those who give themselves to God do everything in God's sight with sincerity and frankness, without any admixture of self-interest, but those who stay in the world cannot avoid having an all too human perspective on even the holiest things. Instead of treating secular things in the spirit of God, they end up treating the things of God in a secular spirit.

"We shouldn't be shocked by this. It's nearly impossible to do otherwise as long as we live in the world, unless God grants us some particular grace. All those we do business with do as much. None of them consider or judge things by any other standard than that of the spirit of the world and of human reason. As a result, they don't even know how to look at things from God's viewpoint. That would be considered just silliness.

"Judge for yourself. Isn't it true that everyone would say that someone would be stupid not to do everything possible to preserve her alleged right to an inheritance? That it would be unthinkable for her just to leave it for someone else? I tell you that it would be difficult to find someone who wouldn't share that sentiment, no matter how tenderhearted she might be. People are so taken with their own self-interest that this becomes their only motive to act. If there is a little charity to be done, they much prefer to do it by their own hands than to let others do it, even though acts of altruism are not all that common. Believe me, worldly people have little inclination to perform acts of charity, because they don't know what it is to live in real need. They've

Worldly people do not understand charity

never undergone it, because they've never really lacked anything. That is why, if I had been here and you had spoken to me of the proposal you wanted to make to your siblings, I would have predicted exactly what would happen, because I have often seen similar situations.

"Look, Sister, when someone has left the world, they consider all the favors we try to give her as a futile gesture. There are only two motives that could make them accept your project: either charity, by sharing your sentiments, or affection, by wanting to oblige you. Now you know very well that the one person who has the greatest interest in this business[5] is still too captive to the world, and even bound by the vanity and the diversions of the world, to prefer the alms you would like to give over his own personal comfort. Can anyone believe he would have enough affection to be considerate of your desires? That would be hoping for something unheard of, indeed impossible. That would require a miracle, a miracle of nature and of the passions. But there's no reason to expect a miracle in such a person. You know very well that we can never expect a miracle to happen."

I couldn't help interrupting her at this point by saying that, although I had made such reflections, I still managed to maintain some confidence in my siblings. I thought that I had the right to hope for one of these miracles, since there had been several examples in my family even more extraordinary than this one. One example was my late father's dealings with one of my uncles, who was already very much in his debt.

She said to me: "I have no problem believing that, but your uncle was a man committed to the world. Didn't you ever hear about a small story in the lives of the desert fathers, which has a clear relation to what you've said, although it might not seem so at first sight? A man of the world went to see one of his brothers who, after leading a very holy life in the world, had retired to a life of solitude. The man was astonished to find his brother eating at the hour of none, because before his retreat he ate only at the hour of vespers. Seeing his brother's astonishment, the recluse said: 'Don't be scandalized, my brother. It's not a matter of being lax. This is a matter of necessity. When I was in the world, I didn't need to do this, because my ears nourished me. The praises that they accorded my austerities so satisfied my mind that the body itself was fortified and strengthened, even if it was still in need. But here no one says anything to me. Self-love has nothing to prop itself up. Despite my inclinations I'm obliged to give some satisfaction to nature, because it is absolutely deprived of pleasure from any other source.'"[6]

5. Blaise Pascal.

6. For the source of this story, see *Les vies des saints pères des déserts*, vol. 2, trans. Arnauld d'Andilly (Paris, 1653), 618–19.

Next she told me: "See, my daughter, it's the same with the case that you are talking about. An honest man in the world feels an obligation, even to the prejudice of his immediate interests, to help a person who like him remains in the world, because this person is an ever-present witness ready to trumpet the donor's actions whenever he is seen. The gratitude of this man and the accolades he brings to his patron are rewards for the generous man that accumulate whenever people hear the congratulations for the great deed.

"But the services you give to someone outside the world are very different indeed. Since it is a pure act of charity, which is more helpful to the one who gives than to the one who receives, no one has any reason to praise you for it. She who has received the benefit cannot publicize it, because she is not around to do so. Those who could know and approve it forget it easily enough, because they have no interest in it. No one is paid to keep a memorial of it. It is because of this that people consider as pure loss anything done for nuns, because there is neither public honor nor temporal gain that acts as a reward in these cases. Consider this a certain truth, which never fails to prove itself. Otherwise you will always be disappointed.

"I've had so much experience of this that I can no longer have any doubts about it. The simple reason that should make us see this truth is that this is the way the world is and the way it acts. It has always acted this way, and it always will. If it acted differently, it would no longer be the world. That is why you should accept that once you leave the world, you no longer have any friends within it. There are none from whom you should expect grand gestures of friendship, except those that are made out of a motive of charity. But if charity is the real motive, you personally will not be singled out for consideration. They could have done as much for a total stranger."

To develop this point, she told me about several incidents similar to my own that she herself had witnessed. One concerned the relatives of a wealthy girl who made her profession in the convent. Despite the appearance of goodwill, the relatives were not faithful to the promises they had made concerning her dowry, which would have been substantial. Further, this occurred at a time when the convent had great need of such resources. The nun in question had always shown the most ardent affection toward these relatives.

She told me: "You can be sure that this injustice took me by surprise and that it deeply disturbed me. I thought that the whole business of the dowry had been completely settled. I thought they would conduct themselves in the way they always had. However, the late Monsieur de Saint-Cyran advised me to accept this difficult trial—because it truly was one—with such tenderness and such peace that he didn't even want me to speak with them

[handwritten margin note, top left:] Charity should not be publicized

[handwritten margin note, middle left:] Once you leave the world, you must be a total stranger to it.

about it. Nor did he want me to give them any indication of how wounded we had been by this action. He just wanted me to act as if I had forgotten everything. He assured me that I had only to place my confidence in divine providence. If I did so, surely God would know how to compensate for this loss and attend to our needs by other means."

Then she added: "God granted me the grace to believe and to follow his advice, because I never believed that it was permitted to do anything against his inspiration. Many subsequent experiences have taught me the truth of this promise, as you can see for yourself. That is why, my daughter, in God's name, don't become carried away against your siblings. Don't show them any bitterness. That will only deepen the current alienation. After all, what is this really all about? A tiny sum of money, that's all. Isn't this less than nothing? Now, it's true that some wealth is necessary just to live. We can't completely renounce it. But honestly, it's quite rare that we fall into real need. It's just greed to accumulate wealth for superfluous needs. When God sends material goods our way by legitimate paths, we can receive them because it's neces-sary to have some wealth to keep on living. But when this doesn't happen, or when someone takes our goods away, we honestly should rejoice about it.

[margin note: necessary to have some wealth to survive BUT... need to reject lavishness]

"The late Monsieur de Saint-Cyran said that riches are to the world what unhealthful humors are to the body. They always concentrate themselves in the part that is weakest and most susceptible to harm. That's why it's danger-ous for someone when she sees wealth coming at her from every side. Instead of rejoicing when you see that people are generous with us, you should fear the very real possibility that the convent might become too wealthy. Please remember this lesson well. You are still young. Someday you might see cer-tain things similar to what is now happening in your own life and in your own situation. I am delighted to see everything that has happened, because at the very least, if in the future someone sought your advice in a similar situation, you could teach others to respond as you yourself have been taught to re-spond."

[margin note: Riches are unhealthy for the spirit]

She added: "So, write again to your relatives, especially to this person who, as you well know, has the greatest affection for you.[7] Show them every possible affection with your heart truly open. Then they can realize that you are sincerely motivated by the unique concern of not hurting their feelings. This is what has driven you to renounce your claim to the disposition of your inheritance. You are no longer even concerned about it. And when the one who should arrive shortly[8] has finally come, speak to him in the same way,

7. Gilberte Pascal Périer.
8. Blaise Pascal.

JP. must
consume
herself that
it is of no
consequence

without making the least reproach and without showing the least chagrin over what has happened. Just show him that you have forgotten this conflict. In fact, you should have already done so by now. I had expected you to have already changed. I remain astonished that you still seem so shaken about something that is of no consequence."

After that she was silent. This gave me a chance to tell her that one of the things that disturbed me the most in this affair was my conviction that I had used my wealth poorly when it was still at my disposition. I gave a good part of it to certain people who would not have received it had I distributed my alms with a more discreet charity. Although I thought I had enough resources both to help the people I did and then to help the others I wanted to, I still felt guilt about these choices. At the very least, my judgments appeared to be too precipitous.

After having reflected a bit on my words, she said: "Don't worry about that. I don't think that when you still had some goods at your disposition, you could have avoided doing what you did when you made a conscientious judgment on the situation at hand. You know quite well that you considered God in all of this and that you considered the welfare of this person[9] who must be more precious to you than all the gold in the world. You didn't do this by some ambition to place him in high society or to give him some worldly splendor. What you gave him didn't even give him the material possibility of doing so. You see that he doesn't have enough left to live up to the standard set by other members of his social circle. So how could you fear that you didn't use your resources properly? How could you have done any less for him?

"Let me be even clearer on this point. Even if it's true that what you gave him only helps him at the moment to live a vain and worldly life, I don't think that in God's sight you would have had any less an obligation to do what you did. If you hadn't made this gift, you would have offended him and done him a great harm by using this wealth in some other way. I'm talking about an offense to his conscience.

"Don't think that I am just saying this to console you in your distress. I must tell you a true story that you will find astonishing. The late Monsieur de Saint-Cyran—who, as you know, was completely given to God—had a brother who was as given to the world as anyone could be. He even died in this worldly state. I don't have to say how much this disturbed him. Still, even though he knew his brother's state well, he didn't hesitate to give him a considerable property that he owned. He wanted to dispose of it so that he could

9. Blaise Pascal.

possess as few worldly goods as possible. Undoubtedly he knew quite well that there were better ways to use this property. He could have made many charitable contributions from its sale. Yet he didn't do so. He gave it to his brother, who would only use it to flatter his own vanity. He did this out of a charitable motive not any less important than the charitable use I talked about earlier. He did this to keep the friendship of this person and to prevent any estrangement, which would have certainly occurred if he had not acted in this way. Had he done otherwise, he clearly would have manifested his low opinion of his brother's state and shown that he considered any gift to his brother a gift wasted or poorly used. By doing so, he would have abandoned any hope of helping his brother in the way he desired. Since he knew how to put a true price on things, he had no problem in sacrificing and even losing some material goods in order to pursue spiritual goods. In other words, my daughter, don't have any regrets about having done the same, since you made this gift for exactly the same reason."

In an admirable act of charity she added: "In order to remove any remaining scruple on this issue, you should know that even if it were true that you had made some error in this affair and that you had dissipated some wealth—which, of course, I don't think you did—and that you had wasted your money, you should consider it as one of the most minor faults anyone could commit. Truly, it's one of the most minor.

"Look, Sister, all external and perishable things are nothing. The smallest loss of the grace of God is a thousand times graver in his sight than is the loss of all the goods of the earth, however well they might be used. He does not respect our goods. He considers them as nothing in comparison with the virtues he places in us. Those are the true goods. We should often examine our conscience to consider the use we make of them for our own profit and for that of others. But we don't think about that at all.

"We show little or no concern when we see that our humility, or our kindness, or some other virtue is declining. We grow scrupulous about how we used a small sum of money, but this is the least of the goods of which God will demand an accounting, because this little sum could only have been used for some temporary relief of a few temporal miseries or for some other work that would quickly fade with time. On the other hand, God's graces and the virtues he gives us are treasures that should eternally assist our own soul and those of others, if we are careful to use them well and to avoid losing them.

"Finally, this business was finished long ago. You shouldn't think any more about it. I say that this is all a temptation trying to divert you from what you have to do now. Don't think any more about all that. Think only about giving thanks to God for having mercifully given you the inspiration to leave the world. He let you come to know this particular convent and gave you the affection for this convent, which made you prefer it to all others. Without this inspiration, you would have undoubtedly entered the Carmelites, who are so popular now and who have such a great reputation for sanctity—and with good reason, because they are women as holy as anyone could desire. They perform extraordinary austerities and follow their rule so exactly that they obey every syllable.

"There is simply no reason to have any concern for the question of the inheritance. Given your current state of affairs, there is no reason to have a quarrel with your relatives or to break off your communications with them. We shouldn't dwell on the details of what they might have hoped to receive from you.

"This affair should make us compassionate. At the same time it should perplex us. It's obvious that these people are holy. They are souls so faithful to the good as they see it. It's obvious that they are doing this because they somehow lack the proper education to understand that what they are doing is evil, indeed a very great evil. We have every reason to believe—I mean, it's morally certain—that if they themselves had the lights with which God has favored us, they would be even more faithful to them than we are. That is why we should admire even more the mercy of God. It is so rare, but he has shown it to us, although we have done nothing to merit it. This should give us so much joy that you forget all the rest. If you were in their situation, do you think you could do anything better than to follow the order of your superiors, as you are doing here? Where would you be otherwise? So aren't you happy that you've fallen into the hands of people who can guide you by pure rules of charity, since they have no personal stake in the conflict?"

I couldn't prevent myself from asking her to take into account that this was the very reason I felt so distressed about this situation. The injustice that my siblings were doing was all the graver because the convent was so genuinely disinterested.

Then she told me: "Now there's a sentiment that shows that you still are not completely a part of the convent. You still haven't lost the habit of considering yourself as belonging more to your family than to the community here. That is why you are so jealous of your family's honor and superiority in comparison with that of your religious community."

Then becoming more serious again, she said: "Look, my daughter, it's certainly true that the charity you owe your relatives obliges you to desire ardently that they become reasonable again. But you should desire this in everything, not just in those things that concern you personally. Otherwise this wouldn't really be charity; it would be a kind of cupidity. If it were nec-

[margin note: Convent has embraced JP]

[margin note: JP must learn to value her new religious community]

essary for your relatives to do some injustice to someone, you should whole-heartedly wish that they did it to us rather than to someone else. After all, you don't know how others would have reacted to this, but you're well aware that we are scarcely concerned about it. Moreover, it's obvious that al-though—thanks be to God—we aren't rich, we aren't so needy that we can't do without this gift.

"You see that we don't really lack anything. We have no great needs. Ac-tually, this is the sort of thing that should perplex us in God's sight, since we have made a vow of poverty. Beyond all this, we think that it's a true benefit for us when we are mistreated by others in everything. Let them despise us. Let them reject us. Let them calumniate us. Let them treat us unjustly. Now, it's not that we wish for all this to happen. We shouldn't actively seek this op-position by some initiative of our own. That would be a lack of charity to-ward those who do it, because there would be some sin on their part. Still, when it happens to us we experience a great happiness. In fact, when God permits this to happen, without our doing anything to cause it, we have good reason to rejoice about it. I say that this is grounds for true joy. This works to our greatest spiritual profit. We must believe this and act accordingly. Oth-erwise we would be unfaithful to the lights God gives us. We would have nei-ther poverty nor detachment. After all, how real would they be if they didn't appear at such moments of opposition? Are they supposed to be just stage speeches and mimes performed to gain the applause of the world?"

She said these words so forcefully that it seemed she doubted I could re-ally put them into practice and wanted to sear them into my heart. But as if she had perceived my own thoughts, she immediately responded to me by softening her words a bit. As she smiled, she said to me: "I have no doubt that you share the same sentiments. I'm quite confident that if someone asked your advice in a similar situation concerning people who are supposed to be indifferent, you would strongly object to any position other than the one we cherish. I am certain that you would show neither displeasure nor any pique toward these people. Surely you wouldn't want to make the least grimace or the least reproach toward them.

"All of this should make you see that there is still a good deal of self-love that clings to you. Whatever you might think, it's neither the convent nor justice that concerns you the most in what has happened. What concerns you is yourself and the distress you experience in not being able to make things go the way you had wanted.

"If by chance thieves had come here last night and carried away all our money, would you weep and wail as you are doing? Of course not. Although such an event would disturb us and we should try to prevent it from occurring, we still wouldn't be that upset by it. We are not that attached to our wealth. Still, it would be an injustice. It would be a transgression against the convent. See, we shouldn't flatter ourselves about our motives. It is for ourselves and for our own self-interest that we weep.

"So forget everything that has happened. Conduct yourself toward your siblings as I've told you to. I beg you to speak to them and to write to them as if nothing had happened, except to tell them that you have renounced your part of the inheritance.

"Still, you should be sincere in everything you write and say. On the one hand, you must avoid speaking out of pride and out of a false courage. You shouldn't say: 'We are more generous than you are.' If that's how we do it, we won't accomplish anything at all. On the other hand, you should be careful not to turn sentimental, not to needle their sense of affection so that they will feel obliged to do what you want. That approach will only take with one hand what you gave away with the other. Your sole intention in all this should be bringing peace to everyone in this affair.

"You should be especially considerate with your female relation.[10] You know how sensitive she is. She could become very disturbed if she thought you were angry with her. This could dangerously intensify the serious illness she faces at present."

Beloved Mother, I am narrating all the details of this small incident with greater freedom than reason might require. It might even violate the rules of politeness to pester others, especially persons in authority, with things that concern only us. But I thought it right to violate custom in this case, since it seemed to me that anyone would be as moved as I personally was to see this concern and this charity from our mother.

Her actions were irrefutable proof that when this divine virtue is as strongly rooted in a soul as it is in hers, it is the virtue of charity that governs everything. It takes care of everything; it authors the least movements and thoughts; in every relationship it gives proofs of the blessed empire it rules. It does this because charity becomes second nature to a person, once charity becomes the mistress of that person's first nature.

You know that this clearly occurs in the conduct of all our mothers. But I must say that I never noticed it as clearly as I did in this interview. I don't know if this is because I've never seen the other mothers act in such a situation or because we are always more affected by what concerns us personally. Beloved Mother, it seems to me that you know me well indeed. So I can share with you all the joy I felt when I saw how, in the midst of all my distress, these

[handwritten margin note: Virtue of Charity governs everything]

10. Gilberte Pascal Périer.

actions forcefully confirmed all the positive impressions I had of the disinterestedness of the convent and the purity of its conduct.

Nonetheless, I was still so proud—I don't dare call it a sense of justice anymore—that I couldn't absolutely resolve to let things alone, as our mother wanted. So I begged her to consider that if we delayed my religious profession for four years, I could then hope to be the mistress of all my affairs. We could even add to the principal of my funds the interest from a considerable pension that my relatives granted me, in consideration of certain services rendered. Their rough treatment of me seemed to release me legitimately from any duty to let them use this interest in the future as they had done until now. Despite my desire to make my religious profession as soon as possible, a desire that burned more ardently than I can possibly express, I still thought myself obligated in conscience to delay this profession. This would place me in a situation where I could do justice to the convent.

JP still felt obligated in conscience to provide $

She said to me: "No, my daughter. On the contrary, you have a clear obligation not to do this. Don't you see that although you have the power to execute your project, you have no power to make them agree to it? I've never had any illusion on that score. I know that in principle no one can prevent you from doing what you want with your personal wealth. But I've never been concerned about what you can do in theory. I'm only concerned about what you should do. That is the entire question.

Change will come on its own accord;

"I have no doubt that you have an obligation, a pressing one, to strengthen their souls as much as you can and to do nothing that would offend them. When you thought that you had complete disposition of these things, you still wanted to have your siblings' approval to do what you wanted to do. That was the right sentiment. Otherwise you would have given them a good reason to feel offended. In fact, you acted this way to avoid offense. Now ask yourself how they would react if you did this against their will and by some kind of violence. If something is going to change here, it must come from them and from their own free will, without any pressure from you at all."

JP should follow her heart; profess

Being neither able to respond to these arguments nor capable of resisting her will, I begged her at least to let me threaten them with legal action and see what effect that might produce. She no more consented to this proposal than to any of my others.

She told me: "No, my daughter, that's out of the question. Don't you understand that by doing this you would be destroying everything you hoped to accomplish by the surrender of your claim? Believe me, leave everything as it is. Remember that your first obligation is to prefer their serenity of spirit and the restoration of peace among you over every other concern. You

Prefer serenity of spirit above all else

shouldn't do here what they tried to do to you elsewhere. I'm especially concerned about the one relative who should be so precious to you.[11] If you had two million francs, I would advise you without hesitation to give them to him, if by that gesture you could reignite the charity between you.

"Let's not talk about this anymore. Don't think about it anymore. When you see them, don't talk about it at all. If they raise the question, tell them they know very well that you've surrendered all these things into their hands. Since you no longer have anything to do with all this, you no longer think about it." With that, she bade me farewell without wanting any reply. This is how the interview ended.

A few days later, the relative with the greatest interest in this affair came to town.[12] I tried to deal with him as our mother had intended. But no matter how hard I tried, it was impossible for me to hide completely the sadness I still had, despite all her efforts to free me from distress. This was so unusual for me that he immediately noticed it. He didn't need an interpreter to tell him the cause. Although I tried to put on my friendliest expression, I was certain that he had concluded that his way of acting had plunged me into this state.

Nonetheless, he wanted to be the first to complain. It was then I learned that they were so offended by my complaints. But he scarcely continued his criticism. He saw that I didn't make any complaint on my own, although I could have demolished his argument with a single word. On the contrary, I told him with all the joy my mood permitted that since the convent had the charity to receive my vows without dowry and that my profession of vows would not be delayed, I no longer had any concerns except making my vows well and asking for the grace to live as a true nun.

If this entire conversation had been as worthy of being recorded as was the preceding one, I would have tried to retain all of its details. I would never complain of the time it would have taken to write it all down. However, it was neither so moving nor so helpful, as I'm sure you can readily understand. So without further ado, it's better just to let the rest pass in silence rather than wasting your time in boring details. To make it short, I would simply say that he was clearly moved by compassion and that on his own initiative he decided to put some order into this confused business. He offered to assume personally all the expenses and the risks tied to the inheritance. He also offered in his own name to give the convent the contribution that justice clearly demanded.

11. Blaise Pascal.
12. Blaise Pascal.

Dear Mother, now I can finish this story. I realize that this whole affair isn't really worth your time. I wrote it down only to preserve the memory of all the debts I owe our mother superiors and of all the profitable instructions I received in these interviews. That is why I have an obligation to finish this narrative, since both the debts and the instructions continued right up to the end of this affair.

After he left me, I gave an account of this interview to our mothers. I wanted them to tell me if I should specify what he owed the convent, as he seemed to expect me to do. But they absolutely forbade me to give him any specific bill. They expressly ordered me to be satisfied with whatever he wanted to offer. I should neither demand nor suggest a particular amount. I should just let him follow his inclinations. Still, knowing the nature of his wealth, they agreed that I could suggest to him that we take what he wanted to give from a certain part of the inheritance that was designated as his own settlement. This was the only concession that I could obtain. The conversation ended on this note.

I didn't have any leeway to try to resolve this problem by obtaining more than he wanted to give, since I had received the express order to accept his first decision as law. The order was so clear and the authority behind it so absolute that I didn't dare to act any further in this business, except in the most prompt and accommodating way. I acted as if it no longer concerned me.

But I still had scruples about this affair. The commands I had received on this matter were supported by so many excellent reasons taken from the very principles of reason itself that I surrendered to them completely. Still, I had to admit that when I contravened them in the slightest, I felt as though I had violated my own conscience as well as the vow of obedience. I could finish this affair entirely only after three or four more interviews, which were completely favorable to my position. When I gave an account of these interviews to our mothers, I recognized their constant concern that everything happen according to God's will and according to the rules of perfect charity. Beloved Mother, I cannot tell you clearly enough how evident was this concern in every meeting we had. I pray God that I may never forget this lesson. I can truly say that I received better instruction from their actions in this affair than from many sermons I've heard on these matters.

Especially admirable here was the diversity of conduct that the same animating Holy Spirit inspired in each one of them.

Our mother, understandably defending the interests of the convent, made it clear that her principal concern was to prevent the impression that the slightest shadow of self-interest, greed, or venality was mixed up with this issue. Finally, she used every bit of energy to underline that we would rather suffer every kind of injustice than permit the least act even slightly contrary to the true spirit of religious life.

Monsieur Singlin, as spiritual father of the convent and of my relatives— some of them are under his exclusive spiritual direction and the others show a boundless respect and affection for him—shared our mother's zeal concerning the reputation of the convent. He also was compassionate toward them in their plight. He lamented the injustice of their actions, but he rejoiced no less in the spiritual profit this brought the convent.

Mère Agnès seemed to leave these particular interests on the shoulders of these two. She in turn was particularly interested in helping her novice profit spiritually from everything that had happened. Every time I saw her, she carefully analyzed what I reported to her in order to point out anything too worldly or too complacent in my manner of acting. By an indefatigable charity, she never ceased to make every effort to anticipate and to counsel against any faults I might fall into. She helped lift me up when her warnings didn't prevent errors. She helped me to embrace every opportunity to practice patience, or tolerance, or humility, or another of the virtues that offer little attraction to the imperfect.

It's not that our mother superior wasn't also committed to this work. But given that her duty was more tied to the conduct of the whole convent than to my personal conduct, she was not informed as frequently on issues that concerned only me. Every time the sight of me made her remember these events, our mother absolutely forbade me to make any effort whatever to try to make this affair come out as I wanted it to. Every time she spoke to me, she never failed to insist that I should remain firm in my resolution not to demand anything from my relatives. She incessantly exhorted me to consider the convent's interests in my way of proceeding.

Once, when I was giving a report to her, she saw that I spoke a bit too critically about what a certain person had proposed doing. She criticized me severely in this firm way that gives such power to the fiery words that so often leave her mouth. She told me that only pride or avarice—or both— could have made me speak this way. I seemed to want to both increase the wealth of the convent and to take the credit for being responsible for this. She spoke so forcefully on the dispositions that the spirit of poverty should inspire in me in this affair that I would have had to have been completely callous not to have some scruple in acting otherwise.

After everything in the conflict had been resolved, I asked to see our mother two days before the day of my profession of vows. The day for profession had been determined a long time before, with no relation to the resolution of this controversy. I asked our mother to come to the parlor for the

[margin note:] JP encouraged to remain firm to her spiritual resolve

purpose of signing the agreement we had settled on. But she could not, since she was very ill that day. Astonishingly, she was delighted with her incapacity to finalize the terms of this agreement because, she told me, "If the agreement is left until after the profession, your relative can act with complete freedom and out of a pure spirit of charity. Understand, my daughter, one must always be firm on basic principles. We know that everything not made by God's spirit and by charity is made by greed, and everything made by greed is sin.

Charity cannot be made in greed — it must be totally free

"That is why I have so often exhorted you not to appeal to his sense of honor or of friendship. I would much prefer that he give you nothing at all than give you a great deal out of all too human motives. If he makes a gift on his own initiative, there's nothing we can do about it. The only thing we two can do is exhort him not to do this. We are not the governors of his conscience. We can't be certain what motive pushes him. He has to make his own examination of conscience. But if our speeches, or our gesture, or anything else we do pressure him to make a bad self-examination, not only would we contribute to his sin, we would be the cause of it.

Do not do charity out of human motives

"That is why, my daughter, in God's name, be careful not to pressure him to do what you yourself would not want to do. If you were the one to make this decision, you wouldn't want to give alms to the convent out of purely human considerations. So why would you try to make him do the same? If he doesn't want to do this out of good motives, it's better that he not do it at all. Perhaps God will touch him at some other moment. But if that doesn't happen, don't worry about it for a minute. This will be a spiritual benefit for the convent.

"So go to him again. Now tell him, but in a cheerful mood, that he should examine his heart to see what is pushing him to make this donation. He shouldn't do anything precipitously. There will be plenty of time after the vow ceremony. I'm not in the state right now that would permit me to finish the formalities for the agreement. You know very well that no one ever talks about a dowry after a girl has made her religious profession."

I executed this command as faithfully as I could. I gave him the details of this small speech, word by word, just as I am giving them to you. He was more than a little surprised by it, although for a long time he had been well informed on how we do things here. But he had with him some businessmen who were astonished by this speech. They couldn't cease expressing their admiration for this way of proceeding. Unanimously they said that they had never heard anything like this and that this was far different from the usual way of conducting such business. But that in no way changed our manner of speaking.

Nonetheless, he didn't want to delay his gift any longer. To show that he was doing from good motives the little that was in his power to do and to persuade me that he regretted not being able to do more—which he always protested was the case—he returned the next day. He had an interview with our mother, which she had to grant because she was feeling better. After he returned from the interview, he explained what she had said.

First, she told him forcefully that she wasn't sure if I had acted in this affair as they had incessantly urged me to. She said: "Sir, because I fear that she might have failed to act properly, I am obliged to say that I beg you, in God's name, not to do anything out of human consideration. If you do not feel inclined to make this charitable contribution out of a spirit of charity, don't do it at all. You see, sir, we learned from Monsieur de Saint-Cyran to receive for God's house only what comes from God. Everything given by a motive other than charity is not a fruit of the Spirit of God, and consequently we cannot accept it." He responded to her passionately but politely. He told her that he wanted no further delay on this gift. So ended this interview.

Next our mother met with me. She told me that there was no reason to worry about this conflict anymore. All was finished. Then, taking me apart, she told me she had been disturbed to see me so agitated in trying to make this person act generously and so angry when I thought he wouldn't do so.

She told me with admirable charity: "My daughter, I really fear that you offended God in this affair. I beg you to think seriously about this. Beyond that, reflect on the fact that you truly have nothing to complain about in your relative, since he has certainly given a substantial portion of his wealth, especially if you compare it with the gifts we received from practically everyone else. I wish you knew how most people respond to the disinterestedness we show them. It's almost impossible to believe!

"But we shouldn't let this misbehavior become an excuse for our not doing our duty. Sometimes people say that if laypeople are so greedy and unjust, we shouldn't be astonished if vowed religious act the same way. But, my daughter, if we don't want to imitate their other vices, why would we imitate this one? They love amusements, gambling, and high fashion. When someone offends them, they avenge themselves and do a number of similar things. Should we do the same? No one is crazy enough to say so. Why then do they want us to imitate them in their avarice? Isn't this as sinful as the other actions? But when you are greedy, it's easy to excuse yourself by saying that everyone acts the same way. You shouldn't be misled by these arguments. You must know evil as it is and where it is."

Dear Mother, these were the last words I heard on this subject and the conclusion of this entire affair. Gratitude has not permitted me to hold it secret any longer, although the little leisure left to me by obedience seemed to take away all the means for making a record of it. Still, great desire can surmount any obstacle. That is what permitted me to surmount this obstacle as well as any others that might have arisen. As you can imagine, one of the obstacles was my fear that I would recount this affair poorly. But everything had to cede to my clear duty. Moreover, I have no pretension to have fulfilled this task well. I claim only to have fulfilled it as well as I could.

If my memory had been sharp enough to recall always the exact words of our mother, I would not have to apologize for this letter. But I wasn't able to report the literal words in many passages, although I'm certain I was faithful to the meaning of these conversations. Because of this limitation, I ask you to disregard anything that I misconstrued and to separate it from the rest. You have the habit of listening to our mother and you can readily recognize her distinctive style.

Dear Mother, I beg you to excuse this letter. It's poorly organized, full of erasures, of ink blots, of addenda, and of so many other disorders. I would have gladly recopied it out of respect for you, but I have so little free time that I don't know when I could have finished it. Moreover, I don't know whether I would have made fewer mistakes in rewriting it. My free time is so limited. The longest blocks of free time give me only enough time to write about twenty-five lines. The usual blocks permit barely five or six. I'm often interrupted by requests or by replies that are not very important but quite frequent. A small brain like mine doesn't need more than that to become upset and to spoil what has to be done. You know how easily this happens to me. I'm especially afraid that our mother would find me in such confusion. That is why I try to do these chores as quickly as possible.

For all these reasons I hope that your goodness will grant me a full pardon for the faults of composition. But I request something more important. With all my heart, dear Mother, I ask you to pray to Our Lord that he may pardon all the faults I committed in this affair. May he especially forgive the little use that I made of so much salutary advice. This was not my intention in writing to you, but since God has offered me this occasion, I do not want to neglect it. I hope to benefit by your charity, which I have experienced on so many occasions. I trust that, without considering what I am, you will not refuse me the assistance I need in order to become what I am not. This would assure that I didn't vainly receive the inestimable grace of being associated with such a holy family, committed to such a wise rule of life and so filled with the spirit of God. It wouldn't be in vain that I became a daughter of such mothers.

Finally, I implore you to offer to the Divine Majesty all those involved in my vocation to this convent. Ask God to give me the grace to avoid from now on this sort of ingratitude that manifests itself in the little use one makes of signal favors. This brief narrative shows you how many particular, as well as general, graces I must render an account of. There are so many of them. That is why with all my heart I implore the help of your prayers, and those of others who might see this narrative one day, to obtain from God the grace I so greatly need: to live and die as a true nun of the Blessed Sacrament and of the convent of Port-Royal (these two titles contain everything I would want to say).

I fear that all the great graces I received for my salvation will serve only to condemn me. I fear that the same consolations that his goodness granted me to dry my tears will become the accusers of my infidelity. I think I have some right to expect you to grant my request, since among these obligations stands the always happy obligation of being all my life and with all my heart,

My dear Mother,
Your most humble and obedient servant and daughter,
Soeur Jacqueline de Sainte Euphémie

P.S. Dear Mother, I thought I had no more apologies to make, but I now remember that I forgot to discuss the scandalous gold-gilt paper I have used in this report. I found it in a box someone left for me. As this was the only thing that remained for me from the world, at least from the external world, I thought that I should sacrifice it to God. It seemed to me that gold could have no better use than to praise the charity of which it is the image. I realize that I can do more than provide a shadow of the truth of the charity that they have shown toward me. In my opinion, letters written in blood would have been more apt than golden paper to preserve the memory of this charity.

A RULE FOR CHILDREN

INTRODUCTION

One of Mère Angélique's reforms at Port-Royal was the revival of the boarding school for girls at the convent. Varying in number from forty to sixty each year, the school's pupils were drawn largely from aristocratic families sympathetic to Jansenism. Composed at the request of Abbé Singlin, her spiritual director, *A Rule for Children* is an educational treatise in which Jacqueline Pascal explains her practice and theory as schoolmistress, starting in 1653. The first part of the treatise explains the mechanics of a typical school day at the convent; the second part dwells on the spirit that should animate teacher and student.

The first part stresses the monastic schedule that structures the school day. In addition to daily Mass, the pupils participate in the Divine Office, the liturgical round of psalms and hymns prayed by monks and nuns at prescribed hours. Other monastic practices characterizing the Port-Royal school day include the "grand silence," a ban on speaking from night prayers until after breakfast; the "chapter of faults," a meeting of teachers and pupils in which the pupils publicly accuse themselves of certain faults and ask forgiveness; and "reading at table," the reciting aloud of the Bible and other religious texts during meals, which are taken in silence. So austere is the daily schedule outlined by Pascal that the nuns who were the editors of the first edition (1665) of *A Rule for Children* cautioned the reader that not all children would be capable of such discipline and that a literal imitation of this program would be unwise.

The first part of the treatise also describes the curriculum at Port-Royal. Pupils are given a basic education in reading, writing, arithmetic, liturgical chant, and catechism. Catechetical instruction is clearly the most elaborate of the classes. The treatise indicates several important pedagogical innova-

(handwritten margin notes: Boarding school for aristocratic girls!; Discipline; Curriculum)

tions. In her discussion of reading and mathematics, Pascal underlines the value of having older pupils teach the younger ones. Each student, therefore, progressively becomes a teacher herself. Similarly, the teaching of catechism minimizes rote memorization. The teacher must provide a thorough explanation of a particular religious doctrine or practice. Such explanation requires application to the pupils' situation and sufficient dialogue between teacher and student on questions about the doctrine.

In the second part of the treatise Jacqueline Pascal evokes the spirit that should animate this structure of education. Since the central goal is safeguarding the child's salvation, Pascal stresses moral transparency as paramount in the relationship of teacher and pupil. The teacher must try to accurately determine the moral temperament of each child under her care. A personal teacher-student conference, which should occur at least biweekly, is one of the means for developing this moral knowledge. The strict surveillance of pupils that Pascal underlines in many passages serves this goal of moral transparency. The public penances, the elaborate preparations for confession, and the counsels on how to deal with recalcitrant students reflect the key purpose of Port-Royal education: the pupils' salvation and moral conversion.

The second part of the treatise also underscores the Jansenist cast of the education championed by Jacqueline Pascal. The major text used in catechism class is the *Théologie familière* of Saint-Cyran, a work censured by the archdiocese of Paris on suspicion of heresy. Especially in the treatment of the sacraments, a certain Jansenist rigorism appears. The elaborate conditions laid down for a good confession and the insistence that a good confession must be followed by a visible improvement in behavior set an unusually demanding standard for confessional practice, especially for young children. The treatment of Holy Communion is dominated by a fear of sacrilege. The strict conditions specified for giving a pupil permission to receive communion clearly discourage frequent reception of the sacrament.

A Rule for Children provides more than an outline of a convent model of education for women. It indicates an emancipation of women on two levels. First, by encouraging laywomen to adopt the liturgical piety usually reserved to priests and nuns, it subverts the hierarchical distinction of clergy/lay and monastic/lay. All members of the church are to enjoy access to Scripture and to the practice of liturgical prayer. Second, the education Pascal proposes spiritually empowers women. The nun-teacher, not only the priest-confessor, will strive to have a complete picture of the moral character of the pupil. Religious education proceeds by interrogation and dialogue, not only by memorization. The nun-teacher, not only the priest-preacher, will offer public commentary on the Gospel, adapting it to the needs of her pupils. In this monastic model of education the intellectual authority of the woman teacher becomes a pronounced spiritual authority.

This translation is based on Jacqueline Pascal, *Règlement pour les enfants*, in the Faugère edition, *LOM*, 228–300. The Faugère edition is based on the Guerrier manuscript, Père Guerrier, Ms. 2e recueil, cahiers-appendix, 1–76. This translation also incorporates material from the Cousin edition of the work: Jacqueline Pascal, *Règlement pour les enfants*, in *Jacqueline Pascal: Premières études sur les femmes illustres et la société du XVIIe siècle*, 8th ed. (Paris: Didier, 1877), 360–424 (hereafter, *JP*). The Cousin edition is based on the first published version of the *Règlements*, when it appeared as an appendix to the Constitutions of Port-Royal: Religieuses de Port-Royal, *Les constitutions du monastère de Port-Royal du Saint-Sacrement* (Mons: Gaspard Migeot, 1665), 421–528. The original print version contains several sections missing in the Guerrier manuscript: the text of prayers for the school day (end of part 1) and the chapter on confirmation (2.7). The Guerrier manuscript contains several paragraphs on confession (2.5.11, 12) absent from the original print version.

It is highly probable that Jacqueline Pascal was the author of these passages on confession, since the Guerrier manuscript incorporates Gilberte Pascal Périer's personal copy of her sister's autographs. It is unlikely that Jacqueline Pascal herself wrote the prayers included in the treatise, although they accurately represent the religious practices of the school under her direction. The authorship of the chapter on confirmation remains ambiguous. All the variant passages have been included and noted as such in this translation of the work.

Glory to Jesus, to the Most Blessed Sacrament
April 17, 1657

Beloved and honored Father,[1]

I humbly ask your pardon for having taken such a long time to write a report concerning my methods for working with children. From the first time you asked me to write such a report, I hesitated because I thought you were asking me to write about the methods that ideally we should use to teach them. Frankly I didn't believe myself capable of writing such a report—or thought it would require great temerity—since I had insufficient knowledge for such a difficult project.

I can assure you that only obedience was capable of making me undertake such a work. If I have achieved anything at all, we should attribute that

---

1. The addressee is Abbé Antoine Singlin, Jacqueline Pascal's spiritual director.

to the influence of the words of our mother,[2] who told me, when she gave me this job, that I should fear nothing and that God alone would do everything. These words so calmed my fears concerning my limitations that I became confident and peaceful. It was as if God himself had made this promise. I must honestly admit that when I become introspective and discouraged—as you know I often tend to do—these words, *God will do everything*, pronounced with confidence, are enough to give peace to my soul.

You also helped to lift the difficulties surrounding this work when you told me later that you were not asking me to write about how we should conduct ourselves with children in general. Rather, you wanted me only to explain how I myself worked with the pupils here. You would then be able to point out the faults that I committed in this work. These faults not only spoil what God is able to do through my agency, but they even place serious obstacles in front of the graces he places in these souls.

In order to keep some order in this report, I will begin by telling you how I organized a typical school day. In the second part I will explain what I do to promote the pupils' spiritual and corporal welfare.

PART 1: DAILY ORDER

Rising of Children

1. The oldest children awaken at 4:00 a.m. The next group follows them at 4:30. The mid-aged children rise at 5:00; the youngest, when their needs and capacities require. As you know, we have pupils of all ages, from four to seventeen and eighteen years old.

2. In waking them, we say "Jesus." They respond with "Maria "or "Deo gratias."

3. They must rise promptly, without taking any time to wake up. Otherwise we might encourage sloth. If they are not feeling well, they should alert those who wake them up, so that they might continue to rest. If some of the older pupils need more rest than the daily order usually provides, they should be given what they need. But when the prescribed hour for rising has been reached, they must arise promptly. It is dangerous to develop a habit of laziness in the first hours of the day.

4. On waking, they say a little prayer that is appropriate for this hour of the day.

5. As soon as they are awake, they worship God and kiss the floor. Then they come into the common room to dress. Once again they worship God as

2. Mère Angélique, the abbess of Port-Royal.

they kneel before their oratory. They pray aloud, to be sure no one has forgotten her duties.

6. The older pupils help each other comb their hair, but this should be done in perfect silence. It is only right that their first words are prayers and thanksgivings reserved for God. If some of them, out of necessity, must say something, they should address themselves to their schoolmistress. She can then ask for what they need from the person with that responsibility. It is crucial to avoid the conversations that might break out during this grand silence of the morning. It is also important to avoid the possibility that they might use the opportunity to speak quietly about some necessity as the occasion to say something unnecessary to others, which could not be heard clearly by the schoolmistress. That could even become the occasion for telling a lie, if someone asked them what they had just said.

This strict silence continues until the Pretiosa of prime.[3] It is also maintained during the Angelus in the evening, when the pupils are walking in the garden.

Dressing of Children

1. We exhort them to comb their hair and to dress as quickly as possible. This accustoms them to giving as little time as possible to decorating a body that must serve as food for worms. This also acts as a reparation for the vanity of society women when they dress and have their hair done.

2. As soon as the older pupils are dressed, they comb and dress the younger pupils with the same speed and in the same silence. We try to have everything finished at 6:15. It is about this time that the bell for the first Mass begins to ring.

3. Each older pupil has the duty to listen to prayers repeated by the younger pupil as she has her hair combed and arranged.

[handwritten margin notes: Dress Quickly.. why Adorn the temporal body-- concentrate on the spirit!]

Morning Prayers

1. At the last stroke of prime, or at the latest at the Pretiosa, they kneel to begin prayers as soon as the signal is given by the schoolmistress. She, or another nun who serves as her companion, always assists at the prayers. The pupils begin by prayers that are their own. They then recite prime from the liturgical office. Every week we choose a child who leads all the prayers said in the common room. That's why I call her "the weekly leader."

3. Prime is a liturgical office of psalms and prayers usually recited at 6:00 a.m.

2. Prime and compline[4] are recited on a midrange tone, neither too high nor too low. This encourages brief meditations. All the pupils stand during all of prime and compline.

3. We teach them that they all remain in this posture to witness to God that they are all ready to accomplish his holy will.

4. All the common prayers said in the common room are said slowly, distinctly, and with proper pauses.

5. At the end of prime, they have a short time, approximately the space of two Misereres,[5] to consider before God what they have to do throughout the day. They may also consider the principal faults they might have committed the preceding day, in order to ask God for the grace to foresee and to avoid the occasions of sin that make them fall.

Making Beds and Breakfast for the Children

1. At the end of prayers, the pupils all go together to make their own beds and those of the youngest, making them in pairs according to their assignment. No one leaves a room unless all the beds are completely made. The only exception is decided by the nun who accompanies them. She might permit some of them to go start making beds in other rooms, if she thinks she can keep an eye on them in several rooms at the same time. Still, we pay careful attention to the children we send. They should be those who are clearly well behaved and obedient.

2. While they are making their beds, one of them prepares breakfast and whatever is necessary for washing hands. She also puts out water and wine for washing the mouth.

3. When the beds are done, they go to wash their hands and take breakfast together. During breakfast, one of them does a reading from the martyrology of the day, so that the pupils know which saints the church commemorates on that day and so that they may honor them and place themselves under their protection.

Work

1. At the end of breakfast, which is about 7:30 at the latest, all the pupils retire to the room set up for needlework. There they must use their time with

---

4. Compline is the liturgical office recited usually before retiring. In addition to psalms and a canticle, it contains an examination of conscience. Like other monasteries of the period, Port-Royal often moved the recitation of part of this night office to the early morning.

5. Psalm 51, a psalm of penitence.

care, keeping a strict silence. If it is necessary to speak, it must be done in a very low voice, not disturbing those mature enough to enter into a silent dialogue with God.

2. We accustom the young pupils not to speak, although we permit them to play after they have faithfully finished their work and observed silence. But in the brief time they are permitted to play, they do so one-on-one. This avoids noise. I have found that this does not create any problems for them. When they are accustomed to it, it does not stop them from really enjoying themselves as they play.

3. We teach the children to avoid making their work useless, but to offer their work to God, making it out of love for God. We give them subjects to keep them in God's presence, according to the seasons and the feasts. From time to time, when the schoolmistress is with them, she tells them a word of God in order to strengthen the soul and to prevent them from drifting off into all sorts of distractions and daydreams.

Nonetheless, we try hard to avoid excess in this area. Given their youth, we do not try to make them too spiritual, unless we recognize that this comes from God. We fear two problems with too great a zeal. The first is that they struggle too hard and end up exhausting their minds and their imaginations rather than uniting their hearts to God. The other is that they grow discouraged when they see that they cannot attain the perfection demanded of them.

4. We try to accustom the children to practice mortification and not to follow their impulse by giving themselves to one work and then to another. That is why we tell them that the work they are doing will please God more if it pleases them less. Thus they must do with more diligence and more joy the work that pleases them less. They must develop the habit of doing their work in a penitential spirit. Still, we always try to take pity on the pupils' weaknesses and to accommodate ourselves to them as much as we can. But we do not want them to be aware of our accommodation.

5. They must not work together as couples unless it is necessary. In that case we choose one who would be good with a more imperfect pupil, so that the strong may support the weak.

6. We exhort them not to be too attached to their needlework, putting it down as soon as the bell rings, ready either to assist at the office in church or to say the office privately. They must always be ready to surrender their tasks to God, attaching themselves to God alone.

7. When the schoolmistress is in the room, she can take some of this time to help the pupils understand how they should hear Mass. She can use the time to explain in particular the ceremonies of the Mass and show them how they can assist at Mass.

[handwritten margin note:] All work is done for God is the girls must be ready to put down what they are doing for God.

8. On those occasions when someone commits some fault, we correct her in front of everyone. We use this occasion to represent to them the horror of vice and the beauty of virtue. I found there is nothing that serves them so well, and that they remember so clearly, as the great lessons one gives them in this manner.

9. We avoid telling them too much out of fear of disturbing their spirit. I've found that the lessons profit them more when the pupils are not overloaded by them.

10. We are vigilant that they are well taken care of, clean, and not neglected. They should be careful to lock everything, to lose nothing, and to be clean and diligent in everything they do.

11. We accustom them to like their needlework and to carry everywhere what they need for their work. In that way they do not lose time in certain meetings that were not planned. The older pupils also sew during recreation, without our obliging them to do so. We exhort them to take up the good habit of never being idle. Once they have developed this habit, it is no longer a burden to them. On the contrary, their work becomes a welcome diversion. I see that some of our pupils, by God's grace, find nothing so long as recreations and feasts. In order to have them develop this habit, I've found that it is good to reserve for them some needlework for which they have particular affection. They can do this work only at the appointed hour. I taught some of our pupils to make gloves of fleece. As they had only the period of recreation to work on them, they became devoted to this work.

12. At each hour of the day, one of the pupils says out loud and kneeling a prayer according to the season we are in, for example, Lent or Passiontide. All the other pupils remain seated. Only the leader kneels down as soon as the bell rings.

13. We insist that they should always be polite when they ask for or receive what they need for their work. They should stand up straight and maintain good posture. They should make a bow on entering and on leaving. That is why, although they wear a veil, they do not curtsey as nuns do, except when they are in front of the Most Blessed Sacrament.

14. In this block of time from breakfast until 8:00, the older pupils who have to sweep rooms or clean up some cubicles will do so briskly and quietly. We are careful not to have two of them working together at these tasks, except for several pupils whose good behavior is beyond question.

15. At 8:00, all those employed in cleaning rooms must leave everything to return to the common room, where they listen to a reading made by the schoolmistress until terce.[6] This office is said at 8:30. The reading is taken

---

6. Terce is a liturgical office of psalms and prayers usually recited at 9:00 a.m.

from a subject that the church emphasizes during the office of the season: for example, the Incarnation in Advent; the birth of Our Lord during the Christmas season; the Passion in Lent. The same is done during the rest of the liturgical year. At the same time, when a feast of some remarkable saint occurs, we take the saint's life as the subject of the reading. This reading then serves as subject matter for personal conversations with the pupils the rest of the day. We always tell them something additional when we do a reading, either to apply the reading to themselves, or to give them information, or to help them better understand what was read.

The Liturgical Office

1. As soon as terce sounds, the pupils kneel down to ask Our Lord's blessing as they say: "Benedicat nos Deus, Deus noster, benedicat nos Deus, et metuant eum omnes fines terrae."[7] They do this every time they leave to go to church, in order to receive from God the grace to avoid distractions and to behave as they should in the convent.

2. Ordinarily we permit those who are at least fourteen years old and who are in good health to assist at all the liturgical offices on the great feasts. We even let those who ask to go to the office of matins[8] do so, as long as they have merited this permission. They go to the offices of terce and vespers[9] whenever we have a feast of double or semidouble rank, and during the octaves of the major feasts. On Sundays and holy days of obligation we also let them go to prime. In general, all the pupils, old and young, go to terce and vespers on Sundays and holy days of obligation. They also assist at these offices on Thursdays and on a few feasts of blessed doctors of the church to which they have particular devotion, although these feasts are not holy days of obligation.

3. Nonetheless, this custom of going to assist at the liturgical office on these days is not observed as a binding rule. Each pupil must request permission to assist at the offices out of her devotion. We grant it to them only as a great favor. We exhort them to go to these offices only if they are inspired by true devotion. It should always be the case that they want to go to these offices more frequently than we permit. There is no reason to tolerate any risk of impiety.

4. We carefully watch to make sure the pupils conduct themselves with great modesty. We do not tolerate pupils' creating a distraction by looking all

7. "Blessed be God, our God, blessed be God, and may all the ends of the earth praise him."

8. Matins is a long liturgical office, including substantial readings from the church fathers.

9. Vespers is a liturgical office of psalms and prayers usually performed at dusk.

around. They should join in the liturgical chant whenever they can. They should always have a book to accompany them, once they have learned the entire office by heart. They should make deep bows and should stand up straight.

5. Those who have the honor to recite something during the office must devoutly fulfill their task, remembering that they are performing the office of angels and that we have shown them great favor in asking them to do this. They must know perfectly what they are to recite. If they make any errors, they must perform a penance. In the refectory, they must say what they had failed to say properly in church. If timidity was the cause of their failure, they sometimes recite the passage several days in a row. This helps to correct this weakness.

Girls
always
supervised

6. A nun always remains in the common room to mind those who are not going to the office, even if only a few remain behind.

7. Every time they go into the convent proper, they line up, as in a procession, even if there are only a few of them. We try to avoid putting together the pupils we think might be tempted to speak with each other. They are chaperoned wherever they go.

8. Ordinarily they never go alone into the convent. Nor do they go in twos or threes. Still, if it is necessary to make a visit to the convent, we send one of the best behaved and most discreet pupils. But even this should be done only on rare occasions.

Holy Mass

1. After terce, all the pupils go to holy Mass, except occasionally the youngest or some others who might still be unruly or garrulous. In that case a nun remains to keep an eye on them and to have them spiritually follow the Mass with the same reverence that is shown in church.

We accustom them from childhood to hear holy Mass kneeling. We have learned that this posture is not so difficult when one is used to it from a young age.

2. We have discovered that when there is no legal obligation to attend Mass, it is better to leave the smallest or most unruly pupils in the common room than to let them develop the bad habit of speaking or joking in church.

3. At the beginning of the Sub tuum praesidium,[10] which is an antiphon of the Blessed Virgin Mary we chant immediately before holy Mass, they

---

10. An ancient Marian prayer (dating possibly from the fourth century), the Sub tuum praesidium asks for the protection of the Blessed Virgin Mary against present perils.

kneel two by two in the middle of the choir. They keep a short distance between themselves. They keep their hands folded in their scapulars. They wear no gloves throughout the Mass. They must maintain a profound and attentive reverence before God. To achieve this, they follow the practices and the *Explanations* of Monsieur de Saint-Cyran on the holy Mass.[11] We instruct them to receive from God himself the prayers they must offer during Mass. We teach them that they cannot be acceptable to God unless the Holy Spirit forms prayers within them. It is the Holy Spirit who sighs and who prays within us.[12]

4. I must add here that we cannot do enough to encourage children to show reverence in church, especially during holy Mass. We must punish forcefully faults committed in this area. Sometimes we must even deprive them of the privilege of going to church on feast days, if we judge that this would truly be best for them. We are talking here, of course, of the oldest pupils. The older they are, the more we must expect in terms of conduct.

Writing

1. After Mass has ended, they all go to the same room to practice their writing. They begin the session with a short prayer to obtain from God the grace to do this action well. We gently try to foster the habit of starting and finishing every action, even the less important, with prayer. They make their prayers according to their own devotion and according to the inspirations God sends them. We tell the youngest to say an Ave Maria at the beginning and at the end of anything of consequence they are doing.

2. They must intensify their silence during the writing lesson. They are not permitted to show each other their papers. Nor may they simply write according to their caprice. They simply imitate the model given or, when they are truly advanced and have been given permission, they transcribe something.

3. The pupils do not write letters, notes, or even sentences to each other without the permission of the schoolmistress. When they have written what was permitted, they place their work in the hands of the schoolmistress, who then gives it to the pupil for whom it was written. The writing lesson lasts three-quarters of an hour.

4. The remaining time until sext[13] is used for learning how to sing with

11. Saint-Cyran composed a manual on the Mass in 1643.

12. Rom. 8:26.

13. Sext is a liturgical office of psalms and prayers usually recited at noon.

the use of notes. A quiet and reverent atmosphere should prevail during the chant lesson.

Prayer before Dinner

1. When the bell for sext rings, the pupil who has been chosen as "the weekly leader" kneels in the middle of the room to help the other pupils renew their attention to God. In this way they can assist at least in spirit in this hour of the liturgical office now being chanted in the choir of the church.

2. Although, except for classes, silence is maintained among the pupils, there are two particular periods when silence is maintained with particular strictness. The first is the "grand silence" of evening and of morning, which I have already discussed.[14] The second is during the masses and other liturgical offices in the convent, when the pupils are not personally assisting. They must have anticipated everything and placed everything in order during these periods. They cannot ask the schoolmistresses for anything concerning their needlework or for any permissions. This strict silence permits them to converse silently with God, and it permits their schoolmistresses to recite their office. At other times, they can more easily ask for what they might need.

3. If one of their classes, such as chant or catechism, occurs during one of the offices, they should not end the class. We ask only that this class be conducted more quietly than is ordinarily done. Still, they should interrupt the class to say the brief prayer said at the beginning of every office recited in the church choir. This helps the pupils to remember and to renew their attention to God.

4. At 11:00, the pupils make their examination of conscience, after having said the Confiteor up to the phrase *mea culpa*.[15]

5. Sometimes during the examination of conscience in the evening and in the morning, we have them examine themselves and ask God's pardon for some fault we believe they haven't noticed but that was committed in front of everyone. This slowly accustoms them to make a good examination of conscience.

6. At the conclusion of the examination of conscience, they all together

14. The "grand silence" is a monastic custom forbidding all conversation from early evening until morning after breakfast.

15. The Confiteor is the church's liturgical prayer of repentance recited by the priest at the beginning of Mass and by all religious and laity who recited the office of compline. In Tridentine Catholicism it was widely used in sacramental confession and in private examinations of conscience.

recite aloud the rest of the Confiteor. Then the weekly leader asks God's pardon for the faults committed and begs for the grace for a more profitable use of the rest of the day.

7. At the end of the examination of conscience, some pupils recite the office of sext in private. We allow this for the older pupils in whom we discern enough real piety to acquit themselves well in this duty. We also permit them to recite the rest of the office, from lauds[16] until compline.

The Refectory

1. Usually the refectory bell rings after sext. The pupils all go to the refectory with the same modesty that they show in going to church. Having arrived, they bow two by two in the middle of the refectory, as they pass in front of a nun. They stand modestly at their places without talking as they wait for the beginning of the Benedicte.[17] They say the grace out loud with the nuns. They maintain their modesty by keeping their hands hidden in their sleeves.

2. After the Benedicte is finished, they sit down at table, not according to their rank, but according to the arrangement we judge to be best. We try to mix the best behaved with those who are less so. This prevents them from speaking among themselves.

3. We take great care to avoid their becoming finicky in their eating habits. We exhort them to eat indifferently, to start with the foods they like least—this fosters a penitential spirit—and to eat enough to keep up their strength. That is why we carefully check to be sure that they have eaten well.

4. They must always have their eyes lowered and avoid glancing around the room. They must listen peacefully to the reading at table. At the end of the meal, they say grace with the nuns and then leave in the same order in which they entered.

Recreation

1. After they leave the refectory, they have recreation. The younger and older pupils are always separated at this moment to give the older pupils the opportunity to converse more quietly. This cannot come about when the younger pupils are present, because their youth inclines them to play at boisterous games that disturb the older pupils.

16. Lauds is a liturgical office of psalms and prayers usually recited in the early morning.

17. Grace before meals.

2. If recreation takes place in the common room, the older pupils gather around their schoolmistress to carry on an informal conversation focused on their interests.

3. We should not require them to limit their conversations to serious subjects. Nor should they always be speaking about God. We can only try discreetly to move the conversations in a more serious direction. If we see that the pupils have taken a liking to that direction, then they will continue on the topic.

4. We can let them play a few innocent games, such as knucklebones or shuttlecock. Actually, our current students do not play such games. Except the youngest pupils, who always play at something, all the pupils work without losing any time. They have developed such good work habits that they find nothing more boring than recreation during holidays, as I have already told you.

Play
Games

5. We do not permit them to be separated from each other, even in the same room. Even less do we permit them to be in groups of two or three. They also cannot speak in such a way that we could not hear them. Everything they say must be heard by their schoolmistress. We always maintain the custom that, wherever we may be, we make them say out loud what they said under their breath. The only exception is if they humbly ask that they divulge this information only in private to their schoolmistress. It occasionally happens that what they have to say could be damaging if said out loud. For this reason, they are carefully instructed to avoid saying out loud what they murmured if it is something bad, if it is something that could disedify others or assault charity. Saying something like this out loud would be considered as much a fault as refusing to say what should be said to the schoolmistress.

All
said
must be
heard by
teacher

6. Although discretion is rare in youth, we try to accustom them to it in all their actions, but especially during recreation, where it might seem that they have the right to say many things in order to divert themselves and to relax. That is why their schoolmistresses take great pains to speak to them and to hold conversations with them. They try to help the pupils say reasonable things that will develop their minds.

Needlework!

7. We do not tolerate their speaking about what they heard in confession or in a private interview, even when they want to point out something edifying. It is possible that there would be someone who had not received such attention, and this lack could drive her to jealousy.

8. They do not speak about the singing of the nuns. They may not say that one nun sings better than another. Nor may they discuss the faults made in choir or the faults made during the reception of Holy Communion. They are carefully trained not to make any judgments on these matters and not to

believe that those who go to communion the most are the holiest or that those who commune the least are the least holy. We tell them in these conferences that each woman must follow the gift of God and what her superior has ordered her to do. They should neither praise those who commune frequently nor condemn those who do it more rarely. They should leave everything to God's judgment.

9. The pupils also do not speak about what happens in the refectory, whether a particular nun performed some penance or even whether they themselves or their companions performed a penance.

10. We forbid them to speak about the penances they often request when we teach them about penance. Otherwise they might turn them into a game or start imitating each other.

11. Nor are they permitted to discuss the dreams they had during the night, no matter how pretty or edifying they might seem.

12. They must say nothing about what they may have learned in the visitors' parlor. If something edifying happened there and if it can be said to everyone, the schoolmistress will not fail to say it. This removes the desire they may have had to reveal it.

13. Sometimes we let them know a little of the news we know, when it is of little consequence. For example, we might reveal the date for the vesture of certain nuns, or the content of a note placed in the choir to request prayers for a particular person, or some affair of piety. This removes the desire to learn about these things by illicit means.

14. If we can avoid it, we never correct the pupils during recreation. We never use this time to speak to them about regulations we have to impose in the common room. It is always possible that during this moment of recreation, the pupils will give their opinion more boldly and that we will then be obliged to correct them even more. It is important to avoid this impasse as much as we can.

15. It is not that we would tolerate the pupils' committing some major fault during recreation. On the contrary, we would correct them with as much vigor, if not more, as at any other time. We must avoid giving the impression that they can follow their passions as freely as they want, on the pretext that they are just amusing themselves. I am only saying that we let the small faults wait for another time and that we never use recreation as a time to speak about faults committed elsewhere.

16. We exhort them to avoid speaking all at once. This permits them to avoid making a lot of noise and to learn how to listen to each other. When one has started to say something, the others should not interrupt her. We try to show them how impolite these violations are.

17. We instruct them to avoid violating charity in anything they say. They should avoid the smallest words that they think their sisters would not like to have said about them. They should even avoid saying things that are not evil in themselves, but that they know some of their companions would prefer not to hear.

18. We also try to inspire them to maintain their honor by a holy politeness that can be produced only by charity.

19. They avoid too great a familiarity with each other. Hugging, kissing, and touching each other are forbidden, whatever the pretext given to justify them. The older pupils do not even use these gestures with the younger ones. If we forbid these gestures during recreation, there are even greater reasons to forbid them at other times. They must never speak except in the presence of their schoolmistresses and, even then, only when there is genuine need.

20. Recreation finishes by a prayer to the Blessed Virgin Mary. Through the intercession of his blessed Mother, it asks Jesus Christ to grant them the grace of spending the rest of the day in a holy way.

Class Instruction

1. At the end of recreation, the pupils divide into two rows in the middle of the common room to receive instruction. They recite the Veni, Sancte Spiritus[18] all together. Their schoolmistress, who must instruct them, says the prayer and versicle that follow the hymn.

2. After the prayer is finished, all the pupils sit down on their stools. Whoever is moved to say one of her faults aloud does it, but we force no one to do so. On the contrary, we let them see that this is made possible by grace but that it is not commanded. Nonetheless, they have the habit of doing so gladly.[19]

3. They must listen with great respect to the admonitions we give them, which must always be charitable. They must be convinced that we are correcting them for their own good and that we are not more lenient with some than with others.

4. They must recognize that we are not acting out of any disordered movement, whether of passion or of self-interest. This concern does not prevent us from correcting them with vigor, so that they truly experience some humiliation and shame. However, if they confess their faults only out of

18. This prayer to the Holy Spirit was frequently used in Catholic schools of the period.

19. The "chapter of faults" is a monastic custom, wherein nuns and monks publicly accuse themselves of certain failings in front of their assembled brethren. The extension of this practice to lay pupils at Port-Royal was controversial.

Handwritten margin note: Forbidden to know each other too well

habit, or so that others will believe them sincere in telling their faults, this will quickly turn into a game or into hypocrisy, which we must try to avoid in everything. That is why we give some penance for each major fault they accuse themselves of. I do not recall that this practice ever took away their freedom to say their faults.

Class begins by expressing one's faults

5. They never say the faults in this way—in front of their sisters—on Sundays and feast days.

6. As soon as all the faults have been said, which always lasts more than a quarter of an hour, we use the rest of the hour to instruct them and to repeat what we had said to them the day before. This repetition consists in making three or four pupils say what they had learned the previous day. We ask first one student, then another, but we do not ask everyone, because that would take too long. Even if the chapter of faults had lasted an entire half-hour, there is still three-quarters of an hour remaining. The repetitions usually take a quarter of an hour.

Repeat previous lesson

7. On the days when there is a proper Gospel, as during Lent, during Ember Days, and on Saturdays (using the Sunday Gospel), all the pupils stand and, folding their hands, reverently listen to the Epistle and the Gospel of the day.

8. After the reading of the Gospel, we explain it to them as simply as we can. The other days when there is no proper Gospel, we instruct them through an explanation of the catechism or through an explanation of the Christian virtues. We also teach them the proper manner to make a good confession, to receive communion, to make an examination of conscience, and to pray well to God. We do not pass quickly from one subject to the other, in order to give them enough time to understand thoroughly what we have told them.

Instruct children in virtue; Gospel

9. The classes where we explain the catechism to them must last for a good while. We begin with the sign of the cross, then the articles of our faith and the commandments of God and of the church. The principal mysteries of faith are reserved for those days near the time when the church solemnly celebrates these mysteries in her feasts.

10. I will tell you how I have taught catechism for the past four years. The first year, I talked to them about the creed, about the sign of the cross, about holy water, about the commandments of God. The second year, I tried to make them clearly understand the manual explaining holy Mass, which is in the new choir of the church. Although the manual explains everything, the pupils could not understand anything, because they read it by rote, without any personal reflection. At least that was the case with most of them, especially the newly arrived pupils.

*Learn what
they are God's
neighbor via
contemplation*

11. I did the same thing for morning and evening prayers, the examination of conscience, and the other duties of a good Christian woman. Since then, I have spoken about the virtues, using the text of Saint John Climacus.[20]

12. For the last and current year, I focused entirely on penance, using works from the Tradition of the Church. I now have the intention, with God's grace, of explaining to them in detail the *Catechism* of Monsieur de Saint-Cyran.[21] This clearly teaches them what they owe to God and to their neighbor, as well as about morals.

13. We finish their instruction by the prayer Confirma Hoc Deus.[22] This lesson ends about 2:30. The pupils may work at sewing during this lesson, on condition that they have nothing to ask from someone else. If one of them needs something, she abstains from work rather than being distracted or distracting the others.

Schedule from None until Vespers; Collation

1. From none[23] until vespers we have a repetition of a lesson of the catechism. On one day we have one pupil ask questions and the other pupil respond. On the next day we reverse the order. At the end of the session, the pupils rehearse a hymn in Latin or in French. These rehearsals do not disturb anyone and do not waste any time, since they are done with each pupil at her place and with each pupil working on her needlework.

*Strengthen
memory*

2. It is necessary to exercise the memory of children. That strengthens their mind, keeps them busy, and prevents them from getting into trouble.

*Encourage
students to
be better
readers*

3. The time remaining between instruction and vespers is used to do some work in complete silence. During this time we only make some of the mid-aged students read aloud. We choose those pupils who need some improvement to become better readers. Those whom we ask to read in the common room must know how to read properly, so that all may profit from what is being read.

20. Saint John Climacus (525–606), a monk of the Sinai peninsula, composed *The Ladder of Perfection*, an ascetic treatise that details thirty virtues in an ascending scale of perfection. Long used in monastic communities, the treatise was popular in Jansenist circles. In 1652 Arnauld d'Andilly provided a French translation. In 1688 a biography of Climacus by Isaac Le Maître de Sacy appeared.

21. Saint-Cyran, *Théologie familière* (1643). Originally composed for use in the Jansenist *petites écoles* for boys, this catechism was condemned by the archdiocese of Paris in 1643. Although the archdiocese lifted the censure when a revised edition (1644) appeared, the work remained suspect because of its treatment of grace, divine election, and moral issues.

22. A prayer asking God to confirm the good work just accomplished, often used during administration of the sacrament of confirmation.

23. None is a liturgical office of psalms and prayers, usually recited at 3:00 p.m.

4. For the youngest pupils, we have come to the conclusion that they learn to read better when they are alone. That is why we assign one of the older pupils to help them. At several moments in the day, in a room set apart for this purpose, one of the older pupils assists them. We choose for this mission one of the older pupils who has the intention of becoming a nun. Moreover, we need to choose carefully one of the older pupils who is well behaved, discreet, and sweet tempered. She needs to do this wholeheartedly and for the love of God.

5. At approximately 3:30 we make a collation for all the young and mid-age pupils. We easily excuse the older pupils when they request it. This meal is not too important for the older pupils, since they dine late and sup early. Moreover, we observe that those who skip it actually seem to feel better. From the age of fourteen years old, we permit them to skip it, unless someone judges that this meal is necessary for a particular pupil. Then we oblige her to take some nourishment at this hour. It is much rarer to exempt the younger pupils, even if they ask for an exemption. We fear that they often ask this permission only to seem grown-up or out of some hypocrisy.

6. At this same moment, when some of the better-behaved older pupils desire to pray to God, we take them to the chapel and remain with them until the end of their prayers.

7. We permit this prayer only for those whom we perceive, as much as we can judge, motivated to request this by a pure motive of pleasing God, and who will profit from it.

Schedule from Vespers until the Meal in the Refectory

1. At 4:00, the older pupils go to vespers, if they have merited this favor.
2. During this time, we instruct the smallest children. Although they are present for everything we say in the common room to instruct all the pupils, they understand nothing. Even if we speak to each of them in private, they still do not understand what we are trying to say.
3. From the end of vespers until the supper in the refectory, one of the older pupils does a reading. As much as is possible, their schoolmistress should be present with them. They do this reading until the refectory bell rings. Then they enter the refectory in the same order in which they had entered it earlier in the day.

From Evening Recreation until Night Prayers and Bedtime

1. Next we have recreation, just as we had it in the morning. In summer we go into the garden in the evening; in winter we visit it in the morning.

2. The children are divided the same way in the evening as in the morning. We do what we can to have two nuns with the older pupils when there are some willing to do so. When one of the nuns walks behind the older pupils, she can detect those who, under the pretext of being uncomfortable, start to walk more slowly in order to speak surreptitiously with others.

3. This evening recreation lasts until the first chimes of compline. But in the hottest times of summer we finish the recreation period later, since they need to spend more time walking outdoors. Nonetheless, we never finish later than 7:30. They start their evening prayers, which they can recite in the garden during the hottest days, by kneeling in a sheltered area. Next they say compline using the same recitative tone they had used in the morning for the office of prime. They may walk as they recite the psalms of the office, on condition that they stop to observe the proper gestures of the office.

4. When the heat is not so great, the pupils begin their prayer at the first sound of the compline bell, so that they will have finished the office before assisting at the Salve Regina[24] in the choir of the chapel. They faithfully assist at the singing of this night hymn throughout the year, with the exception of the three hottest months, which last from the octave of Corpus Christi until the end of the month of August. We make this concession to avoid interrupting their walk, which we think is so helpful for them at that time.

5. At the end of the Salve Regina or of the period in the garden, the pupils go straight to their rooms. There they undress silently and quickly. This is done with such dispatch that in both winter and summer they must be abed no later than 8:15, each pupil in her own separate bed. We never accept any excuse to exempt pupils from this bedtime rule.

6. As soon as they are in bed, we visit not only the pupils in cubicles, but also the pupils in regular rooms. We pass by each individual bed to be sure they have gone to bed with appropriate modesty and to see if they are well covered in winter.

7. After the inspection we extinguish all the lights, except for one lamp that we keep lit all through the night in one of their rooms. This lamp is essential to help them with the needs they may have during the night.

8. A nun or an older pupil in whom we have complete confidence sleeps in each of the rooms.

9. This is the schedule we observe throughout a typical day. Sometimes we do modify the time of certain exercises to accommodate the pupils' needs. For example, during Lent and on the fast days of the church, the morning portion is longer than that of the afternoon.

24. Marian hymn that closes the night office of compline. In Tridentine Catholicism it was widely used by all Catholics as the last prayer before retiring.

Collection of School Prayers[25]

I have saved until now the presentation of the prayers the pupils recite morning and evening.

PRAYERS FOR MORNING

Immediately after waking, they raise their heart to God and say:

My God, I give you my heart. Accept it, my God, by your infinite mercy, so that no other creature may possess it.

Let us pray. My God, by your infinite goodness you awaken me to pull me out of the shadow of death. Give me this day again to adore you and to work on my salvation. Give me your grace, which permits me to know your holy will, which makes me vigilant in executing it, and which lets me pray unceasingly out of the desires of my heart. May the things of this corrupt world and the traps of demons not make me fall into sin.

While they dress, they say:

Let us remember to take off the old man and to dress ourselves with the new.[26]

Let us pray. My God, I realize that the need I have for these clothes is a proof of the corruption I inherited from my ancestors. Let me feel the nakedness of my soul in the humiliation of true penance. After having completely abandoned the old man, may I be completely clothed in Jesus Christ, in his justice, in his innocence, in his light and in his power. Amen.

After they finish dressing, they kneel and adore God:

My God, I adore you with all my heart, with all my soul, and with all my strength. I adore you, O my God! Father, Son, and Holy Spirit, in the unity of your essence, and in the trinity of your persons.

I adore you, O my Savior Jesus Christ! and your sacred humanity, in all its states, its mysteries, its thoughts, its words, its actions, its movements, its internal and external suffering. I adore you risen and glorified. Judge of the living and the dead, give me the grace to adore you in spirit and in truth in honor of the eternal adorations you offer to your celestial Father in heaven and to the Most Blessed Sacrament of the altar.

PRAYERS SAID IN COMMON

Pater Noster. Ave Maria. Credo.

---

25. The following collection of prayers is published only in the Cousin edition of the *Règlement*: *JP,* 382-93. For a discussion of the textual issues, see the editor's introduction above.

26. 2 Cor. 5:17.

We alternate the language in which we say them: one day in Latin, the other in French.

Prayers of petition.

We thank you for having kept us throughout the night. and we beg you to guide us throughout the day. We ask pardon for all the sins we have committed from the moment we reached the age of reason until now. Give us the grace to live and die in a spirit of penance.

We commend to you our fathers and mothers, all our relatives, our friends and enemies, our benefactors, and all those for whom we are obliged to pray.

We commend to you your entire church, our holy father the pope, our archbishop. Please keep and guide our most Christian king and all of his council. May everyone know you, love you, and serve you. Give us peace and we will keep it according to our needs. Console all who are afflicted in soul or in body. Give your grace to the living and eternal rest to the dead.

Our Lord's commandment.

This is my commandment: that you love each other, as I have loved you.[27]
If someone does not love Our Lord Jesus Christ, let him be anathema.
You will love the Lord your God with your whole heart, with your whole soul, and with your whole mind, and your neighbor as yourself. On these two commandments depend the Law and the prophets.[28] Whatever you eat, whatever you drink, whatever you do, do it for the glory of God.[29] May all your actions be done in a spirit of love and of glory.

Give us the grace, O my God! to be among the small number of your elect, who never cease to love you. Always deepen this charity that you have given us as a foretaste of your glory.

Let us pray. O my God! What grace you give us. We are so unworthy of your love. You not only accept our love for you, but you command us to love you with all our strength! So that we may obey this commandment, which is so necessary for our salvation, spread this love in our heart, and give us what you command. May the fire of the charity that you came to earth to bear consume every other love. May it destroy everything opposed to your holy will. May it create one heart and one mind among all the faithful. May it unite us all to Jesus Christ your Son. May it embrace us in him through the Holy Spirit forever and ever. Amen.

Let us pray. O eternal God, living source of all being, I come to you as to my origin and my last end. I seek to find in you what I lack and the power to

27. John 13:34.
28. Matt. 22:37-40.
29. 1 Cor. 10:31.

offer you what I owe you. Infinite goodness, consider your work. Without your grace it is so imperfect and so miserable. Give me this grace by the merits of your Son, my Savior Jesus Christ. Unite my spirit to his. Let me perform all the obligations that our first father refused to do. In this divine union with your Son, my Savior Jesus Christ, may I love you, adore you, and accomplish your holy will forever. Separate me from Adam, from his ways and from his life. May I be inseparably united to Jesus Christ, whom you have given to me to be my way and my life. Amen.

Prayer to the Holy Virgin.

Verse: Holy Virgin, pray for us poor sinners.

Response: Now and at the hour of our death.

Holy Virgin, you were so blessed to find favor before the Lord, to give life, and to be the mother of salvation. Let us be received by your Son, Jesus Christ. Since through you he has been given to us, may it also be through you that he would receive us into his holy company. May the eminence of your purity erase the stains of our corruption in the sight of his divine majesty. May your unequaled humility help us to obtain pardon for our vanity and our pride. May your superabundant charity cover the multitude of our sins and your miraculous fecundity flood us with a fecundity of graces, of merits, and of glory. Amen.

Verse: All saints, intercede for us.

Response: And for all the faithful.

Lord, give us the grace, by the intercession of all the saints, to avoid always the sentiments of pride. May we always progress in the virtue of humility, which is so pleasing to you. May we firmly reject everything opposed to your law, and may we try to do everything just and holy by a divine love that truly makes us free. Amen.

Offering to God.

Lord, we are obligated to offer your majesty all our mind, our body, and all that we have in this world. But since we cannot make this great sacrifice by our own strength, we pray that Jesus Christ, your Son, may do it for us. Lord, grant us this mercy, inseparable from his very person, so that we may become part of his sacrifice. In living and acting only for your glory, may we always be ready to suffer and to die so that your divine will may be done. Finally, may we be like Jesus Christ and with Jesus Christ a living, holy, spiritual host, acceptable in your eyes, in order to be consummated completely in you. Amen.

Let us ask God for the grace not to offend him this day.

Verse: Keep us, Lord, throughout this day.

Response: And preserve us from all sin.

Let us pray. Almighty God, who brought us to the beginning of this day, save us today by the virtue of your grace. May we not fall into any sin in the course of this day. May all our thoughts, our words, and our actions have only one purpose: to observe your commandments. Amen.

May the charity, the truth, and the peace of Jesus Christ be with us.

PRAYERS FOR THE EVENING

Pater Noster. Ave Maria.

Let us ask God for the assistance of the Holy Spirit.

Verse: Holy Spirit, who proceeds from the Father and from the Son, come to us.

Response: Fill our hearts and by your grace warm them by the fire of your holy love.

Let us pray. My God, you have taught the hearts of your faithful by the light of your Holy Spirit. Give us your grace by the same Spirit, so that he may help us to know and do those things that please you. May he also help us to receive a holy and eternal consolation. We ask this through Jesus Christ Our Lord, who lives and reigns forever and ever. Amen.

Let us thank God for all the graces he has given us.

Lord, we thank you for the infinite mercies you have shown to us without any merit on our part. When we were children of your anger, you gave us your Son and, with this blessed Son, every kind of blessing. You gave us his blood to purify us, his death to make us die to sin, his resurrection to make us rise to a life of grace, his body to nourish us, his spirit to sanctify us. We recognize that you alone kept us from all the sins we have not committed. We recognize that if we have ever done something good, it is you who have done this in us. O God of mercy! May this thanksgiving that we offer you not only be in our mouths, but also in our hearts. May we live like those who fear more than anything falling into the forgetting of your gifts. May we be like those who have no desire more ardent than that of living so that all the movements of their heart and all the actions of their hands become acts of thanksgiving. O my God! Help us to make these acts of thanksgiving faithfully throughout our entire life, in order to offer you them with greater holiness in union with all the elect in eternity. Amen.

Thank God in particular for the graces he gave us on this day.

Pause.

Ask God for light in order to know our sins.

Lord, give us this divine light, which alone can truly show us our sins, convict us of our sins, and help us to renounce them. If we only see our sins in our own light, we always excuse them and even hide them from ourselves. If our self-love cannot dissimulate our sins, it only provokes a pointless anxiety, sterile and haughty. But you, Lord, by a glance of your eyes, you reveal our sins and you give us peace. You crush a soul by humbling it in order to destroy its pride. After it has become humble, you raise it up and give it a firm confidence in your protection. It raises its eyes toward you in confidence. By your mercy lower your eyes to gaze upon it. O infinite Light! This is how we desire to see our sins. We ask this grace through Jesus Christ Our Lord.

Confiteor until Mea Culpa.
Let us show God great sorrow for our sins and ask him for pardon and for a cure to our sins:

Lord, we recognize the depth of our offenses before your divine majesty. We ask pardon and a cure for them. Let this body of sin die continually, because it fights your spirit. Separate from us this weight of corruption that inclines us to do the evil we do not want to do and prevents us from doing the good we want to, because we want to do it so weakly. My God, be stronger in saving us than we are in losing ourselves. By your mercy, make charity destroy all the powers of our self-love by a power greater and completely divine. May it grow and reach perfection in our hearts. May it completely destroy sin, so that we may obtain through your goodness complete forgiveness in Jesus Christ Our Lord.

Mea culpa, etc. Miseratur.
Let us ask for assistance from the Blessed Virgin:

Verse: Holy Virgin, pray for us.

Response: That we may be made worthy of the promises of Christ. Holy Virgin, you are our queen, our mediatrix, and our advocate. Reconcile us with your Son. Commend us to him and present us to him. O incomparable Virgin! You were filled with blessings by the singular favor you received by anticipation of Christ, by the extraordinary privileges by which you have been honored, by the countless graces with which you have been adorned. By your intercession, may Jesus Christ, your Son, our master and our God, who deigned to enter our weaknesses and our miseries by your mediation, make us also participants in the glory and in the beatitude he enjoys for all eternity. Amen.

Verse: Saints of God, intercede for us.

Response: And for all the faithful.

Lord, we ask that all your saints help us wherever they may be and obtain holy joy for us by their intercession. In honoring their merits, may we feel the effects of their powerful protection. Give us peace during the time we live on this earth and remove from your church everything that can corrupt the morals of your faithful. Guide our paths, our actions, and our wills in blessedness and sanctity. Reward by heavenly gifts those who shared part of their worldly goods. Eternal rest grant unto all the faithful departed who died in your peace. By Our Lord Jesus Christ.

Prayer to our guardian angel.

Verse: The Lord has commanded his angels.

Response: To guard you in all of your ways.

My God, by your ineffable providence you have deigned to send your holy angels to guard us. By your mercy help your faithful to be always assisted by their help and to enjoy their company in eternal felicity. Amen.

Ask God for his holy blessing.

Verse: May God bless us.

Response: And may all the nations of the earth fear him.

Lord, bless the people you have chosen as your inheritance. Extend your divine hands upon us, since they are full of infinite grace. In your right hand are the blessings of kindness, because you are the God of all consolation. In your left hand are the judgments you impose on those you accept among the number of your children. You make them suffer penalties to purify them. You chastise them for a moment in order to crown them in eternity. By both hands, by consolations and chastisements, you attract them to you, so that they may not find their consolation among sinners and may not be judged with the world. Lord, may we always be your people and may you always be our God. Be with us and we will always walk in your sight. When we must fight, fight for us. When we have finished blessing our crosses and our labors in this world by the crosses and labors of Jesus Christ, may you call us to possess the glory he has prepared for us and to receive eternal blessings. Amen.

Antiphon

Save us, Lord, when we are awake. Watch over us as we sleep, that awake we may keep watch with Christ and that asleep we may rest in peace.[30] Amen.

OTHER OCCASIONAL PRAYERS

In honor of the mystery of the childhood of Jesus Christ.
Become like newborn infants.

Lord, make us ever like children by our simplicity and innocence, as worldly people always are by ignorance and by weakness. Give us a holy

---

30. The prayer is taken from compline, the night office of the church.

childhood which the passage of years may not destroy and from which we may never fall into the senility of old Adam or into the death of sin. May it make us more and more new creatures in Jesus Christ and may it lead us to his immortal glory.

If you do not become like children, you cannot enter into the kingdom of heaven.[31]

Ask God for the grace of a holy and Christian childhood.

Lord, give us the grace to be among the number of these children whom you call, whom you let approach you, from whose lips you elicit your praises. Nourish us with your milk and carry us on your breast to preserve our purity from the corruption of this world. May the angels you have given us to guide us intercede for us before your throne. May we adore you with them in eternity.

Regulations for Feast Days

1. On feast days we fill the entire day with small, special exercises. In this way the pupils do not end up wasting their time in boredom or in the foolishness that inevitably occurs if they are not busy with something. Children simply do not have the strength to devote every hour in the day to God's service.

Feast Days are filled w/ small exercises of devotion

2. They all awaken and dress themselves at the same time as they do on workdays.

3. At 6:00, if the young pupils are almost dressed, the oldest pupils who desire to assist at prime may do so, on condition that they ask permission. This permission is given only when we clearly see that they have requested it out of a pure motive of wanting to please God and of wanting to sing his praises. This rule for permission applies to all the other office hours. Next we assist at the first Mass of the feast. All pupils, old and young, attend this Mass.

4. After Mass is finished, they go make their beds and have breakfast. This lasts until about 8:00, when they all sit down in rows in the common room to listen to the book being read aloud, just as is done on regular workdays.

5. At 8:30, practically all of them go to terce. All of them then go to the High Mass.

6. From the end of High Mass until sext, there is approximately three-quarters of an hour. During this time, they try to memorize what they must know: basic religious truths in *Simple Theology*, *Practice of holy Mass*, and *Treatise on Confirmation*.[32] After that they learn all the French hymns in their book of

---

31. Matt. 18:3.

32. Saint-Cyran published these religious pamphlets in 1643 as appendixes to his *Théologie familière.*

hours. Then they learn all the Latin hymns in the breviary. Many of those who came to the convent school at a young age manage to learn the entire psalter. They have little difficulty with all this memorizing as long as they receive a little encouragement.

7. At the sext bell, they make their examination of conscience. Next, those with permission to say their office recite sext.

8. At the end of sext, they go to the refectory for dinner, and then they have recreation until 1:00.

Children
learn:
teach each
other

9. From 1:00 until 2:00, the oldest pupils learn arithmetic, while younger pupils practice their writing and the youngest children repeat their catechism.

10. From 2:00 until 2:30, the oldest pupils teach arithmetic to the youngest. They then recite none privately until 3:00.

11. At different hours of the day, the oldest pupils rehearse their singing by notes. One of them explains sight-reading to the younger pupils. When they are just working on their singing, they use their time profitably. It prevents them from becoming bored. The pupils never tire of learning more and more about the art of singing.

12. At 4:00 they all go to vespers and to the benediction that immediately follows it.

13. At the end of vespers, those older pupils who are inspired by great devotion, and to whom we have given permission, may remain to pray in the chapel until the time for supper in the refectory. If more than fifteen minutes remain, we bring the rest of the pupils back to the common room. There they can use their time for their devotions, or for some reading in *The Imitation of Jesus Christ*,[33] or for reciting what they have memorized.

14. The rest of the day follows the same schedule as a typical workday.

Pt 2!

PART 2: SPIRITUAL AND PHYSICAL WELFARE

Having reported to you how we organize the daily schedule for our children, it now remains for me to consider the second issue you enjoined me to explain: the spirit in which I respond to all the spiritual and physical needs of the pupils. When I explain what I am supposed to do, it is not because I often fail to do so. But these duties will move you to pray to God for me so that he will make me what I should be in order to safeguard these souls he has committed to the care of one so incapable of serving them. There are many things

---

33. *The Imitation of Christ*, attributed to Thomas à Kempis (1375–1471), was the most popular ascetic work in early modern Catholicism.

that I am not capable of saying in this particular report, since I cannot find the right words to express myself. Still, obedience makes me rise above my difficulties, since you have bound me to tell not only how I work with the children, but also what I believe we should do for their education.

1. In What Spirit We Must Serve Children. Union among the Schoolmistresses. Some General Advice about Their Conduct, Especially toward Small Children

1. If we are truly to serve children, I believe that we should never speak to them nor act on their behalf without considering God and asking for his holy grace. We should want to take directly from God everything that is necessary to instruct pupils in the fear of God.

[margin note: Always consult God]

2. We must have much charity and tenderness for the pupils. We must neglect nothing, internal or external, that they need. On many different occasions we should let them see that there is no limit to our desire to serve them and that we do so with real affection and fervor, because they are children of God. We feel obliged to spare nothing in their service, in order to make them truly worthy of this holy dignity.

[margin note: Serve all needs of child]

3. It is necessary that we give ourselves to their service without stinting. Without some urgent reason, we should never leave their quarters. We should always be present in the common room where they do their studies and their work. We make only brief exceptions to speak to them, or to visit them when they are ill, or when we are taken by other duties concerning their needs.

[margin note: Obligation to children is top priority]

4. We should not be disturbed when we cannot assist at an occasional office, except when the older pupils themselves are present at it. It is so important to mind the children that we should prefer this obligation to anything else, when obedience requires us to assume this task. We should prefer it even to the fulfillment of our own immediate spiritual desires. The charity with which we give them the services they need not only will cover many of our faults, it will take the place of many things we think we must have for our perfection.

5. We should have at least one nun we can count on, without in any way withdrawing her from her other obligations. If possible, this nun should remain as much as she can in the common room. That is why it is desirable to have two nuns who would be inspired by the same zeal and by the same sensitivity toward children. It would be good to have them both in the common room, even in the presence of the headmistress. Seeing the respect the chil-

[margin note: Nuns w/ zeal & passion for children]

dren show toward both of them, each one would have the right in the other's absence to ask the class to show the same respect to her that they show toward the absent nun.

6. We must ensure that the children notice a deep harmony, a perfect union, and a clear trust between the companion nun and ourselves. That is why we must never publicly criticize anything she says or does, so that the children never notice any disagreement. This should be reserved for a private conversation. It is important, indeed necessary, that the nun we are given as an auxiliary have the disposition to approve everything we tell her. This agreement is crucial for the education of children. If this is not the case, we should alert the superior. Still, if her resistance to us only grates against our temperament and causes no wrong to the children, we should ask God to obtain the grace to rejoice in the fact that we had an opportunity to experience adversity.

7. We must implore God to give our children a great respect for the nuns who help us. We must also give them great authority, especially the nun who works with the pupils after us. That is why it is good to witness to the children, and even to tell them on occasion, that this nun shows great charity toward them, that she loves them, and that we are the ones who oblige her to report everything that happens in the common room. In front of the pupils we could even tell the nun that she is obligated by charity and by duty to tell us not only all the serious faults committed, but also the lighter faults, so that they might be assisted in correcting them.

8. We take the auxiliary nuns into our confidence when we tell them about the inclinations of the pupils, specifically those of the youngest and also those of the older pupils who might cause some trouble. Thus they might be even more vigilant. Still, we should not lightly reveal those things that the children told us in private. We should do this only when it is clearly necessary for their welfare. There is always danger in revealing a confidence too easily. I think it is very important that the children trust our discretion. Although they often tell us things that are of little importance, there are occasions when they want to confide something important, especially as they grow older. They will find it difficult to tell us these things if they feel that we had not maintained their confidences concerning small matters.

9. Since it is so important that we have a profound union and mutual comprehension with the nuns given to us as aides, it is even more important that these nuns act only according to the order they find established by the headmistress. They should be so imbued with the sentiments of the headmistress that they speak only through her mouth and see only by her eyes. The children should notice nothing that is not perfectly harmonious be-

tween the nuns. If the auxiliary nuns find anything to question in the conduct of the headmistress they should tell her, if they are confident enough to approach her and if they have permission from their superior to do so. If God does not give them this confidence, they must alert the mother superior so that they can avoid showing any sign of dissension to the pupils.

10. When there are two nuns in the common room at the moment the office bell rings, they can say their office one after the other so that one of them still keeps an eye on the pupils. But she will say nothing about the faults she has seen them do, if they were minor, until her companion has finished her office. It is important to inculcate in the pupils a deep sense of reverence when they see that we are praying to God. However, as soon as the office is finished (which is short enough when we recite it in a low voice), we must punish the pupils in proportion to the severity of the fault. The punishment should be even more severe when the fault was committed during a time of prayer.

Punishment fits the crime

11. When there is only one nun, there should not be any difficulty in keeping an eye on the pupils, but she should not say anything until she has completely finished her office. We have seen by experience how the pupils benefit from this. When we are strict about neither speaking to them nor responding to them during prayer, they become more reverent as they themselves pray and are more fearful about interrupting us. We can never do enough to inspire reverence for God among the young, by our personal example as much as by our words. That is why we should be punctual in saying our office at the very moment that the other nuns chant it in the church choir. We should leave everything we are doing at the second chime of the office bell, and we should never let ourselves absentmindedly finish something that we like. I do not mean to say that, if some real need demanded immediate attention to the pupils, we should not prefer that service to that of our office. Still, it is important that both the children and our conscience be convinced that we act only out of consideration for God. Our example is the greatest lesson we can give. The devil gives them a razor-sharp memory, so that they remember our least faults. He has damaged their memory to prevent them from remembering the little good we are able to do.

Inspire Reverence for God

12. Since obedience has committed us to this work, we can never pray enough, never humble ourselves enough, and never be vigilant enough to give the children what we owe them. I think this is one of the most important missions in the house. We really should tremble as we carry out this mission. Still, we should not be overly fearful. We should place our trust in God and ask him by our sighs to grant us what we do not merit by ourselves. We ask him this grace by the blood of his Son, shed for these innocent souls whom

he has placed in our hands. We must always consider these tiny souls as a sacred deposit entrusted to us and of which one day we must render an account. That is why we should talk to the pupils less than we talk to God about them.

13. Since we are obligated to be always among our pupils, we should conduct ourselves in a way that avoids extremes or inconsistency. There is a danger in treating the children too softly on one occasion, then too severely on another. Ordinarily these two faults accompany each other. When we let ourselves be carried away by making all these little hugs and flatteries, which gives the pupils the freedom to act just as their mood and their feelings desire, it is inevitable that a period of cold reproof will follow. This is what creates inconsistency, which is much more hurtful to a child than always keeping her within the confines of her duties.

14. We should never be too familiar with them, nor should we show them too great a confidence, unless they are quite mature. But we must always show them true charity and a great attentiveness in meeting their needs and even in anticipating them.

15. We should treat them politely and speak to them only with respect. We should accede to their desires in everything that is possible. Sometimes it is a good idea to show some special consideration in things that are indifferent in themselves. This helps to win over their hearts.

16. When it is necessary to correct them for light faults or for their bad temper, we should never mimic or bully them, even if they have shown a bad spirit. On the contrary, we should always speak to them calmly and give them good reasons in order to convince them. This will prevent them from growing bitter. It will also help them to accept what we are trying to say to them.

17. We must frequently ask God to give the pupils a frank simplicity and to work on our end to remove from them any spirit of subterfuge or of cunning. But we have to do this in a subtle way so that we do not end up making them more cunning by exhorting them to be simple. That is why I think we should not complain to them that they already show too much craftiness. Sometimes when we keep telling them they should not be sly, they figure out that they are. They then use everything we warned them about earlier when they need to find some artifice to conceal certain faults they do not want others to know.

18. That is why we must maintain a perfect surveillance of the pupils, never leaving them alone anywhere, whether they are healthy or sick. Still, we should not be so obtrusive that we end up encouraging a spirit of defiance or making the child apprehensive. Overzealousness encourages the pupils,

especially the younger ones, to attempt little pranks in hiding. I also think that our continual surveillance should be done with a certain gentleness and trust, which helps them believe that we love them and that we stay with them only to give them proper company. This helps them to enjoy rather than to fear this surveillance.

19. Even more than with the other pupils, it is important to treat and nourish the youngest as if they were small doves. We should not say much when they commit some major fault that deserves punishment. But when we are certain they deserve punishment, we should punish the pupils without saying a word. We should give an explanation for the punishment only afterward. Still, before we say anything, it is good to ask them if they know why they have been punished. Ordinarily they have some idea of the cause. Done promptly and without words, this punishment prevents them from telling lies to have an excuse for their faults. Young children are all too prone to this vice. I find that this method really helps them to overcome their faults, because they are always afraid of being taken by surprise.

20. I also believe that we do not need to correct them too much about their lighter faults. If we are always talking about their faults, they quickly dismiss it as routine. For every fault we remark, we should turn a blind eye to three or four. Nonetheless, when we have observed a particular fault recurring several times, we should take them by surprise and have them do some reparation for their fault immediately. This helps them to correct themselves more than words do.

21. When there are some young pupils who are completely obstinate and unruly, we should try three or four times to have them perform the same small reparations. When they see that we will not budge, they are completely disarmed. But if we insist on punishment one day, and then forgive their fault or just ignore it another day, that behavior makes no impression on their mind. We will then.have to resort to much stronger methods than those we could have used if we had been consistent in our repeated demands for reparation.

22. Lying is all too frequent among young children. That is why we must do everything possible to persuade them not to adopt this pernicious habit. To help in this area, it seems to me that we must encourage them with great tenderness to confess their faults, telling them that it is obvious to us what they have done wrong. When they themselves confess their transgression, we should pardon them and reduce their penance.

23. Even when the pupils are very young, say four or five years old, we should not let them pass the time with nothing to do. We should organize their day, teaching them to read for fifteen minutes, then to play for another

quarter hour, and then to work a little during another little period. These changes of activity divert them and prevent them from picking up a bad habit common to infants: namely, playing with their book or their yarn as they squirm around, glancing everywhere. When we ask them to use up a good fifteen or even thirty minutes, and when we promise them that if they work hard they can play afterward, they work well and happily during this period to gain the reward afterward. When we make this promise before their work period, but they play all through the supposed work period, we do not say anything to them. However, at the end of the failed work period, when they think they are going to play, it is necessary to assign them a new period to do their promised work. This shows them that we do not always have to talk to them when they do something wrong. But when they use their time only to fritter it away, they must start the work period again. This takes them by surprise and makes them more cautious the next time.

2. What We Discuss with the Pupils in the Conferences and in the Meetings When They Need to Be Lectured and Admonished

1. We help them to understand that perfection consists not in doing many extraordinary things, but in doing their everyday work well. They should do this common work with a stout heart and out of love for God. They should always have a great desire to do his holy will joyfully.

2. We help them to esteem those small occasions when God sends them something to suffer for his love. These could be the times when their sisters make some groundless accusation against them, when there are some privations to endure, or when they must sacrifice their own will because of the orders of the schoolmistresses or some other circumstance. We urge them to accept them as so many gifts of God, as a sign of his greatest love, and as a token of the concern he has to send them occasions to become more perfect every day.

3. We should speak to them frequently of the pleasure and the contentment to be found in giving themselves completely to God and serving him in truth and in simplicity, without any reticence. Nothing is painful when we are doing everything out of love. Continual fidelity to God's inspirations always attracts new graces for us. Some win heaven, while others merit only punishment by the same action. It all depends on the posture of their heart and on the purity or impurity of their intention. It is good to help them understand this by some homely comparisons. A good action made out of the love of God and out of the desire to please him and to fulfill his holy will leads us to heaven. On the contrary, if we performed the same action out of hypocrisy, or vanity, or the simple desire to be admired by other creatures,

that would merit only punishment. Having done nothing for God, we could expect no reward, but only punishments as just payment for our hypocrisy.

4. We should strongly exhort the pupils to know themselves: their tendencies, their vices, their passions—right down to the root of their faults. It is also good for them to know just how their temperament influences them, so that they may remove anything that displeases God and that they may change their carnal tendencies into spiritual ones. For example, if we tell them they have a highly affectionate personality, they need to work at changing their love for themselves and for the creatures of the world into a wholehearted love for God. We proceed in the same way with other tendencies.

5. Sometimes we should help them see that one of the greatest faults of youth is indocility. That is almost second nature to them. If they are not careful, this vice can lead to perdition, because it makes them incapable of accepting any sort of correction. This fault always emerges in a proud spirit. That is why we tell them often that they should gladly accept strict treatment. By the gentleness with which they accept the corrections addressed to them, they witness that they truly want us to destroy everything in them that displeases God.

6. We exhort them not to be ashamed to do what is right. Sometimes those who were somewhat disordered are ashamed to do what is good in front of those who saw them in their earlier disorder. We should tell them to pray to God that he might strengthen them to do the good boldly and, when they fall again at the beginning of their reform, to rise again with even greater generosity. These instructions should be given to everyone, even when there are no pupils who are really so disordered. They can be useful for other occasions, and they can help even the best-behaved pupils apply the lesson to their own needs.

7. We tell them that their difficulties in cultivating virtue come from the fact that as soon as some vice must be combated or some virtue acquired, they turn inward to consult their temperament, their desires, their self-love, their weaknesses, and the fears they must overcome. Rather than being weakened by all these too human perspectives, they should turn toward God, in whom they will find all their strength in the very midst of their weakness. It is really a lack of confidence in God's goodness if we do not hope that he will deliver us by the power of his holy grace. If we told them to try to work their own way out of their misery and weakness, they would only become more discouraged. However, since we tell them that God himself will lift away their difficulties, they only have to pray, to hope, and to rejoice that they can receive all the assistance they need from God.

8. We must encourage them truly to appreciate and to want our assis-

tance to overcome the weaknesses of their corrupt nature by not clinging to it. We should patiently encourage them to want to accept some minor reversals and public admonitions, so that they will slowly learn not to be so delicate in their feelings. Sometimes they should say their faults publicly. This accustoms them to the value of penance and of humiliation.

9. We try to convince them that virtuous acts conceived only in the mind count as nothing before God if there is no practice of virtue when an occasion presents itself. At the hour of death, it will help us very little if we spent our life concocting virtuous intentions that we never put into practice. Far from being rewarded for this, we will merit a just punishment from God.

10. We need not give the pupils extensive information on the vowed religious life, especially not in general conferences. Nor do we have to discuss in detail everything we believe concerning the small number of people who can be saved in the world. It is enough to make it clear that it is very difficult to be saved when you live in the secular world. We should help them to understand all their duties as Christian women and the extent of the promises made at the moment of baptism. We must also show them just what they should avoid when and if they return to the world. Sometimes it might be a good idea to share the feelings we have about our own way of life. It is good not to hide our joy, our happiness, and our peace.

11. If they take the initiative to raise the subject of religious vows in order to share their personal feelings about them, we could profitably use the occasion to tell them about the happiness of a nun who truly lives her vocation. We could cite her constant consolation in thinking about the sublime means God gives her to love him and to make her eternally blessed by obedience and by humility. These virtues are essential on the path to heaven for all Christians, but they have special force in the life of the nun. We should help them understand that religious life is not a burden but one of God's great gifts. It is a solace for those who want to live in strict observance of their baptismal vows. God does not grant this religious vocation to everyone, not even to all those who desire it. Given the excellence of this state in life, we must request it from God with humility and prepare ourselves to receive it through good works.

12. It is good sometimes to witness clearly to the pupils that we love them for God's sake. It is this religious devotion that makes us so sensitive to their faults and so unwilling to overlook them. It is the ardor of this love that sometimes adds bite to our words of reproof. At the same time, we need to reassure them that no matter how we act, we are motivated only by the deep affection we bear them and by the desire to help them become as God wants them to be. Our heart always remains tender toward them. We act forcefully

only when we must confront serious faults. And this force requires some violence against our own inclinations, since we would much prefer to treat them with indulgence rather than severity.

3. How We Should Speak to Children in Private

1. The greatest help in improving the conduct of the pupils is our custom of having private conversations with them. In these interviews we relieve their anguish, we wage war against their faults, we help them to see the hidden roots of their vices and of their passions. I can say without hesitation that when they have complete confidence in their schoolmistress, we can hope for a great deal. I have never seen a situation when this total confidence did not succeed in resolving all problems.

[margin note: Private conversation helps to resolve problems]

2. These interviews with the pupils must be serious in nature. We should show them great charity, but no familiarity. If we realize that one of them sought out this conversation as a type of diversion, we should deal with her more lightly than we would with the others. That is why we must use a great deal of discretion, not only in the interview proper, but during the time of preparation. We hold these interviews with each pupil about once every two weeks, unless some particular need requires it more frequently. But we cannot have a strict rule in this area.

[margin note: Interviews are serious]

3. We need to be very careful not to be fooled by anything. It is a great advantage for them to know from the beginning that we know all the subterfuges of childhood. Then they will conduct the conversations on the path of simplicity and of sincerity. Without this, it is not possible to serve their best interests.

4. It is very important not to let ourselves be taken by surprise. We cannot avoid this without the continual assistance of God. That is why we never speak with them without having prayed to God and having foreseen, right in his presence, what we think we have to say to them and how we might respond to their needs. With tears and sighs, we should beg his divine Majesty to shed light in our shadows and to let the light of his grace help us to discover what the pupils might want to hide from us. If, during our conversation, they tell us something but we are not so sure about the whole truth of their claim, we should tell them that we will take some time to pray before we answer them. On their end they should also pray, so that God will dispose them to receive in true serenity everything we will tell them for their good on behalf of God. We should also use this pause as soon as we realize that the pupils might be bitter about what we might tell them or that they would not receive our admonition in a good spirit. We could tell them that we clearly

[margin note: Pray to God before conversation]

see that they are not in the proper mood to listen, or that perhaps we do not have all the information we need. If each of us prayed humbly to God, surely he would take pity on us. This small consideration for their feelings must not be used with everyone, but it can be very useful in dealing with older and more mature pupils. We must exercise great discretion in determining the time and place for this interview. That is why I must repeat again—I cannot say it often enough—that it is more important to pray than to speak. I think that we must always have our hearts and minds raised to heaven in order to receive from God all the words we should tell them.

5. We must be especially vigilant if we are to notice and to understand the particular temperament and tendencies of each pupil. In learning these, we can understand certain things about them that they themselves may not be able to reveal. It is good to anticipate these things when we see that the pupils are ashamed to tell us their disorders. It gives them a great freedom to discover these defects for themselves. At least at the beginning, it is good to hide from them certain hard truths about themselves that are too intimidating to reveal to them in their immature state.

6. To the extent that God opens their hearts to speak to us with some sincerity, we can speak to them more frankly and explain the commitment they should make to do penance, if we see that they have such a need. We must also show them how narrow is the road that leads to heaven and tell them that only the passionate and the violent bear it away.[34]

7. If they ask permission to do many private things, we grant permission only rarely or not at all. We admonish them that this is not the way to please God. They will please God only by doing things that spring from a heart truly touched by his love and by a sincere desire to please him and do penance. For our part, we judge the pupils not by these special actions but by the faithfulness with which they follow the smallest rules in the schoolroom, by the encouragement they give their sister pupils, by the charity with which they serve their sisters' needs, and by the seriousness with which they attempt to correct their faults. These are the things that convince us they really want to serve God. It is not a multiplicity of private gestures. Thus they should not object when we refuse them permission to engage in these special tasks. We are only trying to ensure their welfare and to help them not to fool themselves.

8. We tell the pupils these things, although sometimes we might have a few meetings where we end up granting their requests, without making any fuss about it. On the contrary, at the moment when they ask for something

34. See Matt. 11:12.

extraordinary, we sometimes pretend not to pay attention to them and do not react to their petition. In so conducting ourselves with them, we can soon discover if they are requesting these things only out of hypocrisy. If they are doing this just to be well regarded, if they see that we have little reaction to it, they will gradually tire of this project and will no longer ask about it. For the same reason, it is important to be quite strict in making them finish what they asked to do. We should conceal what we have realized about their dispositions until another time when they are in a better mood to face this. At that time we can help them to see their true state and to understand the danger lurking in the desire to do extraordinary things for an all too human motive.

9. If some of the pupils are truly licentious, but the superiors for good reason have judged that we must keep them, we try to speak to them privately at a time when their mood is comparatively good. We attempt to have them understand that we can no longer tolerate their infractions. As gently and as charitably as we can, we try to admonish them concerning their obligation to live as Christians. But if we see that these admonitions are not affecting them, we will make them understand that we cannot accept that they continue to commit these transgressions. Although we realize that everything we say and do to them will probably not change the problem, we are still bound in conscience to demand satisfaction for their infractions by some penance. We cannot let them simply grow accustomed to their bad habits. Moreover, God wants us to make these pupils do some reparation in front of their sisters for their bad example. Their defects must not harm others. It is good to show them that our conscience demands we act this way.

4. On the Penances to Be Imposed on the Pupils: General and Individual Penances

1. The pupils must ask forgiveness from the companions they offended by their speech, by their displeasing behavior, or by their bad example.

2. They can ask for this forgiveness in several ways, according to the gravity of the transgression. They can request it in group meetings or in private, in the refectory or during class. We can also tell them to kiss the feet of the companions they offended. We should always take care that, if the fault was witnessed by only a few students, especially if it was a minor fault, the penance for it should be performed in private. Otherwise students who did not witness the fault could be disedified. I take the same position concerning penance for somewhat serious faults committed by several students. If a good number of them were involved in the transgression, it is better to correct

[handwritten margin notes:] Discover pupil motives; Cannot allow pupils to be overcome w/ bad habits; Ask forgiveness ÷; Perform Penance in private/public depending on severity

each guilty party in private or to correct the guilty group together. We should try to avoid disedifying the weaker pupils.

3. As punishment, we could have them wear a gray coat, go to meals without a veil or a scapular, or even remain at the door of the church.

4. Sometimes we could also deprive them of the privilege of going to church for one or several days. We could make them stand at the church door or in some other spot separated from the other pupils. We should be careful that they are not indifferent to this banning from the church.

5. With the younger and mid-aged students, we can make them wear cards that explain their particular fault. They should be written in very large letters and should contain only a word or two. Examples would be "lazy," "careless," or "liar." We could also have them wear a red tongue.

6. We could have them ask their sisters in the refectory to pray for them as they explain the fault they committed or the virtue they are lacking.

7. We must help the oldest pupils repent out of the loving fear of God and out of fear of his judgments. When we discuss their faults with them, we could impose one or another of the penances we use with younger pupils: for example, going to meals without a veil or begging the prayers of their sisters in the refectory. Still, we should carefully weigh whether such penances will really help them reform or whether they might not make them bitter. This obliges us to pray often to God to enlighten us and to guide all of our actions for his glory and for the salvation of the souls he has entrusted to our care.

5. Confession

1. As often as we can, we speak to the pupils about the great importance of making good confessions: confessions that are sincere and frank. We emphasize this both in the group meetings and in the individual interviews. Children have a strong tendency to make bad confessions, either by neglecting to name certain faults or by so disguising them that one cannot understand the true state of their souls.

2. That is why we urge them to ask God for a truly contrite and humble spirit, which permits them to honestly admit their faults and makes it easy for them to accept some embarrassment and to receive the penance they deserve.

3. We often remind them that they must tell the faults they find most humiliating and explain the circumstances that make them even more grave. To do this, they must overcome their natural repugnance. That is why it is helpful to describe often the terrible state of a soul at death's door, when the soul sees itself separated from God and plunged into eternal suffering because it

had wanted to avoid some brief and passing humiliation earlier in life. The pain this soul will receive will be seen by everyone. This contrasts with the humiliation they think they will feel in confession, a humiliation that concerns only one other person, that is secret, and that lasts for only a few moments.

4. When we see that they are a bit stronger and more courageous, we exhort them to spare nothing to recover their friendship with God, if they had broken it. We gently guide them toward the practice of external and especially internal penance. It is good to tell them that the sign of a good confession is a visible change in their moral behavior. It is a great evil to go frequently to confession and then fall again and again into the same faults. This would be a clear sign that they are not confessing as they should and that they do not really regret having offended God.

5. When we see certain pupils who wantonly commit transgressions at every type of meeting, we should tell them that in God's eyes they are more guilty than they think. He will impute to them all the intentions they had formed in their hearts and that they shared with others, even if they never had the chance to execute them. We should tell them that they must confess all these things and examine the recesses of their conscience, so that nothing is hidden from the one who holds the place of Jesus Christ. We should tell them that they might be able to fool other people, but that no one fools God and that the blood of Jesus Christ is applied only to those who sincerely accuse themselves of their sins. In this way we would make them understand that they alone are fooled.

6. It is a good idea not to ask the youngest pupils to discuss the greatest sins in detail. They might end up with less horror for the smaller sins and thus be more easily inclined to overlook them. That is why we should tell them that for a soul who loves God, there is nothing of little consequence. Everything is great, and we should try to scrupulously avoid everything that we think displeases him. After all, he did not spare the blood of his own Son to wash us free of our sins.

7. We should not have the pupils go too young or too frequently to confession. For the youngest, we should at least wait until they attain the age of reason and clearly display their desire to have their small faults corrected. The thing we should fear the most here is sending children to confession and then not perceiving any change whatever. We should at least wait until they are capable of showing some real perseverance in trying to do better.

8. When they are still very young, we should accustom them little by little to telling us all their faults, in order to instruct them how to confess their sins properly. Then they will avoid making up tales or pointing the fin-

ger at their sister pupils. We help them to remember their major faults, if they have forgotten them, and we explain to them the way they should accuse themselves of these faults.

9. We watch carefully to see if the pupils really profit from confession. If they commit several grave transgressions soon after confession, we urge them to make some satisfaction for their faults before they confess again. If they have enough confidence in us to tell us their faults, which is so useful in these cases, we suggest that they perform certain reparations proportionate to the gravity of their faults. We recommend in particular practices that mortify them and that are clearly opposed to their faults. For example, if they have wounded the charity they should show to their sisters, we might tell them to serve these pupils with particular grace and courtesy. If these transgressions were public, we might have them ask pardon from those who were offended and from those who witnessed the offense. We might also ask them to say some prayers for the offended parties. We try to arrange it so that these pupils do not return to confession until their hearts have been truly humbled and until they have real sorrow for having offended God. We should act this way whenever we see the children committing serious transgressions, so that they do not fall into the habit of routine confessions. This is a grave danger for all people, but especially for children.

10. We tell them that it is not enough to confess five or six faults, but that they must also talk about their state in life and their dispositions since their last confession. Faults confessed singly and separate from their state in life give practically no information. For example, if they are subject to pride or to sloth, we would advise them that they need to report it if they believe they have been more inclined to these vices since their last confession. They should say how many times they seemed to be in the grip of these vices. They should be specific about any actual sins, based on these vices, that they committed since the last confession. This is the only way to confess sin truly.

11. It is good not to make them so delicate that they do not want to name those with whom they committed a particular transgression, since they all confess their sins to the same confessor. He should have a full knowledge of all the children. This knowledge permits him to know their tendencies and the gravity of their faults. This knowledge is necessary for the confessor if he is to help the children as he should.[35]

12. We are presupposing here something absolutely essential: that the

---

35. This paragraph is found only in the Faugère edition, *LOM*, 285–86. It is not found in the Cousin edition or in the original print version in the *Constitutions* of 1665. For a discussion of the textual issues, see the editor's introduction above.

schoolmistress accurately describes the general state of the children to the confessor. This helps him to assess whether the children are confessing their faults as one would reasonably expect.[36]

A profound harmony must reign between the confessor and the schoolmistress to help the pupils improve their conduct. The schoolmistress should not permit any serious religious acts to occur without receiving the advice of the confessor. These acts include receiving Holy Communion, performing penances, and saying particular prayers. The confessor should counsel the schoolmistress on what he thinks would be helpful for the welfare of the children. She should not say or do anything he does not find appropriate. The pupils should not notice any difference between the conduct of the confessor and that of the schoolmistress.

13. If one of the pupils had some difficulty in confessing to the priest provided for the occasion, she should not speak about this to her peers, but we permit her to express her reluctance to her schoolmistress. With the superior's permission, the schoolmistress will try to resolve the problem when she believes that the pupil's complaint was reasonable and was not some childish foolishness.

14. We do not discuss here all the necessary spiritual dispositions for confession. Nor will we do so in our treatment of Holy Communion and other pious exercises. In this work we intend only to point out what is especially helpful for the conduct of children.

6. Holy Communion

1. We must ardently ask God to grant us the grace to give the pupils a great fear of making unworthy and sterile communions. We must beg him to give them this fear, because without it everything we tell them will be in vain. We try to make them understand that a single communion must bring about some change in their heart and that this change should be obvious even in their external conduct. Those who are sustained by the body of the Son of God should stand out by the quality of their words and of all their actions. In particular, they should exercise control of their tongues, which had the honor of receiving this bread from heaven. We should also explain to them that they must lead a life completely different from the one they led before receiving this grace. Being so wonderfully nourished, they must become more ardent in the mortification of their drives and in the practice of virtue.

---

36. This paragraph is found only in the Faugère edition, *LOM,* 286. It is not found in the Cousin edition or in the original print version in the *Constitutions* of 1665. For a discussion of the textual issues, see the editor's introduction above.

2. We evaluate their spiritual progress in order to determine the frequency of their communions. We rarely give permission for communion to pupils who are attached to some notable fault and who do not know how to accept the admonitions we give them so as to bring about some correction. We consider in particular whether they truly have the fear of and the love of God. One must avoid going to communion indifferently, simply in imitation of others. Sometimes there might even be some pupils who try to take communion out of pride, out of a desire to act like grown-ups. If we are not careful, all these defects and worse can easily arise in children. That is why it is good to inspire some religious fear in them by words of warning. We need to show them the danger of communing with such insouciance. This is the place where they can receive life or death. They cannot ponder this fact too carefully. We should tell them these truths in group meetings with everyone and then repeat them in private interviews with those pupils who seem to have these particular defects.

3. It is rare to find a pupil who suffers from being too shy and too scrupulous. However, when this does occur, we should try to console and strengthen her during the private interview.

4. Even if we see that a particular pupil is unusually devout and prompt to accept correction, we should not permit her to receive communion more frequently than the pupils who perform the best in the schoolroom and who are exemplary in following the daily order. It is possible that this apparent virtue is feigned. It is important to keep such a pupil tethered to the practices of common life and not to let her see that we have noticed this virtue. We should never tolerate their boasting among themselves for any reason, but especially not for the frequency of their communions. It is even a good idea to refrain from praising the pupils in front of each other, whether in public or in private, on the pretext of trying to edify them or to give them a subject for imitation. We could make an exception to this rule for infants who are only two or three years old. If the pupils perceive that we are making a fuss over their virtue, there will be some who will do good actions to win praise and admiration. Further, they will ask for permission to receive communion more frequently out of the same motives.

5. We need to be aware that there are pupils who start to behave better a few days before the feasts when we usually give permission to go to communion. They clearly are thinking about this permission. This sudden improvement is not enough, if we observe that after receiving communion they quickly return to their former faults and foolishness. That is why we try to convince them as best we can that it is not enough to think about communion several days before the great feasts. We should not even let them go to Holy Communion just because they have not received communion for a

long time. They should receive permission to receive communion only as the consequence of a good life and of sustained good order in all their actions.

6. We should carefully observe in just what spirit the pupils perform their penances. It is possible that some of them do these penances all too easily. Nothing seems difficult to them, because of their pride and their desire to avoid any humiliation. But if we carefully study them in all their various interactions, we soon notice that they really do not have their hearts in these penances. When we realize this, we should rarely give such pupils such a great privilege as Holy Communion.

7. When we judge it proper to deprive a pupil of communion, we should be careful that she does not accept this decision with indifference. On the contrary, we should make her remember what a loss this entails. We should show her that she should be in a prolonged state of mourning to ask God for the grace to recover what she has lost. She needs to pray for what she is lacking in order to return to receiving the Most Blessed Sacrament.

8. We usually do not let very young pupils go to communion, especially not those who are pranksters, jokers, and attached to some serious defect. We should wait for God to bring about some change in them. It is a good idea to take an extended period, like a year or at least six months, to see if their good actions really continue. I have never had any regrets when I delayed a certain pupil's receiving communion. On the contrary, the delays always helped the well-disposed pupils to advance in the path of virtue and underlined the insufficient goodwill in the other pupils who were not advancing. We cannot be too careful in our orchestration of first communion. The quality of all the other communions often springs from the first one.

9. After they have received Holy Communion, we should exhort them not to forget God, who has just given himself to them. They should often adore and pray to him. They must be vigilant to avoid doing anything unworthy in his sacred presence. They must be convinced that God will remain in their hearts as long as he sees nothing displeasing in them and that he will not abandon us until we take the initiative to separate ourselves from him by offending him. On communion day, it is a good idea to see if they really have the sense of God, if they speak to him silently, and if they show a greater recollection.

7. Confirmation[37]

When we are given children who have not been confirmed, we take great care to prepare them to receive this sacrament, whose purpose is to fill them with the fullness of the Holy Spirit.

37. The chapter on confirmation is present only in the Cousin edition of the *Règlement: JP,* 416. For a discussion of the textual issues, see the editor's introduction above.

If they have not made their first communion either, we usually delay communion until after they have received confirmation. Being filled with the spirit of Jesus, they are better prepared to receive his sacred body, which will give them a new share in his spirit. As Scripture says, to those who have much, even more will be given.[38]

Confirmation – Sentiments of the heart

I will not go into the details of this preparation. We adhere generally to the small treatise written about this sacrament.[39] But we do not set great store by what the pupils have been able to memorize. We put a greater stress on the sentiments in their heart, as much as we can judge these sentiments by their external action and by their concern to correct their faults. Our efforts here follow those already presented in our discussion of Holy Communion.

It yields grace

When the unconfirmed pupils are in danger of death, we do everything we can to avoid their dying without this sacrament, as Saint Thomas counsels us to do.[40] Although this sacrament is not necessary for their salvation, it is still advantageous for them not to be deprived of so great a grace.

8. Prayer

1. Since we have discussed prayer in all the passages of this work, I only want to add some general reflections on prayer here. We try to give the pupils a great desire to turn to God for all their needs, especially when they experience weakness and temptation. We help them understand that a single trusting, humble, and persevering glance toward God will sustain them far more than all the grandiloquent resolutions they make by themselves. Moreover, these resolutions will be useless if the goodness of God has not shaped them in their hearts by the power of his holy grace. By our own strength, we can only be lost. God alone can save us.

Prayer + Contemplation sustains

2. We do not overwhelm them with a great number of vocal or mental prayers. We try to inflame their hearts with an ardent desire for the holy presence of God, so that they may ponder him everywhere and in all their activities. They should adore and praise him everywhere, since even inanimate creatures praise him in their own way.

3. We help them to see that all their faults come from the fact that they do not pray as they should. They cannot pray as they should as long as their hearts remain attached to themselves, to their desires, and to the things of this world, no matter how holy these things may appear to be.

38. Matt. 13:12.

39. This is a treatise by Saint-Cyran that serves as an appendix to his *Théologie familière*. See above, note 21.

40. See Saint Thomas Aquinas, *Summa theologica* 3.Q.72.A.8.

4. We are very careful that morning and evening prayers are said as they should be. If the pupils seem to be tepid or negligent in saying them, we should not let them go to Mass for several days. We should tell them that although we cannot hand them internal sentiments of piety, we can and we must make them externally reverent and attentive in God's presence. We should make them understand that there will be penances for those who misbehave or who are negligent. A good type of penance would be setting them apart and letting them say only a Pater Noster or an Ave Maria, then telling them that we will permit them to do more when we see that they act more devoutly.

5. Those to whom we gave permission to pray for half an hour, as we discussed in the first part of this rule, must be those who clearly have a pronounced affinity for prayer. We need to instruct these pupils privately on the way they should conduct themselves during this prolonged quiet prayer. If we see that this prayer time does not make them more humble, more charitable, and more recollected, we should take away this privilege. Even when they clearly benefit from this period, we should occasionally prevent them from going to church. This permits us to see how they react to this privation and to determine whether they are as willing to stay as to go.

6. We frequently recommend that the pupils take the Blessed Virgin Mary as their mother and as their mediatrix for all their needs and in all the difficulties they may face. We tell them that she was raised in the temple from her infancy, just as the pupils are raised in houses consecrated to God in order to learn how to become good Christian women. The house where we live is dedicated to the Blessed Virgin and named Our Lady of Port-Royal. She must be their model of prayer, of humility, of silence, of modesty, and of zeal. She must inspire all their actions. We exhort them to celebrate her feasts with special solemnity, since they have always been so honored in the Cistercian order. They should say their rosary often and recite the litany of Our Lady every day.

7. We also commend to them devotion to the holy angels, especially to their guardian angel. We tell them that God has given them this angel to protect them from the snares of the world, the flesh, and the devil. Their guardian angel watches over them vigilantly and cares for their spiritual and even physical needs. He joyously carries their good works to heaven. If an angel were capable of being sad, their guardian angel would be so when they do something wrong and when they let themselves fall into some improper activity, something unworthy of a Christian woman.

8. We also tell them God has given us the saints to act as our intercessors before him. That is why we teach them to call on them and ask them to ob-

Saints as intecessers (margin note)

tain all the graces they need from God. Each day they should commend themselves to the protection of Saint Joseph, of Saint Augustine, of Saint Benedict, and of Saint Bernard. They should also invoke the patron saints of the convent, their name saints, the patron saints of a particular year or month, and the saint whose feast they celebrate on a given day.

9. Books and Reading

1. The books we use for the education of our pupils include the following: *Tradition of the Church;*[41] *Letters of Saint-Cyran;*[42] *Imitation of Jesus Christ;* works of Grenada;[43] *Introduction to the Devout Life;*[44] *The Heavenly Ladder* by Saint John Climacus;[45] *Simple Theology;*[46] *Christian Maxims,* from the book of hours;[47] *Meditations of Saint Teresa d'Avila on the Pater Noster.*[48] We also use other books whose aim is the formation of a truly Christian woman.

Books call on Religion (margin note)

2. I already discussed the readings at 8:00 a.m. in my earlier exposition of the daily school schedule.

3. For the public reading that one of the pupils performs after vespers, one could use a number of other books. Examples would be *Letters of Saint Jerome;*[49] *Of Christian Almsgiving;*[50] and Saint Teresa of Avila's *Path of Perfection* or *Book of the Foundations,*[51] especially those passages treating the lives of the desert fathers. Other lives of the saints are also helpful.

Nuns explain the texts (margin note)

4. Except for the one after vespers, we teachers ourselves do all the public readings for the pupils as a group. We always take care to explain what we just read and to talk to them about it. We should always try to have them develop the habit of never listening to the readings in a spirit of amusement or

---

41. *Tradition de l'église sur le sujet de la penitence et de la communion,* selected texts, trans. Antoine Arnauld (Paris, 1644).

42. Saint-Cyran, *Lettres de Saint-Cyran* (Paris, 1645).

43. Louis de Grenade, *Catéchisme, ou Introduction du symbole de la foi,* trans. Nicolas Colin (Paris, 1587); *Les sermons sur les principales fêtes des saints,* trans. Jean Charon (Paris, 1602); *Traité de l'oraison et la méditation,* trans. Jean de Chabanel and François de Belleforest (Paris, 1608).

44. Saint François de Sales, *Introduction à la vie dévote,* last ed. (Paris: G. Clopejau, 1640).

45. Saint Jean de Climaque, *Traité des degrés pour monter au ciel,* trans. Arnauld d'Andilly (Paris, 1652).

46. Saint-Cyran, *Théologie familière* (Paris, 1643).

47. *Heures de Port-Royal: Office de l'église en latin et en français* (Paris, 1650). Jacqueline Pascal contributed her translation of the hymn "Jesu, nostra redemptio" to the volume.

48. *Méditations de Sainte Thérèse sur le Pater Noster,* trans. Antoine Le Maître (Paris, [1665]).

49. Saint Jerôme, *Les Lettres de S. Jerôme,* trans. Jean Petit (Paris: Jean Couterot, 1679).

50. *Aumône chrétienne,* selected texts trans. Arnauld d'Andilly (Paris, 1647).

51. Sainte Thérèse d'Avila, *Les oeuvres de sainte Thérèse, divisées en trois parties,* trans. Robert Arnauld d'Andilly (Anvers: H. Van Dunewald, 1688).

of curiosity. Rather, they should listen with a desire to apply their lessons to their lives. To accomplish this, we need to explain the readings in ways that convince the pupils that it is more important to become a good Christian woman and to correct their faults than it is to become a woman scholar.

5. Besides the readings we perform by ourselves, we tell them what they should read. They are permitted to change neither the book nor the passage we have assigned. There are few books that do not contain something that should be avoided.

6. At the reading after vespers, they are permitted, in fact encouraged, to ask questions about what they do not understand, as long as they remain respectful and humble. When we answer them, we teach them how to apply this reading to reform their morals. If, as we do the reading, they keep asking questions about something we think most of them were not listening to, we ask them if they understand it. If it is obvious that they cannot answer, we reprove them for remaining in their ignorance, since they knew they were supposed to acquire knowledge concerning all the subjects they did not yet understand.

7. As soon as the reading is finished, we put the book back in its place. We let the pupils privately own only a few books: their book of hours; *Simple Theology*; an *Imitation of Jesus Christ*, and a Latin-French psalter. All the other books remain in the possession of the schoolmistresses. The pupils are content with this arrangement, since they realize that even the most sacred books are of little benefit to them when they are read simply out of curiosity. The moral effect of this sacred reading is nearly always diminished when they keep their books in private.

8. They are forbidden to open any book that is not theirs. Nor may they borrow books from each other without the permission of the schoolmistress. This permission is rarely given, in order to avoid the small disorders this borrowing may cause.

10. The Sick and Their Corporal Needs

1. We must take great care of those who fall ill. We should serve them zealously, have them see a doctor if the illness is serious, and punctually do everything the doctor prescribes to relieve the affliction.

2. We do everything we can always to be present when the doctor comes to visit the sick. It is a good idea to speak to him before he visits the sick, to describe the illness and how the sick pupils are eating and taking their medications. We ask him not to speak at length to the patients. Otherwise they might become depressed or obsessed with their affliction. After the doctor

has visited the sick, we learn from him what we need to do to provide relief for our patients.

3. We accustom them to avoid making any trouble when they must take the more unpleasant treatments. We are always present with them at these moments so that we can tell them some word of God to encourage them and to help them offer their suffering to God.

4. We exhort them never to criticize the doctor's orders because, as long as they are sick, he should hold the place of God in their lives. That is why they must obey him as if they were obeying God himself, by surrendering their life, their health, or their illness to the order of divine providence, which uses either the success or the failure of different treatments for our good. That is why, whenever something disturbing happens, we should never blame the doctor or the course of treatment. We should simply adore silently and humbly the order that the divine goodness provides for us. To make it as easy as possible for the sick to enter into these dispositions, I presume that we always use, as much as is possible, doctors who are truly good Christians and good doctors.

5. There should always be a sickroom isolated from the rest of the school. We should not let the other pupils enter it unless it is for some grave necessity and with the permission of their schoolmistress. During the recreation period, we could let one of the better-behaved pupils go to the sickroom to entertain the patients. It is essential that the nuns who take care of the sick never leave them alone, unless we use older adolescents in whom we have complete confidence. They could watch the sick, and even attend to their needs, when the illness is a minor one.

6. When there are many sick pupils, we should assign an additional nun, besides the one already designated for health care, to care for the sick. These nuns must be intelligent and gentle. They should be especially skillful in helping the patients follow the proper diet. There is a danger that the sick can lose everything they had earlier gained through hard work when they were healthy. The nursing nuns must help the patients to overcome any repugnance they may have concerning one or more of the prescribed treatments. They must ensure that the patients abstain from certain foods that could damage them further. But these nuns must also be gentle. Their charitable manners and their soothing words can help soften the bitterness of the patients who must renounce certain pleasures for the sake of their health.

7. We are very devoted to the sick, happily leaving the company of the healthy to obtain for them the treatment they need, or to keep their spirits

up, or to teach them how to accept illness as a Christian woman. All of this helps them to avoid being overwhelmed.

8. Beyond this medical treatment and these general visits, we take a certain amount of time to make individual visits to each sick pupil when there is more than one patient. We try to make these visits with the greatest gentleness and cordiality. We use them either to listen to the patients if they have something to tell us or to exhort them to do good and to accept their pain patiently, to offer their affliction to God in honor of and out of love for the sufferings of Our Lord Jesus Christ. Although we certainly must treat the sick gently and charitably, we should not encourage any squeamishness that would only put them in a bad mood or make them more difficult to serve. On the contrary, we should encourage them to accept everything they need to undergo out of a virtuous motive.

9. When the illness is grave, we must take the advice of the mother abbess and of the physician concerning the administration of the sacraments, according to the age and capacity of the sick pupil. We should intensify our spiritual and physical assistance to her, so that she can be as serene as possible. We should try to relieve her as much as possible of any worry she may have about herself. As fully as her age and her virtue permit, she should focus on God as much as on her illness. Still, we should not press her on this. We must be careful that our discussions with her do not become a burden to her. We should take into account her own desires concerning a discussion about God. But even when we visit only to cheer her up, we should be able to interject some pious remarks into the visit.

10. As soon as the pupils have recovered, we have them return to be with the others. Otherwise they might become dissolute. We should fear this especially with the young, who often want nothing other than their own freedom. However, even when they have returned to their rooms, we should be sure they receive all the food and rest they need for the complete recovery of their health.

11. For their minor health problems, we should give them everything they need, but we should not spoil them. Sometimes children pretend to be sick. I have seen some of them like that, although by God's grace it has been a long time since I have seen it among our own pupils. Nonetheless, when that occurs, we should not appear to believe they are trying to fool us. On the contrary, we should commiserate with them and tell them they really are sick. We should put them in an isolated room with a nun to mind them but who never speaks to them. We should tell them that talking would make them worse and that they must have complete rest. We should put them on a

Treatment
done in
part to
prevent
lying

diet of broth and eggs for a day or two. If they are really sick, this diet will be excellent for them. If they are not, they will undoubtedly tell us the next day that they are not sick anymore. Thus we would heal them of their hypocrisy without giving them any reason to complain. But if we tell them that they do not really have the illness they claim to have, we only open the door to further lies and further pretense on their part.

INTERROGATION OF SOEUR JACQUELINE
DE SAINTE EUPHÉMIE (PASCAL),
SUBPRIORESS AND NOVICE MISTRESS

INTRODUCTION

The ecclesiastical interrogation of the Port-Royal nuns took place in two sessions in the summer of 1661: June 26–29, under the direction of Monsieur Louis Bail alone, and July 11–26, under the joint direction of Monsieur Bail and Monsieur Jean-Baptiste de Contes. Monsieur Bail, imposed by Louis XIV as the new superintendent of the convent, was clearly hostile to Jansenism, while Monsieur de Contes, a grand vicar of the archdiocese of Paris, had previously shown some sympathy toward the Jansenists. The interrogation of Jacqueline Pascal recorded in this transcript probably occurred during the June inquest conducted by Monsieur Bail alone.

The clear purpose of the inquest was to investigate the charges of heresy against the Port-Royal nuns. The inquisitor's questions reflect two common charges against the Jansenists: that they believed Christ died only for a small elect rather than for all humanity, and that they believed salvation depends uniquely on predestination and not on any moral effort by human beings. Pascal deftly insists on the unresolvable mystery involved in both theological issues.

This translation is based on Jacqueline Pascal, *Interrogatoire de Soeur Jacqueline de Sainte Euphémie (Pascal), sous-prieure et maîtresse des novices*, in the Faugère edition, *LOM*, 301–4. The text was originally published in Religieuses de Port-Royal, *Histoire des persécutions des religieuses de Port-Royal* (Villefranche, 1733), 167.

After asking my name and loudly praising Saint Euphemia, he asked me whether I had noticed any doctrinal changes in the house since I had arrived there. I told him I hadn't been here such a long time. But I could tell him that no one here had said anything concerning the faith that I hadn't learned in my childhood.

Question: Did you learn in your childhood that Jesus Christ died for all human beings?

Answer: I don't remember that being discussed in my catechism.

Q: Since you've been here, hasn't anyone taught you anything on this matter?

A: No.

Q: What do you think about it?

A: I usually don't think about such matters, since they aren't very practical. Still, it seems to me that we must believe Our Lord died for everyone. I remember two verses in the Book of Hours[1] I possessed when I was still in the world. This is how they spoke about Our Lord: "In order to save the whole world, You did not disdain / To enter the humble womb of a fertile virgin."[2]

He smiled a little at that and then he said: "Now there's a good answer. But how do you explain that there are so many souls that are lost eternally?"

A: Sir, I must admit that this has often disturbed me. Usually, when I am praying, especially when I am before a crucifix, that question comes to mind. Then I say to the Lord: "My God, how is it possible, after everything you have done for us, that so many people perish in misery?" But when these thoughts haunt me, I reject them, because I don't think I have the right to sound out the secrets of God. That's why I just content myself with praying for sinners.

He replied: "That's very good, my daughter. What books do you read?"

A: At present I am reading the *Moralia* of Saint Basil, which was just translated.[3] More often, I read my rule.

Q: What position do you hold?

A: Before they made the novices and postulants leave, I took take care of the ones who were here. But for the moment, we have in the novitiate only several professed sisters, one novice, and several lay sisters.

Q: That must have been a painful test for you when they took away your novices.

In my response, I discussed the issue at length. I didn't appear bitter. I just showed how concerned I was by the suffering they endured and by the dangers they faced in the world.

---

1. The Book of Hours is a simplified, lay version of the breviary, a compilation of psalms, prayers, and hymns that clerics and vowed religious are required by canon law to pray every day.

2. The passage is taken from the Te Deum, the hymn of praise found in the liturgical office of vigils.

3. Saint Basil (329–79) specialized in moral and exegetic issues. His *Moralia* is an anthology of New Testament passages. Le Roy de Haute-Fontaine had recently translated the work: *Les règles de la morale chrétienne recueillies par Saint Basile* (Paris: Savreux, 1661).

He seemed understanding enough, and then he said to me: "Did you teach the novices that Our Lord died for all human beings and why there are both good and bad people in the world?"

A: Since I don't trouble myself about those things, I try to avoid troubling the novices about them. On the contrary, I try to keep them in a state of simplicity as much as I can.

He replied: "That's very good. But do you tell them that when they sin, it's by their own fault? Do you believe that yourself?"

A: Yes, Sir, and I clearly know it through my own experience. I assure you that when I commit faults, I blame only myself. That's why I try to do penance for them.

He said: "That's an excellent answer. Praise God, I think that you've spoken sincerely."

A: Yes, Sir, as if I were before God.

He added: "I believe it. I'm confident of it. God be praised. My daughter, always remain in this faith, whatever anyone else says. Teach it well to the novices. I thank God with all my heart for having preserved you from all error. It's atrocious when people say that God saves some from the corrupt mass of humanity and that he lets others perish, just according to his good pleasure. That's a horrible belief. But God be praised for having spared you from such a great error—Don't you have any complaints to make?"

A: No, Sir. By the grace of God, I am perfectly happy.

He said to me: "But that's strange. Whenever I go to interview nuns, they always take up hours and hours in complaining to me. But I don't find any of that here."

A: Sir, it's true that by the grace of God we live in great peace and in great union. I believe that this comes from the fact that everyone does her own duty without interfering with that of others.

At that he cried out: "Ah! Now that's the right way to do things. May God be praised, my daughter! Have the next sister come in to see me."

A MEMOIR OF MÈRE MARIE ANGÉLIQUE
BY SOEUR JACQUELINE DE SAINTE
EUPHÉMIE PASCAL

INTRODUCTION

Shortly after the death of the abbess Mère Angélique on August 6, 1661, Mère Angélique de Saint-Jean asked members of the Port-Royal community to write their recollections of her words and actions. The purpose of these memorials was to document the sanctity and orthodoxy of the controversial reformer at a moment of heightened anti-Jansenist persecution. In response to this request Jacqueline Pascal composed her *Memoir of Mère Marie Angélique* in the late summer or early autumn of 1661.

This biographical sketch underscores the wisdom of the abbess. In four separate incidents Mère Angélique manifests a penetrating knowledge of the recesses of human character and proposes a clear, firm solution to a moral or religious dilemma. This biography, however, provides more than a moral portrait of one particular nun. It depicts the ideal Jansenist nun. Her moral rigorism categorically condemns such common vices as gambling. Her enlightened piety rejects the least trace of superstition.

This translation is based on Jacqueline Pascal, *Relation de la Soeur Jacqueline de Sainte Euphémie Pascal concernant la Mère Marie Angélique* in the Faugère edition, *LOM*, 223–27. The Faugère edition is based on the manuscript *Relations sur la vie de la Mère Angélique*, BNF Ffr. 17797, 66–69.

Once when I was speaking to Mère Angélique about someone whose father made a living by gambling, she told me with her usual firmness that this person's goods were more ill gotten and more subject to restitution than those stolen by highway robbers. According to her reasoning, the thieves are authors only of the evil they do to passersby, whereas the gamblers are the authors of countless sins they make other players commit: blasphemies, cheating, the ruin of families and all its related evils, murders, often an infinity of crimes. They cause all of this.

"If this person isn't embarrassed by having such a father, she is as guilty as he is and she should be treated as he should be. It's true that children should not bear the iniquity of their fathers, but this is only on condition that they hold this iniquity in contempt. If they don't experience some shame about this, if they don't wholeheartedly condemn it, if they aren't deeply disturbed by this, this evil should be imputed to them as surely as it is to their fathers.

"The judgments of God are a terrible thing. We don't think enough about them. We don't dread them enough. That is why we don't try hard enough to avoid them.

"Look, my daughter, the only way to avoid these terrible judgments is to humble yourself, deeply humble yourself, before God for everything, but especially for the stains in your family. Outside of that, how can we possibly rise? We should ponder only what can humble us, either in nature, or in fortune, or in the order of grace. Of course, we do just the opposite. If there is something a little to our advantage, we take our good time to talk about it and to make sure that others know about it. On the other hand, if there is something a bit shameful—as there always is—we do everything to stifle discussion about it and even to disguise it. The dullest people have enough brains to do that! But what is this really? Isn't it just an insufferable claim of pride?

"Now, I'm not saying that you should criticize your family. No one is obliged to do that. In fact, no one should do anything of the sort. But we also shouldn't go around publicizing the little good we do while we suppress all knowledge of the evil. We should just be completely silent. But this silence shouldn't spring from a fear that we might reveal what we truly are. It shouldn't arise from dread of speaking about it at all. Sometimes we think that we are doing something virtuous in refraining from speaking about our merits. But when we are silent on these matters, we are simply doing our duty."

Once we were speaking about someone who was much taken with a false devotion. Clearly it was going to be difficult to disabuse her of her illusion. Mère Angélique told me: "It's not only difficult. It's completely impossible if God himself doesn't do it, and he will do it only in his own time and in his own way. I'm not saying that we shouldn't do what we can. After all, it might be that God is using us as the means to execute his decrees. Still, trying to solve the problem by our own ingenuity and trying to make immature souls understand certain spiritual truths is like trying to make the sun shine in the middle of the night. All the powerful princes and kings of the earth together cannot make the sun rise an hour earlier than it will in the morning. All human beings together, with every artifice of eloquence and of persuasion imaginable, cannot make the truth manifest to someone who is still un-enlightened by God."

One day in Mère Angélique's presence, someone said that she did not want to be involved in a particular problem. The problem concerned another person who had real afflictions but who was suspected of having serious faults. This person had asked the speaker to help her.

Mère Angélique pondered these words. Then she said that she didn't know anyone who could help someone facing serious peril better than the speaker could. Except for Monsieur Singlin, she saw very few who could do such a good job as could the speaker.

Someone then told her that she should also make an exception for herself, since she never refused to hear or to help anyone in need. She said: "No. For my part, I am only a miserable creature who never does any good. But it is true that on those occasions when aid is requested, I imagine that we've lost a person whom we deeply loved. I imagine that we don't know whether this person is living or dead. We don't know where she is. For example, it might be my sister Catherine of Saint Jean.

"Now, I ask you, how should we act if some unknown and miserable person asks to see us? Wouldn't we run to see her? Wouldn't we then say: 'Alas! My God, perhaps it is my poor lost sister!' What affection and what excitement we would show! I'm moved just by thinking about it. If this person is given to God and is unjustly persecuted, shouldn't we be as touched by this suffering as if it had happened to our own sister? How do we know that this isn't a sister sent by Jesus Christ, that is to say, a person he sends us to love and to assist in whatever way we can?

"That is why we should never refuse to see and to be involved in this sort of thing. Now I'm not saying that we should do anything outlandish or try to take care of everyone without distinction. After all, if our sister were lost, we wouldn't simply take the first person we see for her. Still, we would be very concerned to see if this person might be she. That's just what I'm asking: that we have the desire and the concern to see if this is some person God is entrusting to our care. This doesn't involve indiscriminate commitments."

Someone else told her that the person who had earlier said she did not want to be involved in this business wasn't refusing this out of any hardness of heart. Rather, she had first taken this task on herself, but when she discovered that her help wasn't really necessary she distanced herself from it because she wanted to avoid spending her time on unimportant matters. Mère Angélique now approved the position of the person in question. She said that this was a good motive to disengage, on condition that the person was ready to commit herself to further action if it was really necessary. She said that she understood the spirit in which this person was performing her actions.

One day a nun came upon a phrase in the Gospel that frightened her. To console her, Mère Angélique said to her: "Every time God threatens, it's so that we may humble ourselves. When we humble ourselves, we always avoid what is threatened. This is true even with the most evil among us. Look at the Ninevites who received God's forgiveness and prevented the execution of God's threats because they did penance for their sins.[1] It's true that this was a temporal pardon, but they didn't desire anything more. When God threatens you, humble yourself, and ask him to give you the graces that are eternal. He will grant you them."

1. See Jon. 3:5.

LETTERS OF JACQUELINE PASCAL

INTRODUCTION

Both as a laywoman and as a nun, Jacqueline Pascal conducted an extensive correspondence. Frequent correspondents included family members (father Étienne, brother Blaise, sister Gilberte) and the principals of the Port-Royal convent (Mère Angélique, Mère Agnès, Mère Angélique de Saint Jean). This selection of letters includes works displaying the following traits: commentary on the major events of Jacqueline Pascal's life; exemplars of Pascal's skill as a moralist; defenses of the spiritual freedom of women.

Numerous letters provide Jacqueline Pascal's own interpretation of the major events concerning herself and the Port-Royal community. Her letter on the profession of vows (3) details her difference with her brother Blaise during the prelude to the "crisis of the dowry." Her letter on the "miracle of the thorn" (4) describes the miraculous healing of her niece Marguerite Périer, which momentarily bolstered the convent in the midst of persecution. Her letter on the "crisis of the signature" (6) explains in detail her refusal to submit to the church's condemnation of Jansenius and her chagrin at the moral compromises proposed by Jansenist moderates.

Several letters exhibit Jacqueline Pascal's skill as a moralist, her capacity to etch vivid moral portraits of personalities she had observed. Her letter on Descartes (1) not only describes the celebrated meeting between Descartes and Blaise Pascal but provides the occasion for sharp satire. In Jacqueline's letter the lionized Descartes emerges as vain, unable to tolerate the least criticism, and as pompous, dispensing absurd medical advice to the sickly Blaise. In her elegiac letter on the death of Soeur Anne-Marie de Sainte Eugénie (5), Pascal delicately evokes the virtues of the dying nun: humility, repentance, obedience, compassion, joy, hope, faith.

Several major letters constitute an extended defense of the religious rights of women. In her letters to her father on her desire to make a retreat (2) and to her brother on profession of vows (3), Pascal defends her right to pursue a religious vocation against paternal and fraternal objections. The letters poignantly express the tension between her desire for family approval and her determination to become a nun, but the right to follow one's vocation clearly trumps the pull of family affection. In her letter on the "crisis of the signature" (6), she explicitly defends women's right to refuse to assent to church judgments they consider unjust and to reject the counsel of confessors and theologians if it leads to endorsing such injustice. These letters constitute more than a general defense of the rights of conscience. They are an apology for the religious rights of women to choose their state of life in liberty and to engage in critical theological reflection.

1. To Gilberte Pascal Périer, On Descartes's Visit[1]

Paris
Wednesday, September 25, 1647

Dearest sister,

I delayed writing to you because I wanted to fill you in on everything concerning the meeting between Monsieur Descartes and our brother.[2] Yesterday I didn't have time to write you that Sunday evening Monsieur Habert[3] came here. He was accompanied by Monsieur de Montigny[4] from Brittany.

Monsieur de Montigny came to tell me (because he couldn't tell our brother, who was then at church) that Monsieur Descartes, his close friend, had expressed a strong desire to meet our brother. Monsieur Descartes had the greatest respect for our father and for our brother because of their achievements, which everyone was talking about. To fulfill his wish, he wanted to come see our brother the next day at nine o'clock in the morning, if that wouldn't be an inconvenience for him (because he knew that our brother was ill).

When Monsieur de Montigny proposed this meeting, I found it difficult to respond. I knew that our brother had difficulty working and speaking at any length, especially in the morning. Still, I didn't think it proper to refuse

---

1. This translation is based on Jacqueline Pascal, "Lettre de Jacqueline Pascal à Madame Périer," *LOM*, 309–12.

2. Descartes visited Blaise Pascal on September 23 and 24, 1647, shortly before his journey to the Netherlands.

3. Jacques Habert, sieur de Saint-Léonard, was an amateur scientist and a friend of Étienne Pascal.

4. Monsieur de Montigny was a scientific researcher and a friend and disciple of Descartes.

such a meeting. We agreed that Descartes would arrive at ten-thirty the next day.

Monsieur Descartes arrived at the agreed-on time the next day. He was accompanied by Monsieur Habert, by Monsieur de Montigny, by a young cleric I didn't recognize, by the son of Monsieur de Montigny, and by several other young boys. Monsieur de Roberval,[5] whom my brother had contacted beforehand, was already here.

After several polite comments, they began to discuss the calculating machine. Everyone marveled at it as Monsieur de Roberval demonstrated it.

Then they began to discuss the problem of the vacuum. Monsieur Descartes became particularly serious on this subject. The others explained a recent experiment to him and asked him what he thought entered into the space of the emptied tube. He said that it was his "subtle matter." My brother responded to this theory as best he could. Believing that my brother was having some difficulty in expressing himself, Monsieur de Roberval took on Monsieur Descartes with not a little passion—although he remained civil. Monsieur Descartes responded rather bitterly that he would speak to my brother as long as he desired, because my brother spoke reasonably, but that he wouldn't continue to talk with Monsieur de Roberval, because the latter spoke out of too many prejudices.

With that, he glanced at his watch and saw that it was noon. He stood up, because he had a dinner date in the Faubourg Saint-Germain. Monsieur de Roberval also had a date in the same neighborhood. So Monsieur Descartes led him over to a carriage where the two of them were alone. They appeared to be joking with each other, but there was a bit of an edge to their humor, as Monsieur de Roberval confirmed for us after he returned from dinner to rejoin Monsieur d'Alibray.[6]

I forgot to tell you that Monsieur Descartes, upset by the little progress he had made in the morning's conversation, promised my brother to come see him again at eight o'clock the next morning. Monsieur d'Alibray, whom we informed about this new meeting the evening before, wanted to be there and tried to bring with him Monsieur Lepailleur,[7] whom my brother had asked to be invited on his behalf. But he was too lazy to come over to visit, al-

---

5. Gilles Personne de Roberval (1602–75) was a leading scientist who held a series of professorships in philosophy and mathematics. A member of the scientific circle led by Père Mersenne, Roberval distinguished himself by research in integrated calculus.

6. Charles Vion d'Alibray was an amateur scientist and a frequent visitor to the Pascal household in Paris.

7. Jacques Lepailleur was a family friend and a frequent guest at the Pascal home in Paris. He directed a prominent scientific academy.

though both he and Monsieur d'Alibray had planned to dine not too far from here.

Monsieur Descartes returned in part to examine and to give some advice on the illness of my brother. But he really didn't have much to say about it. He only suggested that my brother remain in bed every day until he wasn't capable of staying there any longer and that he drink some strong bouillon.

They spoke about many other things, because they were together until eleven o'clock. But I don't know what they talked about it, because I wasn't present yesterday.

I couldn't know, because we were busy all day yesterday trying to get my brother to take his first bath. He said that the bath gave him a small headache, but that's because he made it too hot. I think that the bleeding of his foot on Sunday evening did him a lot of good, because on Monday he was able to speak at length with Monsieur Descartes in the morning and with Monsieur de Roberval in the afternoon. He had a long dispute with Roberval over many issues dealing more with theology than with physics. Still, he didn't have any pain other than some night sweat and some insomnia later that evening. He didn't have the headaches that I would have expected after such an effort.

Tell Monsieur Ausoult[8] that my brother wrote a letter to Père Mersenne[9] the other day to ask him about the grounds on which Descartes opposed the theory of the column of air. The response was poorly written (because he had an artery in the right arm cut during a bleeding; this might cripple him). However, I read that it wasn't Descartes who opposed this theory (on the contrary, he believed in it strongly, but for a reason my brother does not accept) but that it was Roberval who strongly opposed it. In this letter my brother also expressed his delight in seeing Monsieur Descartes and in seeing Descartes's admiration for his machine. But we consider all that a simple formula of politeness.

Farewell, beloved sister. I remain your most humble and obedient servant,

J. Pascal.

---

8. Adrien Ausoult was a close friend of Blaise Pascal. Both had assisted at the scientific and religious discussions led by the controversial Frère Saint-Ange.

9. Marin Mersenne (1588–1648) was a Minim priest, philosopher, theologian, and mathematician. He organized conferences for the presentation and encouragement of research by young scientists and was a close friend and defender of Descartes, especially on questions of religious orthodoxy. He published numerous works refuting religious skepticism.

2. To Étienne Pascal, on a Religious Retreat[10]

Paris
Friday, June 19, 1648

Dear Father,

Since ingratitude is the blackest of vices, everything that comes close to it is horrifying. Anyone with the slightest love of virtue would not even consider it. Forgetting the benefits one has received from someone (especially when they are great and when they have been nearly continual) is ordinarily an effect of this vice. The lack of confidence in this person can only be the result of this forgetting. I think it would be a crime for me to have such a lack at this moment, although it's true that I very much wish you to grant me what I am asking of you and that this lack of confidence is quite common in those who have such a wish.

Above all things, Father, I ask you in God's name—whom alone we must consider in all matters, but especially in this one—not to be astonished by the request I am going to make of you. It should in no way offend the goodwill you have shown that you possess on many occasions.

I also beg you by everything that is holy to recall the prompt obedience I showed concerning the thing in the world I prize the most and whose fulfillment I desire with the greatest fervor.[11] Undoubtedly you have not forgotten this obedient submission. You seemed too satisfied with it to let it leave your mind so quickly.

As God is my witness, I think that I did my duty in this act of obedience. I am telling you all this only to help you understand that all my principles incline me to undertake nothing important without your consent. If it were possible, I would never do anything that could anger you. I beg God to imprint this truth as deeply in your mind as it is in my heart.

After all this, Father, I can no longer doubt that you wouldn't do me the honor of agreeing with me and granting me my request.[12]

The ardor with which I desire this favor means that I can't discuss it with you without some preparation. Undoubtedly this will make you think that

10. This translation is based on Jacqueline Pascal, "Lettre de Jacqueline Pascal, à M. Pascal, son père," *LOM*, 318–25.

11. Jacqueline Pascal refers to her desire to enter the convent of Port-Royal as a nun. When her father opposed this vocational decision, she agreed to care for him until he died, on condition that she could pursue a withdrawn, ascetic life at home.

12. The request is for permission to undertake a retreat of several weeks at the convent of Port-Royal under the direction of Abbé Singlin, the convent chaplain. When her father rejected her request, Jacqueline Pascal abandoned her planned retreat. Against her father's commands, however, she continued her visits to the Port-Royal convent.

it's something of consequence, yet it's really nothing at all. It's so small that knowing my intention to obey you in every circumstance, just as I am doing here, and knowing that the issue is urgent, I think that without offending you in any way—and I would never even entertain the thought of offending you—I could have actually done this before discussing it with you. However, such an action might have taken you by surprise. And since it's a foretaste of an even greater commitment, you might have been astonished that I had done this without your permission. Perhaps you might have taken it for an act of disobedience.

Please realize, Father—and I'm sure that you already know this—that it's quite common for all sorts of people, whether they're engaged in worldly affairs or not, to make two or three weeks of retreat in a monastery on the great feasts or even at other times. It's up to their spiritual director to judge. With the permission of the superior you are enclosed in the convent in order to speak to God alone, among people who have given themselves to him alone. That is why those who are the most careful about their salvation do this regularly in the convents following the strictest rule.

I think you can clearly divine my intention and that you agree with me that I could not make a better choice than to cast my eyes on Port-Royal for this retreat. There couldn't be a better time, either, than that of your absence. There are no other services for me to perform at home. In fact, I'm quite useless here at the moment. Since you've left, I haven't written a single word for my brother. This is what he usually needs me for, but he could easily do without me and use someone else's services.

Finally, I don't see any area where I am really essential until your departure from Rouen, especially if you compare this need with the necessity I have to make this retreat, and to make it in that place. God has given me the grace to deepen day by day the sense of the vocation he has deigned to give me and you have permitted me to retain. I have the desire to fulfill this vocation as soon as he makes his will known through your will. As I told you, this desire becomes greater with the passage of every day. I see nothing on the face of the earth that could have prevented me from pursuing this vocation if you had permitted me to. This retreat will serve as a test to discover if this is the place where God wants me.

There I will be able to listen to him one-on-one. It's possible that I could discover through this retreat that I wasn't born to live in this sort of place. If that occurs, I would frankly ask you neither to heed nor to yield to what I told you earlier. On the other hand, if God leads me to understand that I am right for this place, I promise you that I will put all my energy into waiting serenely for the moment you would like to choose for his glory. I think this is all you

are looking for. This is better than our current condition, where I have a continual desire for something that may or may not succeed, even if you desired
it. As a result, my mind is in a confusion I can scarcely express. But after this
test, I would be able almost certainly to assure you that I was attracted to one
option or the other, and I would patiently await the moment that you commanded me to await.

My idea, if you think it good, was to remain in this convent until you
were ready to return from Rouen. Still, if you absolutely want me to return
before that time, I have no problem in assuring you that I would do so. I know
very well that you have no doubts on this subject. So I wouldn't fail to obey
you promptly.

So, Father, here is the humble petition I have to make to you. I have no
doubt that you will grant it, but I ask you to send your response as early as
possible by my sister or by someone else. I'm fearful that the medicines you
take might prevent you from doing this chore by yourself.

Please realize that I have only this one period to make this retreat. It's so
useful and even so necessary for me because of certain circumstances. That is
why I beg you that, if I have ever had the pleasure of satisfying you in something, you would grant me promptly what I ask. These nuns have had enough
goodness to accept my request. Monsieur Périer,[13] my brother, and my faithful servant[14] approve this project and are happy with it as long as you give
your consent. It now depends on you alone.

I have had the boldness to ask you for few things in life. I beg you, as
much as I can and with all possible respect, not to refuse this request. Please
do not leave me without a response, unless you agree that these retreats are
such a minor matter that mine could be made without an express sign of your
will. In that case I wouldn't have any reason to believe that you disagree with
my project unless you clearly indicate that you don't want me to do it.

Since the mail leaves often, since you have ample opportunity to write
back, and since moreover silence gives consent, I plan to start preparations
for my trip if I do not hear from you by a week from Tuesday at the latest. (I
could receive the news earlier.) I plan to make this short trip in two weeks on
Sunday the twenty-first. Before leaving, I would be able to know if there are
any letters from you in the mail. If there aren't any, I would consider myself
confirmed in the belief that you desire this retreat as much as I do. Consequently I would feel free to go ahead with my plans without further permis-

13. Jacqueline Pascal's brother-in-law, Florin Périer.

14. According to Jean Mesnard the term *ma fidèle* in this passage probably refers to Louise
Delfaut, a servant in the Pascal household who often acted as Jacqueline Pascal's chaperone. In-
forming Étienne Pascal of his daughter's movements, Delfaut helped to block Jacqueline's at-
tempts to communicate with members of the Port-Royal community.

sion. I assure you that if I did not believe that this constituted a clear proof of your consent, I would not even think about undertaking it.

If there were some argument stronger than that of God's love to prevail upon you to grant this little request in his name, I would use it at this moment, because I am so attached to this project. In the name of the holy love that God gives us and that we owe him, I ask you to grant my petition. If not for this reason, then grant it out of consideration for my weakness or for my arguments, because you must be certain—and the last test must have proved it to you, if nothing else has—that your commands are my laws. Whenever it is a question of your happiness, even if it compromises the rest of my life, you know how promptly I rush to help you. I do this more out of gratitude and affection than out of duty. When I give you what you request, I do it out of pure devotion to your service. You've told me that this devotion is why you want me to remain at your side.

I hope that God will one day help you understand how I could serve you far better by remaining next to him than by remaining next to you. But in awaiting this moment, I ask that he keep me throughout my life in the sentiments I have held until now: to await patiently the decisions of your will after I have discovered his during my brief retreat. The place I have in mind is ideal for that.

I await your response on this issue with an impatience that you can well imagine. But I also await in a total spirit of submission, although I have such a great desire to have my request granted. Whatever your response contains, it will in no way change my devotion toward you, a devotion that will never stop showing you how much I love you more out of my heart's affection than out of natural obligation.

Father,
Your very humble and very obedient daughter and servant, J. Pascal.

3. To Blaise Pascal, on Profession of Vows[15]

Port-Royal du Saint-Sacrement
May 7–9, 1652

My dearest brother,
I wanted to show you how much I hope you will receive my news with

15. This translation is based on Jacqueline Pascal, "Lettre de la Soeur J. de Sainte Euphémie Pascal à M. Pascal, son frère," *LOM*, 334–43. Although the Faugère edition cites March 7 as the date of the letter's composition, Jean Mesnard argues persuasively that the letter was written on May 7–9, a few weeks before Jacqueline Pascal's clothing and consecration as a nun on May 26.

joy and in a mood that is serene and faithful to God's graces. That is why I chose Monsieur Hobier[16] to bring you this news. You have such respect for his merit and virtue. You so treasure his friendship. I thought that anything you might find disturbing in this news, even though it would be softened by knowing how it contributes to my own happiness, would be more than outweighed by the mediation of this admirable person.

He so charitably accepted this commission that we both should be eternally grateful to him: you, because he will help you to stifle the all too natural sentiments that might oppose the sacrifice God offers you on this blessed occasion in my own person; me, because he will be the instrument God uses to respond to the nearly continual prayers and tears I have offered him for more than four years.

It's true that I am free now to make my own commitments. It has pleased God, who chastises by granting favors and who favors us by chastising us, to take away the last legitimate obstacle that could prevent my making the commitment I want to make. You know, but I dare not name, how God accomplished this, since I don't want to mingle grief with joy.[17]

I still very much need your consent and your approval of my decision. I ask for them with all the devotion of my heart. Of course they are not required for my going ahead with the vows. But I want them to be able to fulfill my vocation with joy, with a good conscience, and with serenity. In that sense they are absolutely necessary for me. Without them I would be making the greatest, the happiest, and the most glorious commitment of my life with a joy mixed with the greatest sadness. I would be in such dreadful consternation. I don't think you could be callous enough to cause me such a great misfortune.

That is why I am addressing you as if you were a guardian of sorts of what will happen to me. I want to tell you clearly: Don't take away from me what you can't give me. Although God used you to help me progress in the first movements of his grace, you know quite well that God alone is the author of all the love and joy we have for what is good. You might be capable of troubling my peace, but you are not capable of giving it back to me if I lose it one day through your fault. You must feel my affection to some extent by your own affection. You must be able to judge that I am strong enough to go ahead despite you but not strong enough perhaps to withstand the anguish that your opposition would cause in me.

Please don't push me to the brink or pressure me to delay what I have

---

16. Monsieur Hobier was a professor at the Sorbonne and a friend of the Pascal family.
17. The death of her father Étienne Pascal.

wanted for such a long time with such fervor. Please don't let there be any risk that I would lose my vocation or that I would have to make my religious profession in some unworthy way. I don't want to undertake halfheartedly, as if I were ungrateful, a commitment that should be full of fervor, of joy, and of charity, whereby I respond to God's commitment to us from all eternity. He chose us as his spouses before we were even created. Don't make me unworthy of the graces that I should expect to follow me all the rest of my life because I would have a divided heart at the very beginning of this commitment. Don't force me to consider you an obstacle to my happiness if you succeed in delaying the expectation of my desires, or the author of my malaise if you are the reason I fulfill this commitment tepidly.

If I had less experience of the power of the natural affection in our family, I would be less concerned to make you consent to something so obviously just and holy. The natural and supernatural graces God has given you should actually incline you to encourage me to be steadfast in my intention if I were unfortunate enough to waver in my resolution. Now I no longer dare to expect this of you, although given your knowledge of the situation, I have every right to hope for it. I only expect you to make a serious effort to avoid doing anything that would make me lose the graces I've received and that would prevent me from making my commitment to God. If that came about, I would protest to God that you alone were responsible for this loss, and I would ask for these graces all over again. May God keep both of us from falling into such a catastrophe!

I know quite well that nature uses every weapon in this sort of crisis. To avoid what it fears, nature finds that every means is just. To support your natural inclinations, everyone will appeal to charity and affection—that is common on such occasions. But these appeals to family loyalty clearly oppose what is good and right.

I didn't leave the world such a long time ago. I haven't forgotten how the world's esteem and applause for virtue are so artfully used by our enemy to weaken virtue in one soul on the pretext that it's being used to help another. He shrewdly sees that what he can't take by violence he might carry away by the caresses the world offers us. He managed to get tyrants to use such a soft torture to shake the faith and the constancy of the martyrs. He has managed to suggest it to his best friends in the interests of the peace of the church to vanquish the perseverance of the faithful.[18]

18. Jacqueline Pascal refers to efforts by some Jansenists to encourage members of the Jansenist party to sign submissions to the church's condemnations of Jansenism out of respect for the peace and unity of the church.

Courageously resist this temptation if it strikes you. When society expresses to you some regret at seeing me no longer, be assured that this is an illusion that would disappear in a minute if it weren't opposed to what is right. It is impossible for the world to have a true friendship with someone who does not belong to it, who never wants to be part of it, and who wants only to destroy the sight of it as far as she is concerned. She abandons it forever through a solemn vow and by her commitment to a way of life completely opposed to the world's principles. She would gladly give up everything she holds most dear to plant this contempt of the world in all the souls she knows. While it's true that I retain some memory of the friendship I had with the world when I belonged to it, may God grant that this memory will never prevent me from leaving it and will never prevent you from consenting to my departure.

My glory and your joy—and that of all of our friends—must spring from this witness of the power of the grace of my God. It's not that the world abandons me, but that I abandon the world. Although the effort the world makes to retain me seems an all too visible punishment for the complacency I once showed toward it, God in his good pleasure has given me the strength to resist it. All the world's efforts only illumine the victory God has deigned to carry out in my heart over all the pomp and works of the world. These are so vain and so small that you need only a small amount of reason enlightened by faith and sustained by grace in order to flee in advance what we should flee by logical necessity after a few minutes of exposure.

Don't oppose this divine light. Don't put obstacles in the path of those who do what is right. Do what is right yourself. If you don't have the strength to follow me, at least don't hold me back. Do not be ungrateful toward God about the grace he has given to a person you love. The dearer she is to you, the more sensitive you should be toward the graces she has received.

If we are counseled not to neglect the chastisements of the Lord, how much less should we neglect his graces—and the greatest and rarest of his graces. Externally he has permitted me to be admitted into the assembly of these visible angels who remain in the world only to adore him. They have no other external occupation nor any other desire in the heart than to serve him as extensively as any mortal creature could. Internally he could turn me into a true angel, if there were some matter disposed toward this transformation within me—I realize I have very little of it—although even this little infinitely surpasses my own merits.

This must increase our acknowledgment of and our gratitude for this infinite and incomprehensible favor of our God toward a creature who is so unworthy of it. I am so struck with this thought as I write this that I think I could make a confession of my entire life to help you better understand how great is God's mercy toward me. But that won't be necessary if you just use your memory a little to recall the time when I loved the world. My knowledge of and love for God at that time made me even more guilty. I shared my heart between two masters with an imbalance that embarrasses me, especially when I remember your frequent exhortations on this subject, when you tried to make me see that I could not yoke together two contrary things: the spirit of the world and the spirit of devotion. This is a solid reason for our eternal gratitude to God, since he not only freed me from this dangerous blindness but established me in a place and in a state of life where I no longer have any reason to fear another fall.

I must finish abruptly. Otherwise, I would go on and on about the topic of my obligations toward you. I beg you not to destroy these obligations and to help me keep them, as I will do even against your wishes and against anything opposed to them. Do not destroy what you helped to build up. There's much more I could say about the incomparable benefits of the religious profession I am going to make and of the convent where I am. There's also much more to say about our shared debt to God, not only our general debt as creatures, but also the particular debt we owe God. If I let myself expand on all these issues, and others as well, I would end up writing a book rather than a letter.

I'm impatient to learn just how you took this news, although it would be an injustice to you to doubt that you would have anything other than a positive reaction. We can easily pardon any disturbances caused by natural affection, but nature should not be the master of your feelings. Let my example help you surmount this temptation. Better yet, follow the example of the apostles, who joyously accepted the separation from Our Lord. There are many things we could say about this example.

Do out of virtue what you must do out of necessity. Give to God what he demands as a personal offering. He wants us to give him what he takes away from us as if we were actually doing what he in fact does in us. I am delighted that you have had the opportunity to merit such a sacrifice. I hope that this necessary offering will dispose you to make the voluntary offering that I hope to witness with all my heart. This is going to be practically my only petition at the very moment when I receive what I have so long desired for myself.

You should be satisfied that it is only consideration for your feelings that has prevented me from professing vows during the sixth months I have been here. Without this consideration, I would have already taken the religious habit. Our mother superiors have accepted my four years of novitiate in the world as all I need as a preparatory period before vows. They've accepted my desire to be governed with all simplicity as sufficient proof of my desire for religious perfection. Only my fear to anger those I love has delayed my ultimate happiness until now.

It's no longer reasonable to continue my deference to others' feelings over my own. It's their turn to do some violence to their own feelings in return for the violence I did to my own inclinations during four years. It is from you in particular that I expect this token of friendship, and I ask for this friendship especially for my betrothal, which, God willing, will take place on the feast of the Holy Trinity. I ask God to send forth his Holy Spirit to put us in the right disposition.

Isn't it odd how you would have a serious pang of conscience and how everyone else would criticize you if for some reason you tried to prevent me from marrying a prince, even if the prince lived in some distant place? Make your own application of this and draw your own conclusion. This letter is already too long to permit any further discussion of this question.

I will write to my faithful servant.[19] I beg you to console her if she needs it and to encourage her. I am telling her that if she feels well enough and believes I could strengthen her, I would be delighted to see her. But if she comes to oppose me, I will warn her that she is wasting her time. I would say the same thing to you and to anyone else who would try to dissuade me.

I have shown enough patience. God wants me to use the penance I desire to do as reparation for the loss this delay has caused me. With all my heart I pray that God will not impute to those who opposed me for four years the sin they committed by their actions. May he pardon them because they truly did not know what they were doing.[20]

It's only as a matter of form that I ask you to attend the ceremony. I'm sure you wouldn't even think of missing it. I would have to disown you if you did. Farewell. Be assured of my affection.

Do gladly what you have to do. Do it in a spirit of charity and please don't lead me into grief. It seems to me that I have given you no reason to do so.

Dear brother,
Your very humble and very obedient sister and servant,
S. J. D. Sainte Euphémie

19. The term *ma fidèle* probably refers to Louise Delfaut. See note 14.
20. Paraphrase of Christ's words from the cross: Luke 23:34.

4. To Gilberte Pascal Périer, on the Miracle of the Thorn[21]

Glory to Jesus and to the Most Blessed Sacrament
Port-Royal
March 29, 1656

Dearest sister,

Lent cannot prevent me from sending you a little note, although I wrote you just last Friday. I have only good things to tell you.

I think you know that we are having a jubilee celebration, which began yesterday. It will last two weeks. Among other good works, we are supposed to receive communion on Sunday, April 2.

I am giving you this preamble to increase the joy you will have in learning that your older daughter will be confirmed and will make her first Holy Communion on that day. She told me so this morning and requested my prayers with such fervor that she began to cry.

Obviously that's good news. But I have another piece of news that is not exactly better but is more astonishing. To tell you what it is, without exaggerating or diminishing its importance, I must simply narrate how this astonishing thing came to pass.

On Friday, March 24, 1656, Monsieur de la Potterie,[22] a priest, sent a very handsome reliquary to our mother superiors, so that the entire community might have the consolation of seeing it. The reliquary holds a small sun of gold-gilt vermilion containing a sliver from a thorn of Christ's crown of thorns.

Before returning it, we placed it on a small altar in the church choir. We showed it the greatest reverence. All the nuns went to kneel in front of it after they had chanted a verse in honor of the holy crown.

After this all the pupils went to venerate the relic, one after the other. Soeur Flavie,[23] their schoolmistress, who was close by, saw Margot[24] come

21. This translation is based on Jacqueline Pascal, "Lettre de Jacqueline Pascal à Madame Périer, sa soeur," *LOM*, 375–79. On Good Friday, March 24, 1656, a pupil at the convent school, Marguerite Périer, the niece of Jacqueline Pascal and the daughter of Gilberte Pascal Périer, appeared to have received a miraculous healing of her eye after venerating a relic of the crown of thorns. On May 30 Marguerite was interrogated on the facts of the case. On June 8-12 a church tribunal gathered testimony. From April 14 to September 25, a committee of physicians examined the medical history. On October 22, 1656, the archdiocese of Paris declared that the miracle was worthy of belief.

22. Abbé Pierre Le Roy de la Potterie was a relative of the Arnauld family and a partisan of the Jansenist cause.

23. Soeur Catherine de Sainte-Flavie Passart later became the head of the small group of Port-Royal nuns who unconditionally accepted the church's condemnation of Jansenius when most of the Port-Royal nuns were placed under interdict and dispersed for refusal to give unreserved assent to the church's condemnation.

24. "Margot" was the nickname for Marguerite Périer.

up to the altar. Soeur Flavie made her a sign to let the relic touch her eye. Margot took the holy relic and applied it to her eye without further reflection. After everyone had left the chapel, we gave the relic back to Monsieur de la Potterie.

That evening Soeur Flavie, who was no longer thinking about what had been done, heard Margot say to one of her little companions: "My eye has healed. I no longer feel any pain in it."

Soeur Flavie came closer and examined her eye. Her eye had been gravely bloated that morning. It had been swollen like the end of a finger. It had been very enlarged and very hard. But now the eye wasn't that way at all. Before the application of the relic, her eye could scarcely see, because it was so filled with liquid. Now it appeared just as healthy as the other one. It was impossible to tell the difference. Soeur Flavie squeezed it. Before, a muddy substance or at least some pasty water flowed out from it, but now nothing flowed. It had healed cleanly.

I leave you to imagine the astonishment into which this plunged us. Still, she didn't publicize the event right away and limited herself to telling Mère Agnès[25] what had happened. She wanted to wait some time to see if the healing was as authentic as it appeared.

The next day Mère Agnès had the goodness to tell me about it. Since we couldn't hope for such a great marvel to be finished in such a short time, she told me that if the girl continued to feel well and it appeared that God wanted to heal her in this way, she would gladly ask Monsieur de la Potterie to grant us the same favor again so that the miracle might be complete.

But up until now this hasn't been necessary. Although it has been a week since this event occurred—because I wasn't able to finish this letter last Tuesday—she doesn't have the slightest trace of her illness. For the moment, we believe she could not have been healed so suddenly except by a miracle as great and as visible as rendering sight to the blind.

Beside her damaged eye, she had several other maladies that sprang from the eye problem. She could practically no longer sleep because of the pain this ailment gave her. There were two places on her head we didn't dare comb because the pain was too great. Only two days before the event, I began to cry when I saw the extent of the damage to her eye. She was beginning to feel ill again.

Now, however, there is nothing like this at all. It's as if there never had been any problem.

25. Mère Agnès, the new abbess of the convent and the sister of Mère Angélique, the previous abbess.

Still, to avoid taking such signal graces too lightly, we thought it proper to have her see Monsieur Dalançay,[26] who saw her not such a long time ago and who saw her often after we had ended the water treatment by Monsieur de Chatillon.[27] He had found her state of health so bad that without hesitation he ordered heat treatment for her and clearly explained to us how he had arrived at that judgment. He should be coming here today without fail. God willing, if he comes early enough, I will tell you what judgment he now makes on the case and why he thought that only heat treatment would have been able to heal her. If not, I will tell you on Tuesday, God willing.

It's a double joy to receive God's favor when one is hated by men. Pray to God for us. May he prevent us from pride in one area and discouragement in the other. May he give us the grace to consider both equally the effects of his mercy.

I have a particular joy because I was in no way involved in this miracle. As a result my joy and my gratitude are in no way mixed with fear. I anticipated your wishes by sending you the verse and the prayer that we had sung before the holy relic. I am going to ask permission to recite this prayer every day in memory of this grace, as long as I am able to say my office. I intend to say it after matins, but if you are inclined to say this prayer also, you might prefer to recite it at three o'clock in the afternoon. This is the hour when it pleased God to effect this healing, just as it is the hour when by his death he gave such a marvelous power to the instruments of his passion.
Farewell.

Since I wrote the first part of this letter, Monsieur Dalançay has examined Margot. He has judged the healing to be complete and miraculous. But he still wants to wait another week to confirm his judgment. We are not to say anything further until then.

5. To Mère de Saint Jean, on the Death of Soeur Anne-Marie de Sainte Eugénie[28]

Port-Royal des Champs
October 7, 1660

Dearest Sister,
    You surely would have a right to complain about me if I didn't seek you

26. Martin Dalançay was a local surgeon who had earlier decided that surgical intervention was necessary to deal with the hemorrhage in the eye and the underlying abscess.
27. Monsieur de Chatillon was a lay medical practitioner.
28. This translation is based on Jacqueline Pascal, "Lettre de Soeur Jacqueline de Sainte Eu-

out for consolation after our shared loss of our poor little child. I assure you that few things have so moved me. I deeply felt the suffering of her illness and even more the pain of her separation. Still, I must admit that both of these were accompanied by so many subjects of consolation that I'm not really sure which is more compelling: the sorrow I felt in losing someone who seemed closer to me than my own flesh and blood or the joy of witnessing the graces God granted someone whom I so desired to receive them.

Her noble character shone most clearly at the worst moment of her illness. It seemed that God sustained her life against all odds during the last week only to make us understand what favor he had accorded her. She was finally convinced that she was dying only two hours before her death. That made it easier to see that her good dispositions ran deep and that they were not born from the fear that an imminent peril often produces. She always hoped to recover, although she never demanded it. Especially since the last visit of Monsieur Singlin, she desired rather than feared death.

The poor child was ailing badly on the feast of the Holy Cross. She went to communion as her viaticum.[29] She feared a little the strength of an illness that began so violently. But she was still in good spirits. She had a special joy in approaching her illness as a penitent. Her greatest fear, after that of death itself, was not using her illness well and not accepting her suffering with enough patience. God gave her the grace in the course of her illness to completely remove the first fear and any concerns she had about the second. She was so kind and such a good patient that she edified absolutely everyone who served her. Her way of dying should lead us to believe that she didn't do this by virtue alone. This was more a work of grace than some effect of nature weakened by illness.

One particular incident leads me to this conclusion. Eight days ago she showed great reluctance to take some herbal tea that, by all appearances, was the last thing keeping her alive. Although she readily drank her ordinary water to receive some refreshment, she took the medicinal tea only drop by drop. So I told her as gently as I could that since God had sent her this illness as a penance, she should wholeheartedly do her part in it by taking all the remedies that were part and parcel of it.

---

phémie à la Mère Saint-Jean, sur la mort de la Soeur Anne-Marie de Sainte Eugénie," *LOM,* 391–96. Faugère's edition is based on the original print version in *Mémoires pour servir à l'histoire de Port-Royal,* vol. 3 (Utrecht, 1742), 596. Soeur Anne-Marie was the youngest daughter of Robert Arnauld d'Andilly. The addressee is Mère Angélique de Saint-Jean (Angélique Arnauld d'Andilly, 1624–84). Raised at the Port-Royal convent school, Mère Angélique de Saint-Jean was a leading chronicler of Port-Royal and the sister of the deceased.

29. The term "viaticum" refers to Holy Communion when it is received by a dying person. Literally meaning "provisions for a journey," the sacramental viaticum provides spiritual support for the soul's journey to divine judgment in the afterlife.

This so impressed her that since that moment, she took everything we gave her. God gave her the grace of such a great desire for penance that she could not tolerate that others lament her plight. Despite the great pain she had in speaking, she said that she was suffering nothing at all. She then compared her illness to the suffering of others she believed had greater burdens. She let it be understood that hers was a trifle.

Right up to the end she showed great gratitude for all the services provided her. She did this out of a spirit of humility and of penance. She truly regarded this care as something she did not deserve. She complained often that her exhaustion prevented her from paying attention to God. Yesterday she told me with great concern: "Won't I even be saying an hour of the Divine Office?" I told her that her illness took the place of everything else. "That might be true if I suffered as I should, but I've made many faults in this."

Concerning this she spoke to me about some movement of impatience, which amounted to nothing. I told her that the same illness that made her make these kinds of faults was just the remedy for them. I told her that for her office it was sufficient for her to make the sign of the cross whenever she had enough presence of mind to realize that it was the habitual moment to say the office. That placed her in peace or, rather, left her in peace, because by God's grace she had never lost it.

She went to confession last evening as usual, because we didn't think she was so close to the end. I think she made her confession with a very special presence of mind. Even when she saw Monsieur Singlin for the last time, she spoke to him in as much detail and with as much light as she had ever done. This morning she spoke in such a carefree way that I was stunned when, as we left High Mass, they told us her death agony had begun. We ran to see her and found she was beginning her death agony, but with such clear awareness that I was afraid the sight and the approach of death might disturb her. But God gave her far more grace than I had dared to hope for.

From that time on neither I nor the prioress left her side. This was a consolation for her, because several times we said a few words to help her think about God. Near noon, she turned toward me, knowing how moved I was by her state. She said to me: "Your poor child is not well." I responded: "True, she suffers a great deal." She was very agitated: "But all of that is nothing, as long as I can hope to satisfy God." I tried to give her some confidence on that point.

A little later she said to me: "How consoling it is to die between your hands!" That made me realize she understood the state she was in. I told her that the mother superior had gone to find Monsieur de Saci.[30] She re-

---

30. Isaac Le Maître de Saci (1613–84) was the spiritual director at Port-Royal. A translator of

sponded joyfully to this news. A little later she told us, "Monsieur de Saci is not coming." Immediately afterward she felt a little better and said that we shouldn't bother him because we might inconvenience him. Still, I had him come, since I saw that she was still sinking.

While they were out notifying Monsieur de Saci, she said to me, "Start the prayers." I did so. The poor child still responded to them, always kissing the cross she held. Her pulse was stronger, and we thought she might live longer. As a result, Monsieur de Saci and the community retired from the sickroom.

After that I asked her if she had great confidence in God's mercy. She responded with great feeling: "I don't know if I'm worthy to have that." I told her that we could never be worthy of this mercy, since it was infinite. She clearly understood.

Next I asked if she didn't find great joy in dying as a nun. She made an effort to indicate to me how deeply she appreciated this grace. A little afterward, the prioress also recited a prayer next to her. She listened very attentively.

Seeing her in this state, we thought we should have her receive once again the holy viaticum, although she had just received it with Extreme Unction on the fourteenth day of her illness. She manifested a great desire for this. I think they are the last words she said to us.

Immediately afterward, as we prepared the room for the service, she passed into death. It was so sudden that we didn't have the chance to alert Monsieur de Saci and the community. Perhaps they would have preferred not to be in the room, since she expired so peacefully that we almost didn't notice it.

Dearest Sister, these are what seem to me to be subjects for great consolation. I cannot tell you more about this because we are busy with the mail and other business.

6. To Soeur Angélique, on the Crisis of the Signature[31]

June 23, 1661

Dearest Sister,[32]

The little interest others have shown concerning what's happening here

classical and patristic texts, he was the interlocutor of Blaise Pascal in *Entretiens avec M. de Saci sur Épictète et Montaigne.* He defended a strict line of resistance during the "crisis of the signature."

31. This translation is based on Jacqueline Pascal, "Lettre de Soeur Jacqueline de Sainte Euphémie Pascal à la Soeur Angélique," *LOM,* 402–14.

32. The addressee is Soeur Angélique de Saint-Jean, subprioress at the convent of Port-Royal de

prevented me from discussing these issues until now. Seeing how poorly this problem is understood at a distance, I had hoped that the resolution of the problem could be delayed.

I should tell you that all the letters I've written so far to our mother concern only the pastoral letter.[33] It fell into our hands by the greatest chance in the world—I would say by the very providence of God, if you take into account our anguish over this question and how the pastoral letter might relieve it.

Everyone here at the moment finds herself sharing the same negative attitude, although we clearly understand the argument that our signature indicates only respect, that is, silence concerning the facts and assent concerning matters of faith.[34] But we no longer have any time left.

Most of us had sincerely hoped that the document would be even worse, since we knew very well that in these times we could not have hoped for a better one. We could have rejected a worse document with complete freedom. Instead, several of us will probably feel forced to accept it as it is. A false prudence and outright cowardice will lead others to accept it as a good way to secure their persons and their conscience.

But as for me, I cannot secure either by this means. It is only truth that will truly deliver us. Incontestably truth delivers only those who freely confess it with as much fidelity as they themselves deserve to be confessed and recognized as true children of God.

I can no longer hide the sadness that pierces the very bottom of my heart when I see that the very people to whom God has confided his truth are so unfaithful to it. If I may dare to say so, they just don't have the courage to risk suffering, even dying, for confessing the truth loud and clear.

I understand the respect that is due to the authorities of the church. I would gladly die to keep that respect inviolate, as I am ready to die with God's help for my convictions in the current controversy. But I do not see how we can easily join one to the other.

When they present the formulary for signing, what prevents us and what prevents all the clergy who know the truth from simply responding, "I know the respect I owe our lord bishops, but my conscience does not permit me to

Paris. A subsequent note, addressed to Antoine Arnauld, indicates Jacqueline Pascal's desire that Arnauld respond to the objections against the signature that she presents in her letter to Soeur Angélique. See Jacqueline Pascal, "Lettre de la Soeur Jacqueline de Sainte Euphémie Pascal à M.***," *LOM,* 414–17.

33. The pastoral letter cited is the *mandement* drawn up by the Parisian archdiocesan vicars Contes and Hodencq to introduce the formulary proposed for signature by the Port-Royal nuns.

34. This passage refers to Antoine Arnauld's *droit/fait* distinction in interpreting the anti-Jansenist church declarations. Arnauld explicitly called for "respectful silence" as the proper attitude of the Jansenist before church rulings that appeared to involve errors of fact.

sign affirmatively that something is in a book I've never seen" and after that, just waiting to see what will happen? What are we afraid of? Exile and dispersion for the nuns, confiscation of our temporal goods, prison and death, if you will? But isn't this our glory and shouldn't this be our joy?

Let us renounce the Gospel or let us follow the counsels of the Gospel. Let us count ourselves blessed to suffer something for justice.

But perhaps they will cut us off from the church! But doesn't everyone know that you can't be cut off against your will? Since the spirit of Jesus Christ is the tie that unites its members to him and to each other, we can be deprived of the external marks, but never of the effects, of this union. This is true as long as we conserve charity, without which one is no longer a living member of this holy body. Further, isn't it obvious that as long as we don't set up altar against altar, we are not trying to make some sort of separate church? As long as we remain in a simple condition of respectful grievance during our persecution, the charity with which we treat our enemies will keep us inviolably attached to the church. The only people who will separate themselves from the church will do so by breaking the bonds of charity that should unite them to Jesus Christ and that made them members of his body.

Alas! dear Sister, we should be joyful if we have merited suffering some great reversal for Jesus Christ! But they work so hard to prevent it, when they so skillfully paint the truth in the colors of deceit that it can no longer be recognized and that even the sharpest observer can hardly see it. I admire the subtle mind behind the pastoral letter and I admit that there is nothing more clever. I think it's difficult to find any work made with such art and such aplomb.

Like a father praising his spendthrift son, I could praise a heretic who cleverly managed to escape condemnation without renouncing his error. Without denying the truth, he would feign a lie. But to see the faithful, the people who know and support the truth—to see the Catholic Church use such disguises and such deception! I don't believe this was ever seen in centuries past. May God permit us all to die today rather than permit that such an abomination start in the church.

Truly, dear Sister, I find it very difficult to believe that this wisdom comes from the Father of Light. Rather, I believe it's a revelation of flesh and blood.

I ask you to pardon me, Sister. I am speaking out of an intense suffering I sense will consume me if I don't have the consolation of seeing at least a few people voluntarily make themselves victims for the truth and clearly protest what the others are about to do. They need to preserve the truth in their own persons.

It's not that I want people to speak out loudly against the arrogance and the power of the enemies of truth. But I think you know only too well that what we are dealing with here isn't only the condemnation of a holy bishop;[35] it clearly entails the condemnation of the very grace of Jesus Christ. If our century is so miserable that it can't find anyone willing to die to defend the honor of a just man, it is even worse if it can't find anyone who would be willing to die for justice itself. Still, I am not asking for any militant declarations of faith. Given the current situation, where God seems to have abandoned so many people to their passions and their feelings, it is obvious that unless a miracle occurs, the truth will be condemned. But I would hope that, while we respectfully refuse to engage in insults or reproaches, we would firmly refuse to give any reason to believe that we had condemned or had seemed to condemn the truth. Dear Sister, in God's name I ask you, What difference do you find between these verbal disguises and giving incense to an idol on the pretext that you have a cross in your pocket?[36]

Perhaps you will tell me that this doesn't concern us, because our particular formulary is such a small affair. But I would like to say two things in response to that.

First, Saint Bernard teaches us, in his admirable way of putting things, that the least persons in the church not only may but must shout with all their strength when they see that the bishops and the pastors of the church are in a state such as we see them now. He says: "Who could object when I, only a small lamb, cry out and try to wake up my shepherd when he's asleep and about to be devoured by a cruel beast? Even if I were ungrateful enough not to do it out of the love and thanksgiving I owe him, shouldn't I still do it out of fear for my own survival? Because, who will defend me once my shepherd has been devoured?"[37] I'm not saying this for the benefit of our fathers and for our friends. I know they are as horrified by these disguises as I am. But I am saying this to address the general state of the church and to justify my interest on these issues.

The other point concerns the fact that until now I have not been able to approve entirely your formulary as it stands. I would like to see changes in

35. Saint Augustine or Jansenius.

36. This is a clear allusion to Provincial Letter 5 of Blaise Pascal, wherein he condemns Jesuit missionaries in China who permitted Catholic converts to appear to pay external veneration to pagan idols while they internally directed their veneration toward the crucifixes hidden in their pockets. Both Blaise and Jacqueline Pascal opposed the casuistry of the Jesuits, especially that concerning mental reservation. See Blaise Pascal, "Cinquième lettre," *Les provinciales,* in *L'oeuvre de Pascal,* ed. Jacques Chevalier (Paris: Gallimard-Pléiade, 1950), 475.

37. Paraphrase of Saint Bernard of Clairvaux, "Lettre CCXXXVIII; to Pope Eugenius," in *Oeuvres complètes de Saint Bernard,* vol. 1, ed. Abbé Charpentier (Paris: Vivès, 1865), 335–39.

two places. The first is right at the beginning. Given our captive situation, it really seems outrageous to say that we are being offered an opportunity to freely state our faith. I might still be willing to do this if there were a brief preamble that removed this inference and its scandal. Have no doubt that this entire procedure of signature and of declaration of faith is a usurpation of power with the most dangerous consequences. This derives from the fact that this is being done principally by the power of the king—whom, I believe, his subjects should not resist. Still, it's necessary to add some indication that we are doing this not because we are ignorant or because we think it's proper, but because we're surrendering to force in order to avoid scandal.

The second is at the end. I would prefer that we didn't speak about the decisions of the Holy See there. Although it is true that we submit to these decisions inasmuch as they concern matters of faith, most people ignore these nuances; and our opponents in this quarrel want so passionately to confuse the "right/fact" distinction that you know they will claim it's all one thing. So what is the real effect of your formulary except to make the ignorant believe and the malicious insist that we agree with everything condemned and that we condemn the doctrine of Jansenius? After all, he's clearly condemned in the last bull.[38]

I know very well that it's not up to girls to argue the cause of truth. Still, we can say in the sad present circumstances that since the bishops are showing the courage of girls, the girls should be showing the courage of bishops. Nonetheless, if it's not up to us to defend the truth, it's up to us to die for the truth and to suffer everything rather than abandon it.

To better explain my views on the decisions of the Holy See, here is a comparison that comes to mind. Although everyone knows that the mystery of the Holy Trinity is one of the principal points of our faith and that Saint Augustine would gladly confess it and sign a statement to that effect, we could imagine a situation where he might refuse his signature. Imagine that his country was occupied by a heathen prince who wanted people to deny the unity of God and wanted to make people believe in the multiplicity of the gods. Imagine that some of the faithful, in order to calm the tense situation, drew up the following formulary of faith: "I believe that there are several persons to which one can give the name of God and to which one can offer adoration," without further explication. Would Saint Augustine sign such a statement? I certainly don't think so. I think even less that he should do so.

---

38. Pope Alexander VII's bull *Ad sanctam Beati Petri sedem* (1656) underlined that Jansenius had indeed held the five heretical propositions and that the church was condemning these theories precisely in the sense that Jansenius had given them.

Although this is a truth that no believer could doubt, it would not be right to say this truth in this way at this time.

You can easily make an application of my comparison. Perhaps they will say that our authority is not that of Saint Augustine, that it is nothing at all. I would answer that objection by saying that I spoke of Saint Augustine only in response to how you've treated all my difficulties during the past days. Our fears were laughed at, and the officials said that Saint Augustine would sign the document we feared. But what I say about Saint Augustine, I say about you and about myself and about the least members of the church. The little authority they have doesn't make them any less guilty if they use it against the truth.

Everyone knows—and Monsieur de Saint-Cyran says it in a thousand places—that the least truth of faith must be defended with the same fidelity that we owe Jesus Christ. Imagine a believer present at the council of Pontius Pilate when they discussed the question of putting Jesus Christ to death. What believer would not be appalled by himself if he settled for an ambiguous way of expressing his opinion that let others believe he agreed with those who convicted him, although in his own mind and according to his own nuanced meaning his words actually tended toward acquittal?

Isn't the sin of Saint Peter infinitely less than such extreme timidity? Nonetheless, how did he consider his sin during the rest of his life? What is so striking is that, although he was destined to become head of the church, he wasn't the head yet. It was only the sin of a simple believer, who didn't say what the imaginary believer did: "He's a villain. He has merited death. Crucify him." Peter only said "I do not know this man." I beg you to push the comparison as far as it will go.

My letter is already too long. So, dear Sister, these are my views on the formulary. I wanted to understand clearly just what it contained, although I understand that it cannot contain everything.

Given our current state of confusion, the most they can hope to obtain from us by our signature is a witness of the sincerity of our faith and of our perfect submission to the church: to the pope, who is its head, and to the archbishop of Paris, our superior. Although we don't believe that anyone has the right to demand a statement of faith in this matter from people who have never given cause to doubt their good faith, we still would be willing to give it in order to avoid the scandal and the suspicions our refusal might create. By this act, we would only witness that we want to live and to die as humble daughters of the Catholic Church, believing everything that she believes and being ready to die for the least of her truths.

If they are content with that, fine. But, for myself, I would not do anything else. This is all we should be willing to concede. If that's not enough, then let the worst arrive: poverty, exile, prison, death. All of that seems to me nothing compared with the anguish in which I would pass the rest of my life if I made a cowardly covenant with death on the very occasion when I should publicly render to God the vows of fidelity that our lips have pronounced.

Dear Sister, let us pray to God for each other. May he strengthen us and humble us more and more. Strength without humility and humility without strength are both just as pernicious. More than ever, now is the time to recall that the cowardly deserve the same fate as the mendacious and the abominable.

Please don't be scandalized by my criticism of the little concern they have shown about our quandaries. Personally I haven't had the least difficulty. I have long accustomed myself to receive these things in a spirit of childhood. May God permit me to continue in this way for the rest of my life! Unintentionally my words wandered into this point. My only concern is that if something similar happens again, they should know that they cannot satisfy us simply by laughing at our difficulties without giving us any reasons for this dismissal.

Farewell, dear Sister. Given the delicate state of our beloved patient,[39] I would not have said a word about it had I not felt the matter was so urgent.

I think, my dear Sister, that I don't need to tell you my primary concern is not the precise words to be used in our formulary. I am indifferent to the words used, on condition that no one could have the least ground to believe we are condemning either the grace of Jesus Christ or the one[40] who has so well explained this grace.

That is why in writing the words "believe all that the church believes" I omitted "and condemn all that the church condemns," although it is true that I condemn everything that the church condemns. However, I don't think it's the right time to say so, since someone might confuse the church with the current decisions. As the late Monsieur Saint-Cyran used to say, "When the pagans set up an idol in a place where there was already a cross of Our Lord, the faithful didn't go there for adoration anymore. They feared it might appear that they were worshiping the idol."

39. This is a reference to Mère Angelique, former abbess of Port-Royal. Gravely ill at the moment of the letter's composition, she died on August 6, 1661.
40. Saint Augustine or Jansenius.

SERIES EDITORS' BIBLIOGRAPHY

PRIMARY SOURCES

Alberti, Leon Battista (1404–72). *The Family in Renaissance Florence.* Trans. Renée Neu Watkins. Columbia: University of South Carolina Press, 1969.

Arenal, Electa, and Stacey Schlau, eds. *Untold Sisters: Hispanic Nuns in Their Own Works.* Trans. Amanda Powell. Albuquerque: University of New Mexico Press, 1989.

Astell, Mary (1666–1731). *The First English Feminist: Reflections on Marriage and Other Writings.* Ed. and introd. Bridget Hill. New York: St. Martin's Press, 1986.

Atherton, Margaret, ed. *Women Philosophers of the Early Modern Period.* Indianapolis: Hackett, 1994.

Aughterson, Kate, ed. *Renaissance Woman: Constructions of Femininity in England: A Source Book.* New York: Routledge, 1995.

Barbaro, Francesco (1390–1454). *On Wifely Duties.* Trans. Benjamin Kohl.In *The Earthly Republic,* ed. Benjamin Kohl and R. G. Witt, 179–228. Philadelphia: University of Pennsylvania Press, 1978.. Translation of the preface and book 2.

Behn, Aphra (1640–89). *The Works of Aphra Behn.* 7 vols. Ed. Janet Todd. Columbus: Ohio State University Press, 1992–96.

Boccaccio, Giovanni (1313–75). *Corbaccio, or The Labyrinth of Love.* Trans. Anthony K. Cassell. 2d rev. ed. Binghamton, N.Y.: Medieval and Renaissance Texts and Studies, 1993.

———. *Famous Women.* Ed. and trans. Virginia Brown. I Tatti Renaissance Library. Cambridge: Harvard University Press, 2001.

Bruni, Leonardo (1370–1444). "On the Study of Literature (1405) to Lady Battista Malatesta of Moltefeltro." In *The Humanism of Leonardo Bruni: Selected Texts.* Trans. and introd. Gordon Griffiths, James Hankins, and David Thompson, 240–51. Binghamton, N.Y.: Medieval and Renaissance Studies and Texts, 1987.

Castiglione, Baldassare (1478–1529). *The Book of the Courtier.* Trans. George Bull. New York: Penguin, 1967.

Cerasano, S. P., and Marion Wynne-Davies, eds. *Readings in Renaissance Women's Drama: Criticism, History, and Performance 1594–1998.* New York: Routledge, 1998.

Clarke, Danielle, ed. *Isabella Whitney, Mary Sidney and Aemilia Lanyer: Renaissance Women Poets.* New York: Penguin Books, 2000.

Crawford, Patricia, and Laura Gowing, eds. *Women's Worlds in Seventeenth-Century England: A Source Book.* New York: Routledge, 2000.

Daybell, James, ed. *Early Modern Women's Letter Writing, 1450–1700.* New York: Palgrave, 2001.

Elizabeth I: Collected Works. Ed. Leah S. Marcus, Janel Mueller, and Mary Beth Rose. Chicago: University of Chicago Press, 2000.

Elyot, Thomas (1490–1546). *Defence of Good Women: The Feminist Controversy of the Renaissance.* Ed. Diane Bornstein. Facsimile Reproductions. New York: Delmar, 1980.

Erasmus, Desiderius (1467–1536). *Erasmus on Women.* Ed. Erika Rummel. Toronto: University of Toronto Press, 1996.

Female and Male Voices in Early Modern England: An Anthology of Renaissance Writing. Ed. Betty S. Travitsky and Anne Lake Prescott. New York: Columbia University Press, 2000.

Ferguson, Moira, ed. *First Feminists: British Women Writers 1578–1799.* Bloomington: Indiana University Press, 1985.

Galilei, Maria Celeste. *Sister Maria Celeste's Letters to Her Father, Galileo.* Ed. and trans. Rinaldina Russell. Lincoln, Nebr.: Writers Club Press of Universe.com, 2000.

Gethner, Perry, ed. *The Lunatic Lover and Other Plays by French Women of the 17th and 18th Centuries.* Portsmouth, N.H.: Heinemann, 1994.

Glückel of Hameln (1646–1724). *The Memoirs of Glückel of Hameln.* Trans. Marvin Lowenthal. New introd. Robert Rosen. New York: Schocken Books, 1977.

Henderson, Katherine Usher, and Barbara F. McManus, eds. *Half Humankind: Contexts and Texts of the Controversy about Women in England, 1540–1640.* Urbana: Indiana University Press, 1985.

Humanist Educational Treatises. Ed. and trans. Craig W. Kallendorf. I Tatti Renaissance Library. Cambridge: Harvard University Press, 2002.

Joscelin, Elizabeth (1596–1622). *The Mothers Legacy to Her Unborn Childe.* Ed. Jean LeDrew Metcalfe. Toronto: University of Toronto Press, 2000.

Kaminsky, Amy Katz, ed. *Water Lilies, Flores del Agua: An Anthology of Spanish Women Writers from the Fifteenth through the Nineteenth Century.* Minneapolis: University of Minnesota Press, 1996.

Kempe, Margery (1373–1439). *The Book of Margery Kempe.* Trans. Barry Windeatt. New York: Viking Penguin, 1986.

King, Margaret L., and Albert Rabil Jr., eds. *Her Immaculate Hand: Selected Works by and about the Women Humanists of Quattrocento Italy.* Binghamton, N.Y.: Medieval and Renaissance Texts and Studies, 1983; 2d rev. paperback edition, 1991.

Klein, Joan Larsen, ed. *Daughters, Wives, and Widows: Writings by Men about Women and Marriage in England, 1500–1640.* Urbana: University of Illinois Press, 1992.

Knox, John (1505–72). *The Political Writings of John Knox: The First Blast of the Trumpet against the Monstrous Regiment of Women and Other Selected Works.* Ed. Marvin A. Breslow. Washington, D.C.: Folger Shakespeare Library, 1985.

Kors, Alan C., and Edward Peters, eds. *Witchcraft in Europe, 400–1700: A Documentary History.* Philadelphia: University of Pennsylvania Press, 2000.

Krämer, Heinrich (1430–1505), and Jacob Sprenger (1436–95). *Malleus Maleficarum* (ca. 1487). Trans. Montague Summers. London: Pushkin Press, 1928; reprinted New York: Dover, 1971.

Larsen, Anne R., and Colette H. Winn, eds. *Writings by Pre-Revolutionary French Women: From Marie de France to Elizabeth Vigée-Le Brun.* New York: Garland, 2000.

Lorris, Guillaume de (fl. 1230), and Jean de Meun (d. 1305?). *The Romance of the Rose.* Trans. Charles Dahlbert. Princeton: Princeton University Press, 1971; reprinted University Press of New England, 1983.

Marguerite d'Angoulême, Queen of Navarre (1492–1549). *The Heptameron.* Trans. P. A. Chilton. New York: Viking Penguin, 1984.

Mary of Agreda. *The Divine Life of the Most Holy Virgin.* Abridgment of *The Mystical City of God.* Abr. by Fr. Bonaventure Amedeo de Caesarea, M.C. Trans. from French by Abbé Joseph A. Boullan. Rockford, Ill.: Tan Books, 1997.

Myers, Kathleen A., and Amanda Powell, eds. *A Wild Country Out in the Garden: The Spiritual Journals of a Colonial Mexican Nun.* Bloomington: Indiana University Press, 1999.

Russell, Rinaldina, ed. *Sister Maria Celeste's Letters to Her Father, Galileo.* New York: Writers Club Press, 2000.

Teresa of Avila, Saint (1515–82). *The Life of Saint Teresa of Avila by Herself.* Trans. J. M. Cohen. New York: Viking Penguin, 1957.

Weyer, Johann (1515–88). *Witches, Devils, and Doctors in the Renaissance: Johann Weyer, De Praestigiis Daemonum.* Ed. George Mora with Benjamin G. Kohl, Erik Midelfort, and Helen Bacon. Trans. John Shea. Binghamton, N.Y.: Medieval and Renaissance Texts and Studies, 1991.

Wilson, Katharina M., ed. *Medieval Women Writers.* Athens: University of Georgia Press, 1984.

———, ed. *Women Writers of the Renaissance and Reformation.* Athens: University of Georgia Press, 1987.

Wilson, Katharina M., and Frank J. Warnke, eds. *Women Writers of the Seventeenth Century.* Athens: University of Georgia Press, 1989.

Wollstonecraft, Mary (1759–97). *A Vindication of the Rights of Men and a Vindication of the Rights of Women.* Ed. Sylvana Tomaselli. Cambridge: Cambridge University Press, 1995.

———. *The Vindications of the Rights of Men, The Rights of Women.* Ed. D. L. Macdonald and Kathleen Scherf. Peterborough, Ont.: Broadview Press, 1997.

Women Critics, 1660–1820: An Anthology. Edited by the Folger Collective on Early Women Critics. Bloomington: Indiana University Press, 1995.

Women Writers in English, 1350–1850: 15 vols. published through 1999 (projected 30-volume series suspended). New York: Oxford University Press.

Wroth, Lady Mary (ca. 1586–ca. 1640). *The Countess of Montgomery's Urania.* 2 parts. Ed. Josephine A. Roberts. Tempe, Ariz.: MRTS, 1995, 1999.

———. *The Poems of Lady Mary Wroth.* Ed. Josephine A. Roberts. Baton Rouge: Louisiana State University Press, 1983.

Zayas y Sotomayor, Maria de (1590–1650). *The Disenchantments of Love.* Trans. H. Patsy Boyer. Albany: State University of New York Press, 1997.

———. *The Enchantments of Love: Amorous and Exemplary Novels.* Trans. H. Patsy Boyer. Berkeley: University of California Press, 1990.

SECONDARY SOURCES

Ahlgren, Gillian. *Teresa of Avila and the Politics of Sanctity.* Ithaca: Cornell University Press, 1996.

Akkerman, Tjitske, and Siep Sturman, eds. *Feminist Thought in European History, 1400–2000.* New York: Routledge, 1997.

Backer, Dorothy Anne Liot. *Precious Women.* New York: Basic Books, 1974.

Barash, Carol. *English Women's Poetry, 1649–1714: Politics, Community, and Linguistic Author-ity.* New York: Oxford University Press, 1996.

Battigelli, Anna. *Margaret Cavendish and the Exiles of the Mind.* Lexington: University of Kentucky Press, 1998.

Beasley, Faith. *Revising Memory: Women's Fiction and Memoirs in Seventeenth-Century France.* New Brunswick: Rutgers University Press, 1990.

Beaunier, André. *Visages de femmes.* 4th ed. Paris: Plon-Nourit, 1913.

Beilin, Elaine V. *Redeeming Eve: Women Writers of the English Renaissance.* Princeton: Prince-ton University Press, 1987.

Benson, Pamela Joseph. *The Invention of Renaissance Woman: The Challenge of Female Indepen-dence in the Literature and Thought of Italy and England.* University Park: Pennsylvania State University Press, 1992.

Bilinkoff, Jodi. *The Avila of Saint Teresa: Religious Reform in a Sixteenth-Century City.* Ithaca: Cornell University Press, 1989.

Bissell, R. Ward. *Artemisia Gentileschi and the Authority of Art.* University Park: Pennsylva-nia State University Press, 2000.

Blain, Virginia, Isobel Grundy, and Patricia Clements, eds. *The Feminist Companion to Lit-erature in English: Women Writers from the Middle Ages to the Present.* New Haven: Yale Uni-versity Press, 1990.

Bloch, R. Howard. *Medieval Misogyny and the Invention of Western Romantic Love.* Chicago: University of Chicago Press, 1991.

Bornstein, Daniel, and Roberto Rusconi, eds. *Women and Religion in Medieval and Renais-sance Italy.* Trans. Margery J. Schneider. Chicago: University of Chicago Press, 1996.

Brant, Clare, and Diane Purkiss, eds. *Women, Texts and Histories, 1575–1760.* New York: Routledge, 1992.

Briggs, Robin. *Witches and Neighbours: The Social and Cultural Context of European Witchcraft.* New York: HarperCollins, 1995; Viking Penguin, 1996.

Brink, Jean R. *Female Scholars: A Tradition of Learned Women before 1800.* Montreal: Eden Press Women's Publications, 1980.

Brown, Judith C. *Immodest Acts: The Life of a Lesbian Nun in Renaissance Italy.* New York: Ox-ford University Press, 1986.

Bynum, Carolyn Walker. *Holy Feast and Holy Fast: The Religious Significance of Food to Me-dieval Women.* Berkeley: University of California Press, 1987.

Cervigni, Dino S., ed. *Women Mystic Writers.* Annali d'Italianistica 13 (1995) (entire is-sue).

Cervigni, Dino S., and Rebecca West, eds. *Women's Voices in Italian Literature.* Annali d'I-talianistica 7 (1989) (entire issue).

Charlton, Kenneth. *Women, Religion and Education in Early Modern England.* New York: Routledge, 1999.

Chojnacka, Monica. *Working Women in Early Modern Venice.* Baltimore: Johns Hopkins University Press, 2001.

Chojnacki, Stanley. *Women and Men in Renaissance Venice: Twelve Essays on Patrician Society.* Baltimore: Johns Hopkins University Press, 2000.

Cholakian, Patricia Francis. *Rape and Writing in the "Heptameron" of Marguerite de Navarre.* Carbondale: Southern Illinois University Press, 1991.

————. *Women and the Politics of Self-Representation in Seventeenth-Century France.* Newark: University of Delaware Press, 2000.

Clogan, Paul Maruice, ed. *Medievali et Humanistica: Literacy and the Lay Reader.* Lanham, Md.: Rowman and Littlefield, 2000.

Crabb, Ann. *The Strozzi of Florence: Widowhood and Family Solidarity in the Renaissance.* Ann Arbor: University of Michigan Press, 2000.

Cruz, Anne J., and Mary Elizabeth Perry, eds. *Culture and Control in Counter-Reformation Spain.* Minneapolis: University of Minnesota Press, 1992.

Davis, Natalie Zemon. *Society and Culture in Early Modern France.* Stanford: Stanford University Press, 1975. Especially chapters 3 and 5.

————. *Women on the Margins: Three Seventeenth-Century Lives.* Cambridge: Harvard University Press, 1995.

DeJean, Joan. *Ancients against Moderns: Culture Wars and the Making of a Fin de Siècle.* Chicago: University of Chicago Press, 1997.

————. *Tender Geographies: Women and the Origins of the Novel in France.* New York: Columbia University Press, 1991.

Dixon, Laurinda S. *Perilous Chastity: Women and Illness in Pre-Enlightenment Art and Medicine.* Ithaca: Cornell Universitiy Press, 1995.

Dolan, Frances, E. *Whores of Babylon: Catholicism, Gender and Seventeenth-Century Print Culture.* Ithaca: Cornell University Press, 1999.

Donovan, Josephine. *Women and the Rise of the Novel, 1405–1726.* New York: St. Martin's Press, 1999.

Erauso, Catalina de. *Lieutenant Nun: Memoir of a Basque Transvestite in the New World.* Trans. Michele Ttepto and Gabriel Stepto. Foreword by Marjorie Garber. Boston: Beacon Press, 1995.

Erickson, Amy Louise. *Women and Property in Early Modern England.* New York: Routledge, 1993.

Ezell, Margaret J. M. *The Patriarch's Wife: Literary Evidence and the History of the Family.* Chapel Hill: University of North Carolina Press, 1987.

————. *Social Authorship and the Advent of Print.* Baltimore: Johns Hopkins University Press, 1999.

————. *Writing Women's Literary History.* Baltimore: Johns Hopkins University Press, 1993.

Ferguson, Margaret W., Maureen Quilligan, and Nancy J. Vickers, eds. *Rewriting the Renaissance: The Discourses of Sexual Difference in Early Modern Europe.* Chicago: University of Chicago Press, 1987.

Fletcher, Anthony. *Gender, Sex and Subordination in England 1500–1800.* New Haven: Yale University Press, 1995.

Frye, Susan, and Karen Robertson, eds. *Maids and Mistresses, Cousins and Queens: Women's Alliances in Early Modern England.* Oxford: Oxford University Press, 1999.

Gallagher, Catherine. *Nobody's Story: The Vanishing Acts of Women Writers in the Marketplace, 1670–1820.* Berkeley: University of California Press, 1994.

Garrard, Mary D. *Artemisia Gentileschi: The Image of the Female Hero in Italian Baroque Art.* Princeton: Princeton University Press, 1989.

Gelbart, Nina Rattner. *The King's Midwife: A History and Mystery of Madame du Coudray.* Berkeley: University of California Press, 1998.

Goldberg, Jonathan. *Desiring Women Writing: English Renaissance Examples.* Stanford: Stanford University Press, 1997.

Goldsmith, Elizabeth C. *Exclusive Conversations: The Art of Interaction in Seventeenth-Century France.* Philadelphia: University of Pennsylvania Press, 1988.

———, ed. *Writing the Female Voice.* Boston: Northeastern University Press, 1989.

Goldsmith, Elizabeth C., and Dena Goodman, eds. *Going Public: Women and Publishing in Early Modern France.* Ithaca: Cornell University Press, 1995.

Greer, Margaret Rich. *Maria de Zayas.* University Park: Pennsylvania State University Press, 2000.

Hackett, Helen. *Women and Romance Fiction in the English Renaissance.* Cambridge: Cambridge University Press, 2000.

Hall, Kim F. *Things of Darkness: Economies of Race and Gender in Early Modern England.* Ithaca: Cornell University Press, 1995.

Hampton, Timothy. *Literature and the Nation in the Sixteenth Century: Inventing Renaissance France.* Ithaca: Cornell University Press, 2001.

Hardwick, Julie. *The Practice of Patriarchy: Gender and the Politics of Household Authority in Early Modern France.* University Park: Pennsylvania State University Press, 1998.

Harth, Erica. *Cartesian Women. Versions and Subversions of Rational Discourse in the Old Regime.* Ithaca: Cornell University Press, 1992.

———. *Ideology and Culture in Seventeenth-Century France.* Ithaca: Cornell University Press, 1983.

Haselkorn, Anne M., and Betty Travitsky, eds. *The Renaissance Englishwoman in Print: Counterbalancing the Canon.* Amherst: University of Massachusetts Press, 1990.

Herlihy, David. "Did Women Have a Renaissance? A Reconsideration." *Medievalia et Humanistica,* n.s., 13 (1985): 1–22.

Hill, Bridget. *The Republican Virago: The Life and Times of Catharine Macaulay, Historian.* New York: Oxford University Press, 1992.

A History of Women in the West. Cambridge: Harvard University Press, 1992–93.

Vol. 1: *From Ancient Goddesses to Christian Saints,* ed. Pauline Schmitt Pantel (1992).

Vol. 2: *Silences of the Middle Ages,* ed. Christiane Klapisch-Zuber (1992).

Vol. 3: *Renaissance and Enlightenment Paradoxes,* ed. Natalie Zemon Davis and Arlette Farge (1993).

Hobby, Elaine. *Virtue of Necessity: English Women's Writing, 1646–1688.* London: Virago, 1988.

Horowitz, Maryanne Cline. "Aristotle and Women." *Journal of the History of Biology* 9 (1976): 183–213.

Hufton, Olwen H. *The Prospect before Her: A History of Women in Western Europe.* Vol. 1, *1500–1800.* New York: HarperCollins, 1996.

Hull, Suzanne W. *Chaste, Silent, and Obedient: English Books for Women, 1475–1640.* San Marino, Calif.: Huntington Library, 1982.

Hunt, Lynn, ed. *The Invention of Pornography: Obscenity and the Origins of Modernity, 1500–1800.* New York: Zone Books, 1996.

Hutner, Heidi, ed. *Rereading Aphra Behn: History, Theory, and Criticism.* Charlottesville: University Press of Virginia, 1993.

Hutson, Lorna, ed. *Feminism and Renaissance Studies.* New York: Oxford University Press, 1999.

James, Susan E. *Kateryn Parr: The Making of a Queen.* Aldershot and Brookfield: Ashgate, 1999.

Jankowski, Theodora A. *Women in Power in the Early Modern Drama.* Urbana: University of Illinois Press, 1992.

Jansen, Katherine Ludwig. *The Making of the Magdalen: Preaching and Popular Devotion in the Later Middle Ages.* Princeton: Princeton University Press, 2000.

Jed, Stephanie H. *Chaste Thinking: The Rape of Lucretia and the Birth of Humanism.* Bloomington: Indiana University Press, 1989.

Jordan, Constance. *Renaissance Feminism: Literary Texts and Political Models.* Ithaca: Cornell University Press, 1990.

Kagan, Richard L. *Lucrecia's Dreams: Politics and Prophecy in Sixteenth-Century Spain.* Berkeley: University of California Press, 1990.

Kelly, Joan. "Did Women Have a Renaissance?" In *Women, History, and Theory,* by Joan Kelly. Chicago: University of Chicago Press, 1984. Also in *Becoming Visible: Women in European History,* ed. Renate Bridenthal, Claudia Koonz, and Susan M. Stuard, 3d ed. (Boston: Houghton Mifflin, 1998).

———. "Early Feminist Theory and the *Querelle des Femmes.*" In *Women, History, and Theory,* by Joan Kelly. Chicago: University of Chicago Press, 1984.

Kelso, Ruth. *Doctrine for the Lady of the Renaissance.* Foreword by Katharine M. Rogers. Urbana: University of Illinois Press, 1956, 1978.

King, Carole. *Renaissance Women Patrons: Wives and Widows in Italy, c. 1300–1550.* New York: Manchester University Press (distributed in the U.S. by St. Martin's Press), 1998.

King, Margaret L. *Women of the Renaissance.* Foreword by Catharine R. Stimpson. Chicago: University of Chicago Press, 1991.

Krontiris, Tina. *Oppositional Voices: Women as Writers and Translators of Literature in the English Renaissance.* New York: Routledge, 1992.

Kuehn, Thomas. *Law, Family, and Women: Toward a Legal Anthropology of Renaissance Italy.* Chicago: University of Chicago Press, 1991.

Kunze, Bonnelyn Young. *Margaret Fell and the Rise of Quakerism.* Stanford: Stanford University Press, 1994.

Labalme, Patricia A., ed. *Beyond Their Sex: Learned Women of the European Past.* New York: New York University Press, 1980.

Laqueur, Thomas. *Making Sex: Body and Gender from the Greeks to Freud.* Cambridge: Harvard University Press, 1990.

Larsen, Anne R., and Colette H. Winn, eds. *Renaissance Women Writers: French Texts/American Contexts.* Detroit: Wayne State University Press, 1994.

Lerner, Gerda. *The Creation of Feminist Consciousness: From the Middle Ages to Eighteen-seventy.* New York: Oxford University Press, 1994.

———. *The Creation of Patriarchy.* New York: Oxford University Press, 1986.

Levin, Carole. *Extraordinary Women of the Medieval and Renaissance World: A Biographical Dictionary.* Westport, Conn.: Greenwood Press, 2000.

Levin, Carole, and Jeanie Watson, eds. *Ambiguous Realities: Women in the Middle Ages and Renaissance.* Detroit: Wayne State University Press, 1987.

Lindsey, Karen. *Divorced, Beheaded, Survived: A Feminist Reinterpretation of the Wives of Henry VIII.* Reading, Mass.: Addison-Wesley, 1995.

Lochrie, Karma. *Margery Kempe and Translations of the Flesh.* Philadelphia: University of Pennsylvania Press, 1992.

Lougee, Carolyn C. *Le Paradis des Femmes: Women, Salons, and Social Stratification in Seventeenth-Century France.* Princeton: Princeton University Press, 1976.

Love, Harold. *The Culture and Commerce of Texts: Scribal Publication in Seventeenth-Century England.* Amherst: University of Massachusetts Press, 1993.

MacCarthy, Bridget G. *The Female Pen: Women Writers and Novelists, 1621–1818.* Preface by Janet Todd. New York: New York University Press, 1994. (Originally published by Cork University Press, 1946–47.)

Maclean, Ian. *The Renaissance Notion of Woman: A Study of the Fortunes of Scholasticism and Medical Science in European Intellectual Life.* Cambridge: Cambridge University Press, 1980.

———. *Woman Triumphant: Feminism in French Literature, 1610–1652.* Oxford: Clarendon Press, 1977.

Matter, E. Ann, and John Coakley, eds. *Creative Women in Medieval and Early Modern Italy.* Philadelphia: University of Pennsylvania Press, 1994. (Sequel to Monson, below.)

McLeod, Glenda. *Virtue and Venom: Catalogs of Women from Antiquity to the Renaissance.* Ann Arbor: University of Michigan Press, 1991.

Meek, Christine, ed. *Women in Renaissance and Early Modern Europe.* Dublin-Portland: Four Courts Press, 2000.

Mendelson, Sara, and Patricia Crawford. *Women in Early Modern England, 1550–1720.* Oxford: Clarendon Press, 1998.

Merrim, Stephanie. *Early Modern Women's Writing and Sor Juana Inés de la Cruz.* Nashville: Vanderbilt University Press, 1999.

Messbarger, Rebecca. *The Century of Women: The Representations of Women in Eighteenth-Century Italian Public Discourse.* Toronto: University of Toronto Press, 2002.

Miller, Nancy K. *The Heroine's Text: Readings in the French and English Novel, 1722–1782.* New York: Columbia University Press, 1980.

Miller, Naomi J. *Changing the Subject: Mary Wroth and Figurations of Gender in Early Modern England.* Lexington: University Press of Kentucky, 1996.

Miller, Naomi J., and Gary Waller, eds. *Reading Mary Wroth: Representing Alternatives in Early Modern England.* Knoxville: University of Tennessee Press, 1991.

Monson, Craig A., ed. *The Crannied Wall: Women, Religion, and the Arts in Early Modern Europe.* Ann Arbor: University of Michigan Press, 1992.

Newman, Karen. *Fashioning Femininity and English Renaissance Drama.* Chicago: University of Chicago Press, 1991.

Okin, Susan Moller. *Women in Western Political Thought.* Princeton: Princeton University Press, 1979.

Ozment, Steven. *The Bürgermeister's Daughter: Scandal in a Sixteenth-Century German Town.* New York: St. Martin's Press, 1995.

Pacheco, Anita, ed. *Early [English] Women Writers: 1600–1720.* New York: Longman, 1998.

Pagels, Elaine. *Adam, Eve, and the Serpent.* New York: HarperCollins, 1988.

Panizza, Letizia, ed. *Women in Italian Renaissance Culture and Society.* Oxford: European Humanities Research Centre, 2000.

Panizza, Letizia, and Sharon Wood, eds. *A History of Women's Writing in Italy.* Cambridge: Cambridge University Press, 2000.

Perry, Mary Elizabeth. *Crime and Society in Early Modern Seville.* Hanover, N.H.: University Press of New England, 1980.

———. *Gender and Disorder in Early Modern Seville.* Princeton: Princeton University Press, 1990.

Petroff, Elizabeth Alvilda, ed. *Medieval Women's Visionary Literature.* New York: Oxford University Press, 1986.

Perry, Ruth. *The Celebrated Mary Astell: An Early English Feminist.* Chicago: University of Chicago Press, 1986.

Pizan, Christine de (1365–1431). *The Book of the City of Ladies.* Trans. Earl Jeffrey Richards. Foreword by Marina Warner. New York: Persea, 1982.

———. *The Treasure of the City of Ladies.* Trans. Sarah Lawson. New York: Viking Penguin, 1985. Also trans. and introd. Charity Cannon Willard, ed. and introd. Madeleine P. Cosman. New York: Persea, 1989.

Rabil, Albert. *Laura Cereta: Quattrocento Humanist.* Binghamton, N.Y.: MRTS, 1981.

Rapley, Elizabeth. *A Social History of the Cloister: Daily Life in the Teaching Monasteries of the Old Regime.* Montreal: McGill-Queen's University Press, 2001.

Raven, James, Helen Small, and Naomi Tadmor, eds. *The Practice and Representation of Reading in England.* Cambridge: Cambridge University Press, 1996.

Reardon, Colleen. *Holy Concord within Sacred Walls: Nuns and Music in Siena, 1575–1700.* Oxford: Oxford University Press, 2001.

Reiss, Sheryl E., and David G. Wilkins, ed. *Beyond Isabella: Secular Women Patrons of Art in Renaissance Italy.* Kirksville, Mo.: Turman State University Press, 2001.

Rheubottom, David. *Age, Marriage, and Politics in Fifteenth-Century Ragusa.* Oxford: Oxford University Press, 2000.

Ricard, Antoine. *Les premiers Jansénistes et Port-Royal.* Paris: E. Plon, 1883.

Richardson, Brian. *Printing, Writers and Readers in Renaissance Italy.* Cambridge: Cambridge University Press, 1999.

Riddle, John M. *Contraception and Abortion from the Ancient World to the Renaissance.* Cambridge: Harvard University Press, 1992.

———. *Eve's Herbs: A History of Contraception and Abortion in the West.* Cambridge: Harvard University Press, 1997.

Rose, Mary Beth. *The Expense of Spirit: Love and Sexuality in English Renaissance Drama.* Ithaca: Cornell University Press, 1988.

———. *Gender and Heroism in Early Modern English Literature.* Chicago: University of Chicago Press, 2002.

———, ed. *Women in the Middle Ages and the Renaissance: Literary and Historical Perspectives.* Syracuse: Syracuse University Press, 1986.

Rosenthal, Margaret F. *The Honest Courtesan: Veronica Franco, Citizen and Writer in Sixteenth-Century Venice.* Foreword by Catharine R. Stimpson. Chicago: University of Chicago Press, 1992.

Sackville-West, Vita. *Daughter of France: The Life of La Grande Mademoiselle.* Garden City, N.Y.: Doubleday, 1959.

Schiebinger, Londa. *The Mind Has No Sex? Women in the Origins of Modern Science.* Cambridge: Harvard University Press, 1991.

———. *Nature's Body: Gender in the Making of Modern Science.* Boston: Beacon Press, 1993.

Schutte, Anne Jacobson, Thomas Kuehn, and Silvana Seidel Menchi, eds. *Time, Space, and Women's Lives in Early Modern Europe.* Kirksville, Mo.: Truman State University Press, 2001.

Shannon, Laurie. *Sovereign Amity: Figures of Friendship in Shakespearean Contexts.* Chicago: University of Chicago Press, 2002.

Shemek, Deanna. *Ladies Errant: Wayward Women and Social Order in Early Modern Italy.* Durham, N.C.: Duke University Press, 1998.

Sobel, Dava. *Galileo's Daughter: A Historical Memoir of Science, Faith, and Love.* New York: Penguin Books, 2000.

Sommerville, Margaret R. *Sex and Subjection: Attitudes to Women in Early-Modern Society.* London: Arnold, 1995.

Spencer, Jane. *The Rise of the Woman Novelist: From Aphra Behn to Jane Austen.* Oxford: Basil Blackwell, 1986.

Spender, Dale. *Mothers of the Novel: 100 Good Women Writers before Jane Austen.* New York: Routledge, 1986.

Sperling, Jutta Gisela. *Convents and the Body Politic in Late Renaissance Venice.* Foreword by Catharine R. Stimpson. Chicago: University of Chicago Press, 1999.

Steinbrügge, Lieselotte. *The Moral Sex: Woman's Nature in the French Enlightenment.* Trans. Pamela E. Selwyn. New York: Oxford University Press, 1995.

Stephens, Sonya, ed. *A History of Women's Writing in France.* Cambridge: Cambridge University Press, 2000.

Stuard, Susan M. "The Dominion of Gender: Women's Fortunes in the High Middle Ages." In *Becoming Visible: Women in European History,* ed. Renate Bridenthal, Claudia Koonz, and Susan M. Stuard. 3d ed. Boston: Houghton Mifflin, 1998.

Summit, Jennifer. *Lost Property: The Woman Writer and English Literary History, 1380–1589.* Chicago: University of Chicago Press, 2000.

Surtz, Ronald E. *The Guitar of God: Gender, Power, and Authority in the Visionary World of Mother Juana de la Cruz (1481–1534).* Philadelphia: University of Pennsylvania Press, 1991.

———. *Writing Women in Late Medieval and Early Modern Spain.* Philadelphia: University of Pennsylvania Press, 1995.

Teague, Frances. *Bathsua Makin, Woman of Learning.* Lewisburg, Pa.: Bucknell University Press, 1999.

Todd, Janet. *The Secret Life of Aphra Behn.* New York: Pandora, 2000.

———. *The Sign of Angelica: Women, Writing and Fiction, 1660–1800.* New York: Columbia University Press, 1989.

Van Dijk, Susan, Lia van Gemert, and Sheila Ottway, eds. *Writing the History of Women's Writing: Toward an International Approach.* Proceedings of the Colloquium, Amsterdam, 9–11 September. Amsterdam: Royal Netherlands Academy of Arts and Sciences, 2001.

Waithe, Mary Ellen, ed. *A History of Women Philosophers.* 3 vols. Dordrecht: Martinus Nijhoff, 1987.

Wall, Wendy. *The Imprint of Gender: Authorship and Publication in the English Renaissance.* Ithaca: Cornell University Press, 1993.

Walsh, William T. *St. Teresa of Avila: A Biography.* Rockford, Ill.: TAN Books, 1987.

Warner, Marina. *Alone of All Her Sex: The Myth and Cult of the Virgin Mary.* New York: Knopf, 1976.

Warnicke, Retha M. *The Marrying of Anne of Cleves: Royal Protocol in Tudor England.* Cambridge: Cambridge University Press, 2000.

Watt, Diane. *Secretaries of God: Women Prophets in Late Medieval and Early Modern England.* Cambridge, U.K.: D. S. Brewer, 1997.

Weber, Alison. *Teresa of Avila and the Rhetoric of Femininity.* Princeton: Princeton University Press, 1990.

Welles, Marcia L. *Persephone's Girdle: Narratives of Rape in Seventeenth-Century Spanish Literature.* Nashville: Vanderbilt University Press, 2000.

Whitehead, Barbara J., ed. *Women's Education in Early Modern Europe: A History, 1500–1800.* New York: Garland, 1999.

Wiesner, Merry E. *Women and Gender in Early Modern Europe.* Cambridge: Cambridge University Press, 1993.

———. *Working Women in Renaissance Germany.* New Brunswick: Rutgers University Press, 1986.

Willard, Charity Cannon. *Christine de Pizan: Her Life and Works.* New York: Persea, 1984.

Wilson, Katharina, ed. *An Encyclopedia of Continental Women Writers.* New York: Garland, 1991.

Woodbridge, Linda. *Women and the English Renaissance: Literature and the Nature of Womankind, 1540–1620.* Urbana: University of Illinois Press, 1984.

Woods, Susanne. *Lanyer: A Renaissance Woman Poet.* New York: Oxford University Press, 1999.

Woods, Susanne, and Margaret P. Hannay, eds. *Teaching Tudor and Stuart Women Writers.* New York: MLA, 2000.

INDEX